The changing shape of the Balkans

The changing shape of the Balkans

Edited by

F. W. Carter
H. T. Norris

WestviewPress
A Division of HarperCollins*Publishers*

Copyright © 1996 F. W. Carter & H. T. Norris

Published in 1996 in the United States of America by Westview Press, Inc., 5500 Central Avenue, Boulder, Colorado 80301-2877. First published by UCL Press Limited, University College London, Gower Street, London WC1E 6BT, UK. The name of University College London (UCL) is a registered trade mark used by UCL Press with the consent of the owner.

Library of Congress Cataloging-in-Publication Data available on request.

ISBN: 0-8133-6954-1

The paper used in this publication meets the requirements of the American National Standard for Permanence of Paper for Printed Library Materials 239.48-1984.

10   9   8   7   6   5   4   3   2   1

Contents

Preface

This publication has been inspired by a seminar organized by the Geopolitics and International Boundaries Research Centre and held at the School of Oriental and African Studies in December 1991. The book's aim is to enlighten the reader on the more specific aspects of changes in the northern and western parts of the Balkan peninsula resulting from the break-up of Yugoslavia, a country concocted as a home for all southern Slavs after the First World War. Authors have undertaken considerable revision of their papers to produce an analytical account of the contemporary Balkan scene.

The broad canvas covered by the book highlights recent changes in the northern and western Balkans, a region of continuing warfare, since the demise of the former communist Yugoslav regime. The ethnic quilt of this previous state contains about 20 different groups, some of whom have a desire to express their own ambitions at the expense of others, which led to an explosive cocktail once the shackles of the former regime had been removed. The geographical concepts of international and national boundary changes involved here also engage the reader in a deeper appreciation of history's role in leading up to this transformation. Political heritage, historical aspects and current geographical reality are bound together to give insights into this complex and sometimes confusing picture. Indeed, "to Balkanize" has entered the English language as synonymous with partition and the division of an area into small antagonistic states.

A special kind of ethnic conflict exists in the former Yugoslavia, because of the many racial/religious groups residing there and the demise of the former state following the death of Tito in 1980. The sheer complexity of over 20 ethnic groups living in a country of nearly 260,000 km^2 has encouraged animosity between sections of society.[1] During the 1950s and 1960s the impressive material gains made under the communist regime inspired large elements of the population to forsake traditional ties and accept the ideologies of the widely popular Tito regime.[2] Increasing difficulties in the

---

1. L. A. Kosiński, "Changes in the ethnic structure in East-Central Europe, 1930–1960", *The Geographical Review* **49**(3), 388–402, 1969; C. Thomas, "Ethnic minorities in Yugoslavia", *Irish Slavonic Studies* **8**, 59–85, 1987.
2. G. K. Bertsch, "The revival of nationalism", *Problems of Communism* **22**(6), 1–15, 1973.

1970s and 1980s, experienced in economic development, decentralization and nationality, meant that individuals reassessed their position and were driven back to old ethnic and religious legacies. Separatist sentiments expressed by the Croats contrasted with the unitarist preoccupations of the Serb majority, whose aspirations equated Yugoslavia with a "Greater Serbia". Slovenes (the third largest ethnic group) and the Macedonians also began thinking of independence, and Hungarians in Vojvodina and Albanians in Kosovo (the former Serbian heartland) expressed their wish for greater autonomy. The Montenegrins (ethnically Serbs) were more amenable to the idea of "Greater Serbia", whereas the Muslim Slavs in Bosnia were treated with suspicion by many of the other mainly Roman Catholic and Orthodox Christian, groups. The majority of the smaller ethnic groups were either located near to their mother country (i.e. Romanians in the east, Italians on the Adriatic coast) or were the result of eighteenth-century Habsburg policies restoring settlements and economy after about four centuries of warfare with the Turks (e.g. Poles and Czechs). The Illyrians (alleged ancestors of present-day Albanians) in the west, and Vlachs in more mountainous areas, can trace their presence in this part of the Balkan peninsula to the days of the "barbarian" invasions of the sixth–seventh centuries and even earlier.[3]

The above discussion provides a background scenario to the ethnic composition of this part of our continent. The attitudes and aspirations of the indigenous assorted ethnic minorities vary considerably. They have taken on a new lease of life since the collapse of the erstwhile communist regime, in which class was seen as more important than ethnic origin, rule through fear was customary, and political elitist (nomenclature) organizations were commonplace. Release from this omnipotent strait-jacket has encouraged old ethnic and religious differences to re-emerge.

Identity, whether ethnic or national, as framed within a clearly defined and fundamental (as opposed to "fundamentalist") religious faith, sect or denomination, is a marked feature of the Balkans today. It is a factor of major importance in Bosnia and Herzegovina, Bulgaria, Croatia, Greece, Macedonia and Serbia. The presence of substantial or predominant communities of Catholics in Croatia and Herzegovina, and of Orthodox Christians in Greece, Serbia – and indeed, throughout the Balkans – is of crucial significance in the defining of frontiers, whether ethnic or political. In the particular instance of Transylvania, the opposition of Catholic to Orthodox is enhanced by linguistic and cultural cleavage between Hungarians and Romanians. Even within a single religious community, tensions (for example, between Gypsies and non-Gypsies) may cause stresses that

---

3. G. W. Hoffman, "The evolution of the ethnographic map of Yugoslavia: an historical geographic interpretation", in *An historical geography of the Balkans*, F. W. Carter (ed.), 437–91 (London: Academic Press, 1977).

divide rather than unite. In the city of Braşov for example, there are two Baptist churches – one Hungarian-speaking, the other Romanian – within a short walking distance of each other. Yet their Sunday services clash and their collaboration exists on parallel lines rather than with an identical common objective. Where unity is shown at an evangelical rally at a stadium, this is, to a degree, incidental. The preacher is an American evangelist and English is the language he uses in his appeal from the pulpit.

The "European" identity of relatively large Muslim communities in Bosnia and Herzegovina, Bulgaria, Macedonia and, partly, Sunni-orthodox and partly Shiite heterodox, in Albania, is probably the most acute ethno-religious problem facing a long-term resolution in the Balkans today. Some of the reasons why this should be so may be read in Chapters 4, 6 and 10. The Serbian onslaught against Islam in Sarajevo in 1992 has been likened by some Muslim writers to the Reconquista and the fall of Granada in 1492. However, there are marked differences between the two events, 500 years apart. In 1492, Muslim al-Andalus was in a state of terminal decline and the city of Granada and its hinterland was a foothold of the faith, which, over the centuries, had shrunk to a pocket within the Iberian peninsula. On the contrary, 1992 marked Sarajevo as being one of the principal Balkan cities where one could find an Islamic resurgence and renaissance in the former Yugoslavia. It was the focus for what Alexandre Popović has described as "une étonnante renaissance".[4] It has been perceived as a potential, if not actual, threat by the Balkan Christian communities, Catholic and Orthodox alike. In the case of the former, a curb and a rebuke may have come from the Vatican and the wider Catholic community, yet within the Balkans themselves – and events around Mostar have sadly proved this to be so – the local historical and cultural prejudices and paranoia can only be tempered, barely curbed, so emotive is the religious memory among the local Balkan populations. Once communism was no longer an ideological cement of substance, it was to be replaced by a manipulated historical memory, an archive of animosity composed of a cultural nationalism had arisen out of religious roots. The religious hierarchy, even if they had so wished it, were not up to the task of tempering the zeal that was to spread rapidly in the Balkan peninsula since the mid-1980s. Where Islam is concerned, it should be emphasized that the impetus for renewal comes from outside the Balkans as much as it does from within the peninsula (Turkey included). In a recent article,[5] Helena Smith, discussing Albania, remarks that "only the mullahs, and the men building the mosques that have mushroomed as the ex-atheist state eagerly embraces Islam, want to stay. The ethnic Greeks, Christian Albanians and Latin-speaking Vlachs are sure

---

4. A. Popović , *L'Islam Balkanique*, 366 (Berlin: Harrassowitz, 1986).

5. H. Smith, "Lurching along a potholed road to the 20th century", *The Observer*, 18 (12 June 1994).

they want to leave". She does not point out that the funding for the rebuilding comes from Iran, or from Libya, or from the Arabian peninsula or Turkey.

Hence, shifting ethnic groups, reshaped and redrawn borders, and new alliances of convenience are not simply determined by facts on the ground within the Balkan peninsula. They are influenced, sometimes dramatically, by such surrounding (or more distant) countries and regions as Russia (historically backers of Serbia) and the Ukraine, Austria and Slovenia, Italy, the Muslim Middle East, and especially Turkey, which is now weighing anew its Ottoman and post-Ottoman identity. The resolution of this latter dilemma could be crucial to the future of the Balkans.

In a recently published article in Arabic,[6] the Albano–Syrian scholar Muhammad Mūfākū al-Arnaut has argued the case for the creation of two peoples in the Balkans (obsessed by the current creed of "one state, one faith, one language") by the religion of Islam. The first of these is Albania (Shqipëria) as we know it. Despite its linguistic cohesion, he argues that, had it not been for Islam becoming the predominant faith of a community without a church, the Albanians would have been absorbed by the surrounding peoples. He remarks that such a view is shared by some Albanian Christians.[7] The second case which he cites is that of the "Muslimanski narod" in Bosnia and Herzegovina, the fate of which hangs in the balance before our eyes. He perceives it as an example where Islam, as it had done elsewhere in the world of Islam in the past, had created a Shaʿb from a Qawm.[8] Such a radical change of identity amid the communities of Muslims and non-Muslims in the Balkans could be of long-lasting significance. It behoves the West in particular, amid an increasingly uprooted, ejected and "cleansed" population, to pay some heed to those agents that are not merely geographical or ethnic, to those other and wider factors currently determining the Balkans' changing frontiers.

From the onset of the present civil war it was obvious that Bosnia was a tinderbox.[9]Conflicts between Serb, Muslim and Croat interests were sharpened when the Bosnian government wished for independence; some Bosnian Croats aligned themselves with the Serbs, insisting on a confederal

---

6. Muhammad Mūfākū, *al-Islām waʾl-qawmiyya fiʾl-Balqān (dawr al-dīn fi tashakkul al-shuʿūb)* (*Islam and nationalism in the Balkans – the role of religion in the shaping of peoples*), Yarmuk University, published in Syria, in *Dirāsat Tāʾrīkhiyya*, September–December, nos 47 and 48, 121–40, 1993.

7. Ibid., 129–37, citing in particular Jacov Milaj, *Raca shqiptarë*, 78 (Tirana, 1944); H. Kokalari, *Kosova djep i shqiptarizmit*, 16 (Tirana, 1943).

8. E. W. Lane, *Arabic–English lexicon* (London: Williams & Northgate, 1863) defines Shaʿb (narod) as "a nation, people, race or family of mankind" and Qawm as "a body of persons composing a community".

9. Lord Carrington, "Turmoil in the Balkans: developments and prospects", *The RUSI Journal* 137(5), 1–4, 1992.

structure, whereas the Muslims preferred a unitary state. Inevitably, any agreement reached between these major differences was sure to be frail. Further, the spatial pattern of Serb, Muslim and Croat communities discouraged the creation of three separate units on a geographical basis, that is, one nationality; nor would it be possible for them to constitute self-contained blocks. No political settlement of Bosnia can be accomplished unless it commands the support of all three groups and, until this is achieved, no long-term peace can return to Bosnia. In the meantime the Muslimized Slavs have the most to lose in partitioned Bosnia, and a permanent ceasefire is impossible until, in their view, all Muslim territory is returned.

The distinctive features of the book are characterized by the clarity and depth of penetration that the authors have managed to inject, and the interest evoked from discussion in their particular fields of Balkan interest. These are supported by cartographic illustrations, tables and figures, which help the reader to follow the complex arguments and debates related to contemporary events. It provides an essential reference book and analytical tool for those wishing to familiarize themselves further with this contentious part of Europe. All the authors are Balkan specialists who have written widely in their various chosen disciplinary domains.

Acknowledgements

As editors of this work we would like to acknowledge the efforts of several people who have been involved in its production. These include Greg Englefield and Richard Schofield, who originally conceived the idea for a seminar on the changing shape of the Balkans, Bjorn Roberts and Richard Schofield, again, for resolving the book's considerable organizational problems, Nicholas Esson and Roger Jones from UCL Press, and Guy Baker from the Cartographic Unit of the Department of Geography, University College London.

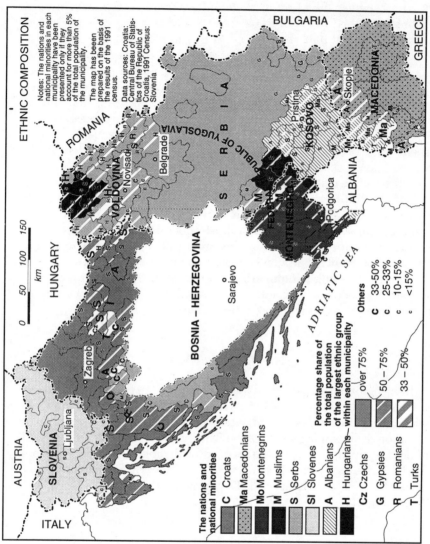

Ethnic composition of former Yugoslavia.

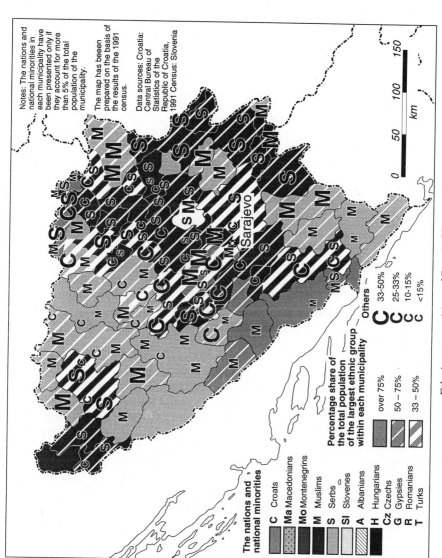

The nations and
national minorities

C   Croats
Ma Macedonians
Mo Montenegrins
M   Muslims
S   Serbs
Sl Slovenes
A   Albanians
H   Hungarians
Cz Czechs
G   Gypsies
R   Romanians
T   Turks

Percentage share of
the total population
of the largest ethnic group
within each municipality

over 75%
50 – 75%
33 – 50%

Others

C   33-50%
C   25-33%
C   10-15%
C   <15%

Sarajevo

km

0   50   100   150

Ethnic composition of Bosnia Herzegovina.

CHAPTER ONE

Not so black as it's painted: the Balkan political heritage

MARK WHEELER

Perverse as it may seem, this chapter will not argue that the political heritage of southeastern Europe is one of unrelieved darkness. Although the murk may nowadays be palpable, with the Yugoslav wars continuing and threatening to spread, and with the other Balkan states still either lagging behind the rest of eastern Europe in making their transitions from communism or, in the case of Greece, in failing to live up to its membership of the European Union, nearly as much of the gloom emanates from the eyes and ignorance of outside beholders as it does from the objects of their censorious gaze. Thus, the assumptions of Western politicians and journalists – that the peoples of the Balkans inhabit a realm of preternatural barbarism, ludicrous ambitions, congenital perfidy, inveterate cruelty and unfathomable complexity with which the civilized world is both ill equipped and ill advised to cope – will find scant endorsement here. For to accept such stereotypes is not only intellectually lazy, it is also to partake of just that mode of thought of which southeastern Europeans stand accused.

That the peoples of the Balkans confront enormous difficulties stemming from their recent and not-so-recent pasts, and that these are often different in degree or nature from those of other Europeans, cannot be denied. If it were otherwise, there would be little point in a volume such as this. But it ill behoves Westerners, beset by their own post- Cold War disorientations and security dilemmas, and by their own increasingly "Balkan" obsessions with issues of nationality, sovereignty, and economic and moral decline, to dismiss southeastern Europeans as unworthy either of serious attention or of sympathetic consideration. Balkan politicians may still be tiresome; Balkan imbroglios may remain difficult to comprehend; and Balkan failures may be as frequent as in the past. Yet, as the international community's own failures to prevent, mitigate or stop the Yugoslav wars have shown, the region retains the capacity to affront the equanimity, upset the security structures and shatter the unity of the West.

The BBC journalist Misha Glenny gave his account of the East European revolutions of 1989 the arresting title *The rebirth of history*.[1] The same idea is conveyed by Joseph Rothschild's pre-revolutionary history of eastern

1

Europe after the Second World War: *Return to diversity.*[2] For well before the communist monolith cracked, the countries of eastern Europe had begun to exhibit a variety of political styles, social attitudes and economic aspirations that owed more to their inter-war and pre-1914 pasts than they did to "real existing socialism".

In the Balkans, in fact, history and diversity never died. The four communist states were, after 1948, both as different from one another as they were from non-communist Greece – and as similar. Each demonstrated features that could be traced to a common Byzantine, Ottoman and semi-colonial legacy. It is likely, for example, that in the 1960s and 1970s Albanian and Romanian colonels shared both a xenophobic world view and a barely suppressed resentment of their political marginalization and institutional impoverishment under their countries' respective potentates. It is certain that Greek and Serbian colonels continued as in pre-war days to believe that they knew best how their countries should be run.

Each Balkan state also exhibited traits that belied either its bloc membership or its repudiation of blocs. Tito's Yugoslavia was a communist dictatorship for all its relative liberalism and much-touted non-alignment. Enver Hoxha's Albania was a chauvinist prison despite the ardent socialist internationalism of Radio Tirana. Bulgaria under Todor Zhivkov turned its ostentatious obeisance to Moscow to it own advantage, much as King Boris had in his day profited from his subordination to Hitler's Germany. Greece, on the other hand, failed after the 1960s to capitalize on American support against Turkey, just as the patronage of David Lloyd George had proved inadequate to permit Eleftherios Venizelos to maintain a Greek empire in Asia Minor after the First World War. Finally, under Causescu, Romanian autarchy and independence were as much charades as they had been in the reign of King Carol II; and Romanian socialism was as phoney as the monarchical corporatism of the late 1930s. The spoils of each were restricted to the dynasty and its courtiers.

Throughout the Balkans, nepotism and corruption, patronage and clientage, overt submission and covert rebelliousness, were as characteristic of domestic politics after 1945 as they had been before. Whether the practitioners were communists or capitalists, the peddling of influence, the mobilization of connections, and the urge to promote personal, local, and narrow party interests would produce in recent years such equally notable "affairs" as Bosnia's Agrokomerc and Greece's Bank of Crete. However, neither scandal would long embarrass its principal putative malefactor. Andreas Papandreou would come again in glory; and Fikret Abdić would

---

1. Misha Glenny, *The rebirth of history: eastern Europe in the age of democracy* (London: Penguin, 1990).
2. Joseph Rothschild, *Return to diversity: a political history of east central Europe since World War II* (New York: Oxford University Press, 1989).

return to do business as usual and with everyone in his besieged Bihać pocket.

In foreign affairs, too, dependency on Great Power allies and Great Power alignments remains a Balkan constant. Yugoslavia turned out to need the Cold War as much as it needed Tito. Nowadays Albania, Bulgaria and Romania pursue American, NATO and European Union favour as eagerly as they once eschewed it. Meanwhile, the Yugoslav wars have intermittently produced constellations remarkably reminiscent of the alignments of the Great War: with the former Central Powers backing Croatia and the former Entente Powers indulging Serbia. But if the Serbs' and Croats' respective attempts to conjure up an Islamic fundamentalist bogey in Bosnia have failed to win either of *them* much Western sympathy on that account, it has certainly not helped the Bosnian cause in the West for it to have been identified so exclusively with that of the Muslims.

If there is any one practice that has come to epitomize the horror of the Yugoslav wars, and to damn its authors, perpetrators and their region, it is "ethnic cleansing". But this abomination is neither new nor exclusive to Balkan barbarians, as the remnants of native peoples all over the world can readily attest. In southeastern Europe it has been a natural concomitant of war and state-building for centuries. What shocks, is that such a thing should be happening now, and so brazenly. That similar impulses animate large parts of the racist Right in western Europe, and that restrictive immigration controls exist to disarm them, is rarely noted, perhaps because Western governments have been at such pains to avoid seeing themselves as possessing any community of interest with the embattled defenders of pluralism in Bosnia. Instead we hear endlessly about "ancient ethnic hatreds" – an oxymoron and a lie – the purpose of which is to depict the Yugoslav wars as being beyond the power of civilized states either to assuage or to comprehend.

It would be a mistake, however, to assume that all Balkan continuities are unhelpful, sleazy or barbarous. The continuing strength of family solidarity is a notable plus, even if it has too often been traduced by extension to the less worthy ideal – or myth – of the nation. The egalitarianism of most of the Balkan peoples is another positive trait. So, too, are resourcefulness, self-reliance and a genius for saving. Few observers, for example, would have imagined, before Slobodan Milošević hit upon hyperinflation as a means of extracting Deutschmarks from his people, that Serbs possessed either such reserves of hard currency or so much resilience. Social and psychological attributes such as these are also parts of the Balkan political heritage.

The original Third World

For more than a century before most of the Balkan states joined or were annexed to the communist Second World, they constituted the original Third World. It was they who, newly freed from the "Ottoman yoke", pioneered the processes that came to be known as "modernization", "westernization", and "Europeanization". Their leaders' development strategies – however unexamined – were broadly similar. They aimed to "rejoin" Europe, even if their territorial models were medieval in origin: that is, the re-creation of their long-lost empires. Yet if their respective national programs were both inherently implausible and mutually contradictory, the political path on which they embarked in order to achieve them was more effective than is commonly assumed. Economically, on the other hand, their experiences were as frustrating as those of any contemporary, debt-ridden Third World country.

Of the four Balkan states that emerged as autonomous or independent in the nineteenth century – Serbia, Greece, Romania and Bulgaria, in that order – only Greece won full independence at a stroke. The others attained it gradually, by degrees, utilizing at various times revolt, negotiation, bribery, and Great Power sponsorship or disarray as circumstances warranted. But whenever between 1817 and 1878 they achieved statehood, they confronted analogous difficulties stemming from their Ottoman pasts.

In the first place, they had to establish frameworks of government, and in particular to settle relationships between the anarchic elements in the countryside, which had flourished as the Ottoman imperium decayed, and the would-be central authorities in the capital. Secondly, they had to order their foreign relations so as to preserve and/or assert their independence and to "liberate" those of their co-nationals who remained outside their borders. Thirdly, they endeavoured to modernize, and especially to equip themselves with those appurtenances of modern life such as no self-respecting country could be without: armies, bureaucracies, railways, opera houses and law faculties.

It was unsurprising that they should have had more success in settling the issues of domestic politics and defining their programs of national expansion than they had in developing their economies and modernizing their societies. Political and nationalistic goals were fairly clear-cut. The key question inherited from their struggles for independence was "Who ruled?" – monarch or oligarchy, capital or village, bureaucracy or parliament? This question was necessarily capable of resolution, even though the rapidity of dynastic and government changes throughout the century indicated that different answers were regularly being offered.

For example, in both autonomous Serbia and independent Greece the main issue was whether the Crown or the local notables who had led the liberation wars would prevail. Would the prince or king succeed in imposing his writ on the countryside and its traditional leaders, or would the latter continue to rule their own bailiwicks and make a mere figurehead of him? The crown won this struggle, although Prince Miloš Obrenović of Serbia made a better job of it than did Greece's King Othon. Miloš turned himself into an Ottoman-style pasha, tamed the local oligarchs, and made himself one of Europe's richest men in the process, although he continued to sleep on the floor like any Serb peasant and never learned to read or write. He made the state his provider and the government his instrument. In this achievement, Miloš was advantaged over Othon by having only one protecting power – Russia – with which to deal, rather than the three that claimed the right to superintend Greece's affairs. After 1839 in Serbia and 1843 in Greece, however, the balance shifted in favour of the oligarchies. Using the rhetoric of constitutionalism, the notables contrived by coups d'état to impose limits on the crown and to take power for themselves. Their aims, though, were no longer what they had been. Increasingly, the monarchs' rivals represented the state bureaucracies that they had themselves called into existence. As a consequence, the struggle for power gradually became one between two centralizing forces, rather than between the palace and the defenders of local interests. This happened because, in small and impoverished countries, the only sure path to security, riches and modernity led from the provinces to the capital.

From the 1860s in Greece and Serbia (and from the start of Bulgaria's autonomy in 1878) more liberal constitutions, increasingly ideological political parties, occasionally real elections, and something approximating mass politics all made their appearance. Agrarian and socialist parties followed, even if the main players continued to represent the Crown, the state machine, the army, and the personal or regional followings of various strongmen. The peasant masses were integrated, indoctrinated, and subordinated, albeit less on a class than on a national and nationalistic basis. Yet despite the material gulf that continued to widen between the Balkan states and those of western and central Europe, these political processes were neither all that dissimilar nor all that retarded in comparison with those in the rest of the continent.

Romania, it has to be said, was different. Politics there, like the independence movement before it, remained the preserve of the landed elite, reflecting a much less equitable social structure. In fact, the jacquerie (or its threat) was still the principal means of peasant mobilization long after it had vanished elsewhere. Albanians, for their part, had a national movement after 1878, but no politics until this century.

In their foreign relations the nineteenth-century Balkan states had much in common as ell. They were all born as rumps. Each possessed only a small portion of the territory that its statesmen, savants and swineherds regarded as properly theirs. Not only was Greek, Serbian, and Bulgarian political life dominated by the lust for land, but – after 1878 – by a struggle for the same land: Macedonia. Romania, again, was different. It inspired to incorporate areas held not by the Turks, whose obvious destiny was expulsion from Europe, but by two Great Powers, Russia and Austria–Hungary. Although the Balkan states, like Italy, could be accused of having enormous appetites but weak teeth, there may have been more method in their territorial madness than met the eye of condescending foreigners. Certainly, Greece and Serbia were too small, too resource-poor and too underpopulated to make economic breakthroughs on the basis of peasant agriculture.

The Balkan and First World Wars largely completed the processes of state formation and aggrandisement (or diminution) for three-quarters of a century. The big winners – Serbia (as the Kingdom of the Serbs, Croats and Slovenes) and Romania – were naturally more inclined either to continue or to initiate experiments in parliamentary government than were the losers. Large-scale land reforms were an equally natural concomitant, particularly as most of those who were to be expropriated could be classed as anti-national elements.

As elsewhere in eastern Europe, however, it proved impossible to maintain simultaneously the fiction of the unitary nation-state, a highly centralized administration, and a semblance of parliamentary democracy. Balkan teeth had turned out to be strong enough; but their digestive systems failed, especially as it was the less developed ex-Ottoman kernel states that attempted to dominate and assimilate their more advanced, ex-Habsburg acquisitions. In the Kingdom of Serbs, Croats and Slovenes, the Yugoslav idea was contaminated by its identification with Serbian hegemonism, and more than ever after King Alexander proclaimed a personal dictatorship in 1929 and attempted to force Serbo-centric "Yugoslavism" down his subjects' throats. In Romania, King Carol took longer to assert his mastery over both the politicians and the region's one genuine fascist movement (the Iron Guard), but then there had been little to esteem in Romania's pseudo-democracy from the start.

Albania, Bulgaria, and Greece were also monarchical dictatorships by the mid-1930s, although they had arrived there by various routes. Bulgaria's defeats in 1913 and 1918, and Greece's wartime divisions and postwar debacle in Asia Minor, unleashed revolutionary currents. Alexander Stamboliski's Bulgarian peasant regime was the most interesting Balkan innovation in the 1920s; but its domestic vengefulness, socio-economic archaism, and irenical foreign policy made it repugnant to those elements (dynasty, army, political establishment, and Macedonian refugees and hit-men) that had long run the state and were able to combine in 1923 to reclaim their property. Simultaneously, the so-called national schism in Greece between monarchists and republicans, each blaming the other for the catastrophe in Anatolia, produced coup and counter-coup until General Ioannis Metaxas seized power in the name of King George II in 1936.

Finally, in Albania, the runt of the Balkan pack, the in-fighting among clans was curbed only when one of their chiefs, Ahmed Zogu, enlisted foreign help to make himself their master in 1925 and their king in 1928.

The little royal dictators of inter-war southeastern Europe each justified his regime by reference to the failures of the politicians and parliaments to put their countries on secure foundations, to govern honestly and competently, to quell separatism or communism, and to make any economic headway. They and their minions often mouthed the mumbo-jumbo of fascism, but their very existence was its negation. They were traditionalists who ruled through the army, the bureaucracy, and such political collaborators as they could co-opt. Yet in their efforts to cope with the depression and to accommodate the diplomatic revolutions of Mussolini and Hitler, they paved the way for real fascists, Nazis, and communists. They had plenty of company in inter-war Europe.

The empires strike back

As should by now be plain, contemporary Balkan distempers, disputes and dependencies cannot all be laid at the door of the region's departed or repackaged communists. Yugoslavs may be re-fighting the Second World War, but elsewhere in the region the domestic and international agendas appear to bear a closer resemblance to those of the inter-war years, or to the 1870s, or even to the time of Philip of Macedon.

It may, in conclusion, be helpful to identify those aspects of the Balkan political heritage that either never disappeared or which have lately re-emerged. The first and most important is integral nationalism. The peoples of southeastern Europe, like those of eastern Europe generally, remain wedded to national mythologies, ideologies and programs that give pride of place to solidarity, homogeneity, and an all-powerful state. The Balkan strongman – as the embodiment of all these alleged virtues – can be expected to reappear beyond his current domains in Serbia, Croatia and Albania.

National and religious minorities will continue to be required to accommodate themselves to the majority. If they are Muslims, they must expect short shrift, as the partition of Bosnia and Herzegovina appears likely to impose upon that republic's one-time plurality. Multiculturalism, local autonomies, and more or less genuine expressions of what the Yugoslav communists used to hail as "brotherhood and unity" are out. Pluralism – never strongly developed – can now be political, but not ethnic or religious. Irredentism is back, with a vengeance in ex-Yugoslavia, but potentially greater elsewhere as Greater Serbia reaps the whirlwind that Milošević has sown. The break-up of Macedonia might easily ignite an all-Balkan war from which a Greater Albania, a Greater Bulgaria, and a Turkish regional superpower could well emerge.

7

Balkan dependency – strategic, psychological, and economic – will also be to the fore. This will foster resentment and autarchic urges that will limit the dismantling of state controls over the economy as much as the fear of social unrest. Populism and chauvinism can be expected to proliferate, the new or retreaded leaders benefiting from their communist predecessors' successes in creating mass societies that are largely urban and amenable to media manipulation. There is, therefore, little scope for peasantist revivals. Political elites, intellectuals, clerics, and probably the military, will maintain or resume their accustomed roles in defining and implementing national goals. The construction of civil societies will progress but falteringly. The Europe of the Twelve will continue to attract, but the Europe of the Ottomans will provide the cognitive dissonance.

CHAPTER TWO

Kosova, and the Kosovans: past, present and future as seen through Serb, Albanian and Muslim eyes[1]

H. T. NORRIS

The purpose of this chapter is to present several contrasted, dissenting, or seemingly irreconcilable, points of view on historical claims to Kosova[2] and to the glittering prize of the possession of its true cultural identity. To do so, I have selected recent statements and opinions, which may be said to represent fairly the diverse and current strongly held opinions and/or political aspirations or nationalist posturings. Conflict between Serb and Albanian is probably by far the best documented of such differences, displayed with a baffling exhibition of varied shades of opinion. Less well known are those views and comments that are to be read in the writings of some Albanian Albanians. Far less documented, and least known of all until the last year or so, have been the views of the Muslim umma, the religious community, in regard to the Albanians in Kosova. Until recently the latter figured relatively rarely, in the Islamic media. The Albanians in Kosova are overwhelmingly Muslim. Only a tiny minority (some 50,000) are Catholics, or are Orthodox. However, in the current contest, the eyes of the Muslim umma are fixed upon the Kosovan Albanians principally as Muslims. Much the same situation is applicable to the Albanians and Turkish minorities in adjoining Macedonia.

If this Muslim viewpoint has not been well enough articulated, or has been insufficiently appreciated, this is in part because regular reporting

---

1. For the most comprehensive survey of Islamic institutions in Kosova, in recent times, the reader is referred to Alexandre Popović, *L'Islam Balkanique* (Berlin: Harrassowitz, 1986). For the historical background, see the article on Kosovo (Kosowa) by M. Munir Aktepe in vol. V of the *Encyclopedia of Islam* (2nd edn), 275–77 (Leiden). Hugh Poulton, in *The Balkans, minorities and states in conflict*, 57–73 (London: Minority Rights Publications, 1991), provides a contemporary assessment of the Albanian position in Kosova. Two further articles of relevance are S. K. Pavlowitch, "Kosovo: an analysis of Yugoslavia's problem", *Conflict Studies* **137–8**, 7–21, 1982; and E. Biberaj, "Kosovo: the struggle for recognition", ibid., 23–43.
2. Kosova is spelt in the Albanian way throughout, with the exception of the Battle of Kosovo and in quoted text.

and commentary have only of late been augmented and forcefully and coherently presented. A second factor is that much of this expression has been in Arabic, Persian, Turkish, Urdu and other Oriental languages. What they have said has not been made available to the Western media of which, Britain is oversensitive (dare one say paranoiac?) on such issues, particularly where the frank and often highly emotional expression of "Muslim sentiment" is involved. Nonetheless, this Muslim voice deserves to be heard, for were the situation in Kosova to deteriorate catastrophically to a point where, as in Bosnia, bloody strife and mass expulsions were to take place, there is little doubt that it would provoke an increasingly violent reaction within the world of Islam at large.

Did the Albanians invade Kosova?

I have chosen to begin with the considered view of a leading Western scholar and authority on the history of Albania, namely Alain Ducellier, in whose articles (collectively bound together in a *Variorum* volume, *L'Albanie entre Byzance et Venise (Xe–XVe siècles)*[3] appeared a response to the question "Les Albanais, ont-ils envahi le Kosova?" At the end of his investigation he concludes and remarks: "In Kosova, it is evidently the Slavs, or the Slavized peoples, Bulgars then Serbs, who occupied, from the seventh century, a region the population of which was solidly Illyro–Albanian since Antiquity. Indeed, the slow implanting and the inevitable slavization of a part of the original population allowed the Serbs, at the beginning of the thirteenth century, to make of Kosova their principal political and economic centre, but no one will ever be able to know what, at this epoch, constituted the respective proportions of the two elements, the co-existence of which seems to have been no major problem. Finally, the Ottoman conquest and the progressive enfeeblement of Serbia, allowed the Albanian population, at once due to an internal reaction, and thanks to the pacific emigratory influx of Christian Albanians from the north, to weigh more and more heavily on Kosova. Much study is still needed to be able to affirm it, but it is probable that, even before the Slav migration of 1690 and 1738, the Albanians constituted an important minority in Kosova, if not the majority of the population. Furthermore, it would be unjust to forget that Serbs were not the only ones to flee from the zones at that time, or to be Islamized. At the very moment of the great Serb emigration of 1737–8, several thousand Christian Albanians left the mountainous zones of the region of Shkodra (Shkoder) and went to establish themselves in the neighbourhood of Karlovac in Croatia, where the Austrian government utilized them

---

3. Published in London 1987, *Variorum reprints*, section X. His article was originally published in *L'Albanie*, vol. 2, **13**, 10–15, 1981.

within the framework of its policy of military colonization. Now, these "Klementiner", as they are so named in the Austrian texts, found themselves there to be intimately mixed into Serbian elements that had emigrated at the same moment and had become installed in the same manner: they maintained their traditions and their language there until about 1910, the date of their definitive "slavization".

The "de-Slavization" of Kosova is therefore a false problem. It is only the result of these immense convex movements that have always characterized the history of the Balkan peoples, supported and based upon an old substratum that remained Albanian. This movement took place without violence all through the Middle Ages and up to the beginning of modern times in such a way that the episodes of 1690 and 1738 should be viewed only as its outcome. This time-honoured movement has clearly nothing to do with the vast projects of the Yugoslav government, when, between the two wars, it sought to combine the division of Albania with fascist Italy and the massive expulsions of Albanians towards Turkey'.[4]

Kosova, the source of Serbia's sorrows and the country at the heart of Serbia's recovery of its identity

The year 1989 marked the 600th anniversary of the Battle of Kosovo (Kosovo Polje). It was a unique occasion, in modern times, for a Serbian mass demonstration of reaffirmation of identity, and lament for a loss of sovereignty, symbolized by this traumatic historic event. A publication appeared in Belgrade entitled "The Battle of Kosovo (1389–1989) (Boj na Kosovu),[5] and in it were printed some 120 articles in English and Serbo–Croat. The Serb viewpoint is made clear on every page. The collection is a peculiar blend of, at times superficially academic, articles (though usually without source references, in any detail, and, at times, of doubtful scholarly quality). The articles embrace such topics as Serb epic, the relics of Saint Lazar, the cultural heritage of Serbian Orthodoxy, alleged Albanian desecrations, Byzantine and Serbian art (often of a higher quality) and quotations from Ottoman sources. The Albanian contribution to the Kosova "saga", al-though not totally neglected, is not conspicuous in the text. As a whole, the book makes ominous reading. The world of Islam is exclusively perceived in an Ottoman context. "Fundamentalism" of an Iranian or a Sudanese type appears nowhere. It is principally the Albanians, as

---

4. Ibid.
5. Časopis Matice, Iseljenika Srbije, year XXXVI, May–August 1989, pp 344–47 [English language editors: John Martlew & Thomir Vuckovic]. For a highly critical Croat review of the Serb Kosova "Obsession", see Branka Magas, "The curse of Kosovo", in *New Internationalist* (September), 8–9, 1993.

Muslims, who are painted in the darkest hues. Dušan T Bakatović 's article, "Migrations from Kosovo" (pp. 89–91), in contrast to Ducellier's conclusions, for example, on the migration of 1690, does not see the events that occurred then as other than a calculated process of Albanization and Islamization.[6]

The demographic disturbance that the Great Migration of the Serbs in 1690 had brought about affected the future of these parts: aggressive mountain tribes arrived from the barren Arbanian (arbanaški) plateaux, and Arbanians (Arbanasi) gradually populated the valleys of Kosova and Metohija. With the support of Turkish authorities, the Arbanians, many of whom were already largely Islamized, settled down in the abandoned regions, slowly pushing out the native Serbian population and attacking their property. The inflow of the Arbanian people, a powerful population with a strong central tribal organization, which Islamization had only strengthened even more, added a new stimulus to the already initiated fermentation. Finding themselves surrounded by the Arbanians to quite a considerable extent, the Serbian people of Kosova, after having converted to Islam, were forced to accept the customs, traditional dress and, eventually, even the language of the Arbanian immigrants. In time, the Islamized Serbs became Arbanians, entering, through inter-marital relations, into their tribes. Thus, Drenica, a one-time central foothold under Bankovic, now became a central Arbanian stronghold. From the beginning of the seventeenth century, the influence of the Arbanian population in Dakovica, the heart of all their uprising grows. To which is added: the Albanians encouraged the colonization of their fellow tribesmen in Kosova and Metohija. They went into the fertile flatlands of Metohija and being Muslims, entered the privileged ruling circles, from which, in turn, personnel were recruited for the ruling Turkish hierarchy. The first mosques built in the villages of Kosova at the beginning of the seventeenth century bear witness to the intensifying presence of Albanians.[7]

However, it is not only the Islamicized Albanians who were then (and presumably now) a threat that proved intolerable to the Serbs, but Catholicism (a secret ally of Islam and a traitor to the Cross) as is made plain in the following passage:[8]

> The policies of the Roman clergy greatly added to the pushing back of the Serbs from Kosova and Metohija. After the founding of the Congregation for Religious Propaganda (Congregation de propaganda fide) in 1622, Serbia, of which Kosova and Metohija are but one part (according to all maps dating from the sixteenth century to

---

6. Within the section "Expulsion of the Serbs".
7. Ibid.
8. Ibid.

the nineteenth century), was a missionary country in which the Orthodox "schismatic" needed to be converted into the Roman Catholic faith. The Roman clergy used the Catholic tribes of northern Albania in the spreading of its influence on Kosova and Metohija. Around the middle of the sixteenth century, from among these tribes, who were either trying to escape "revenge in blood" or were in search of new "living space", came certain numbers of families that settled on the borderline of Metohija, in Pec, Dakovica, and Prizren, and where, almost immediately, they began attacking the Serbian population. In order to weaken the Serbian Orthodox population, missionaries of the Roman clergy encouraged the Muslim Albanians in their attacks upon the Serbs. As sources show, Catholic bishops from Skopje, who were mainly of Albanian descent, helped in the Islamization and Albanization of the Serbs.

Records regarding the strengthening of Catholic oases indicate their increase around the middle of the sixteenth century, though their number, in comparison to the total population, was insignificant. Despite all trials, Serbian people of the Orthodox were still the majority population. Reports made by Catholic "inspectors" and foreign travellers who wrote of their journeys, show that Prizren was considered the capital of Serbia, and that there were still many Serbs in Peć, Priština, and smaller towns, as well as in most of the villages.

The closing down of the Patriarchate of Peć in 1776, put the Serbian population through the most difficult trials; it was suddenly caught between Catholic propaganda and the Islamization forced upon it by the Muslim Albanians, who now had more and more representatives in the Turkish ruling hierarchy in Metohija and Kosova. In 1767, the papal inspector, Matija Masarek, an Albanian by descent, noted that the demographic map of Kosova was changing due to the fact that every possible nook and hideaway was full of "damned Moslemised Albanians, bandits and murderers, who killed among themselves, and caused trouble for Catholics".

Similar statements of lost ethnicity are to be read, however disguised, in one or more of the prestigious contributions. Among them is the speech delivered in the Swedish Royal Academy, "Traditions and ideologies in the historical fate of the Serbian people" (pp. 10–11). It was made by Dobrica Cošić (former President of Yugoslavia), who, although conceding the fact of a "myth" of Kosova in the Serb historical memory, in no way disowns or even queries it, nor underestimates its value as a spur to dynamic rebirth. He compares the Serbs to the Ancient Greeks, confronted on all sides, yet a victim of their own *hubris* (as he puts it). Not only is Kosova the preferred setting of a confrontation, but Croatia and Bosnia–Herzegovina likewise. No ethnic or denominational distinction is to be made between those whom the Serbs oppose.[9]

13

Its aim was liberation from the Turks and the creation of an independent state. That ideology, permeated with Serbian national myths and the morale of the Christian eschatology and the folk epic, was based on the defeat at Kosova and the Serbian heroes who, in the national spirit and soul *do not cease* (my italics) fighting against the Islamic half-moon and for "the honourable cross and golden freedom", so that with that spiritual energy becoming the native tradition of the Serbs, this people would begin uprisings and would lead liberation wars throughout the whole of the nineteenth century and right up to the end of the First and the Second World Wars. The result of these uprisings and wars would be the foundation of two Serbian national states in the nineteenth century – Serbia and Montenegro – that would *at first* (my italics) include only the mainstream elements of the Serbian Diaspora. Later Cošić remarks:

> With its negative dialectic, history has again expressed itself on our soil, in a paradoxical result of human aspirations: in the denial of an ideal. With a will for liberty and democracy the Serbian people has been fighting for its national identity and union for almost two centuries. Nevertheless, even after several uprisings and wars, after the revolution, that people is nowadays, according to the Constitution of 974, in the Yugoslav multinational state, for the creation of which it sacrificed the most, nationally unequal, politically, economically and culturally disintegrated, exposed to Albanian violence and persecution in Kosova – its homeland, subjected to assimilation in Croatia, to Islamic pressures in Bosnia and Herzegovina, paralysed by the split of the particular bureaucratic oligarchies, overwhelmed by depression and hopelessness. Following two great ideologies, under the banner of national and under the banner of socialist ideology, the Serbian people has experienced fatal defeats in the twentieth century.

The above remarks do not take into account the real fear of genocide or expulsion that was felt by the Yugoslav Muslims – the Albanian Kosovars among them – before the Second World War. Such fears were forcibly expressed in the following statement of opinion, which was published in Sarajevo as recently as 1991:

---

9. Note such choice expressions as the "Islamic half-moon", or Islamic "pressures" in Bosnia–Herzegovina. Here, Ivo Andrić set a precedent, "The Turks could bring no cultural content or sense of higher historic mission, even to those South Slavs who accepted Islam; for their Christian subject, their hegemony brutalized custom and meant a step to the rear in every respect", in *The development of spiritual life in Bosnia under the influence of Turkish rule*, p. 38 (Durham & London: Duke University Press, 1990). See also Hugh Poulton, op. cit., 19.

In the thirties of the nineteenth century in the Kingdom of Yugoslavia different plans were made for the displacement of the Muslims, particularly the Albanians from so-called Southern Serbia. Quasi-scientific discussions about it, initiated by the government and the general-staff office, were held in the Serbian Cultural Club. One paper was written by Dr Vasa Ćubrilović, the university professor and the other by Ivo Andrić, the well known writer, academician and diplomat. Above all, Ćubrilović regretted that after 1918 they did not do what once had been done by Karađorđe, Miloš, Mihailo and Jovan Ristić, who cleared Serbia of the foreign element and populated it with their own people. In addition to some discriminating and even insulting statements about the "Arnauts", Ćubrilović held that the only solution to the problem was to make them leave the country. When it is possible for Germany to force tens of thousands of the Jews to emigrate, for Russia to transfer millions of people from one part of the continent to another, a world war will not break out just because of some hundreds of thousands of displaced Arnauts.

In his paper, Ivo Andrić was much more cautious, more analytical and intelligent. After a detailed historical analysis he came to the conclusion that an independent Albania would best suit Yugoslavia, whereas its possible division between Italy and Greece would be a necessary but inevitable evil. Of the two evils, Andrić remarked at the end, the lesser should be chosen. On 9 February 1934, the Balkan Alliance between Yugoslavia, Turkey, Greece and Romania was signed in Athens with the aim of the preservation of the established territorial order in the Balkans, which was threatened by the revisionist policy of the countries defeated in the First World War, among which Bulgaria, backed by Germany, was the greatest threat. Within that agreement, Yugoslavia signed a special Convention with Turkey about moving the Muslim, mostly Albanian, population out to Turkey with adequate financial compensation. Thus, the Royal Government did not try to find a solution to the Muslim–Albanian issue in a versatile development of those peoples, but in their migration. However, that plan was not carried out because the Yugoslav government was afraid of submitting the Convention for the ratification, suspecting a public scandal. Yet, regardless of that fact, the migration of about 40,000 families was anticipated between 1939 and 1944. The plan failed only because of the shortage of funds as well as of the April war and the fall of the Kingdom of Yugoslavia in 1941.[10]

---

10. "Preglad Istorije Genocida nad Muslimanima u Jugoslavenskim Zemljama" (A survey of the history of genocide against the Muslims of Yugolsav lands), published by the Supreme Islamic Authorities in sfr Yugoslavia, in *The Herald (Glasnik)* (6), 71–2, 1991.

An Albanian view of Kosova and Kosovar identity

Although all Albanians would hotly maintain that Kosova is a part of the Albanian "homeland", and – in common with the vast majority of world opinion – would protest at the current total suppression of Albanian human rights there, they are not of one mind whether Kosova is a part of a "Greater Albania", or whether it should enjoy, as it once did within limits, an autonomous, or semi-independent, status within some "Balkan federation" (a "Yugoslav federation" was a pre-1991/2 possibility, if only their dream). Many Yugoslav Albanians sincerely held this view. John Halliday (in Appendix 1: "The Kosovo question") included within his memoirs of Enver Hoxha,[11] remarked:

> Kosovo represents two quite different things for the two states. For Belgrade it is a backward region, populated mainly by an unwelcome national minority, bordering on a state (Albania) with which relations are frosty and difficult. For Tirana, Kosovo is not only the historical centre of Albanian nationalism and resistance to the Turks, but also where some 1.7 million ethnic Albanians live – one third of all the Albanians in the world."

Nothing has changed, except that the total of Albanians has risen substantially since these words of his were penned. But, in happier days (certainly not today), Albanians in Kosova viewed a future in Yugoslavia as a possible choice. As Ramadan Marmullaku (himself a Yugoslav Albanian) wrote, in the mid-1970s:[12]

> The Albanians in Yugoslavia do not regard themselves as second-class citizens. Nationalism and separatism do exist among them but less than ever before. Their attitude towards Yugoslavia has altered considerably due to their national, political and cultural emancipation and through the general economic progress of Kosovo and the other areas that they inhabit in the federation. Foreign observers who regard the Albanians as one of the weak points of the Yugoslav federation base this assessment on the preoccupations of the Albanians before the socialist revolution, when bourgeois Yugoslavia was a prison for them. It was natural then that the demand for secession should be strong. However, in the multinational federal Yugoslavia of today, in which they enjoy equal rights and cultural, political and

---

11. Edited and introduced by John Halliday, *The artful Albanian: the memoirs of Enver Hoxha*, 34–343. (London: Chatto & Windus, 1986).
12. Ramadan Marmullaku, *Albania and the Albanians*, 151 (London: Hurst, 1975). Chapter 10 is one of the best surveys of Albanians in Yugoslavia, especially in Kosova.

economic emancipation, they feel at home and are committed to maintain the security and integrity of their homeland. The Albanians as well as the other Yugoslav peoples are aware who would profit from a possible conflict in this part of the Balkans.

What would he write today?

The individuality of the Kosovan Albanians has been commented upon and sometimes even criticized by other Albanians on historical, cultural and linguistic grounds. One such commentator is Arshi Pipa, born in 1920,[13] writer, scholar and linguist, whose family originates from Shkodra (Shkodër), the heartland of Gheg culture in the past. To him, Kosova is a region of Gheg resistance to the cultural authoritarianism of the Tosks, particularly so in language and culture. But his views extend far wider than this. Unlike the Serbian view, he assesses Albanian allegiance to Islam (as a belief system) to be but skin deep:[14]

The Albanians have no innate religious vocation of the theistic type. Going back to their ancestors, Diocletian persecuted the Christians; and Julian, a nephew of Constantine 1, was called Apostate because he tried to restore Roman polytheism. Scanderbeg was born an Orthodox and raised as a Moslem while a hostage in the Ottoman court, then acted as a Catholic for the rest of his life. Albanian Bektashism is essentially a pantheistic religion (sic). Sunnite Moslems used religion to gain privileges. Kosovars became attached to Islam the better to differentiate themselves from Orthodox Slavs, their foes. No longer than a generation ago, extended families in secluded cantons (such as that of Lura) could still be found in which both Bairam and Easter were celebrated. Nor were the Orthodox conspicuous for religious fervour. The princely dynasties of central and Southern Albania embraced Islam to a man. Those who resisted conversion, mostly peasants, paid for their religious freedom with the lowering of their social status to that of declassed rayah-s.

At the same time, he concedes that the Kosovars were, for long, instinctively loyal to the Islam they shakily professed, while playing a leading part in the Albanian national movements:[15]

The case of the Muslim Kosovars is different. They remained faithful to Islam and the Sultan (as shown also by their epic songs) until the

---

13. For a brief biography of Arshi Pipa, see Robert Elsie, *Dictionary of Albanian literature*, 111 (Westport, Connecticut: Greenwood Press, 1986).
14. *The politics of language in socialist Albania*, 195–6 (New York: Columbia University Press, 1989).
15. Ibid., 119.

League of Prizren, in which however, their role, after the Great Powers decided that Plave and Gusinje should go to Montenegro, was paramount. Prizren rebelled against paying higher taxes in 1885, rebellion subsequently spreading through the entire Kosova province vilayet. Kosovar irregular troops in the service of the Turkish government repressed the Macedonian revolt (1901–02) while also committing atrocities against Serbs. Their pro-Turkish stance in general gradually changed when some of their more enlightened leaders (Hasan Prishtina, Nexhip Draga, Dervish Hima) realized that the Ottoman Empire's days were numbered. A protest in Ferizovic against the construction of a railway line through Kosova by the Hapsburg Empire (1908) spared an insurrectional movement that toppled the Turkish government, bring the Young Turks into power. Among them were many Albanians, including a main founder of the Young Turk organization, Ibrahim Temo. And it was the Kosovars assembled in Prishtine in 1912 who, disappointed by the chauvinistic policies of the Young Turks, exacted the dissolution of the Turkish Parliament, followed by the demise of the Young Turk government. And when Albanian independence was proclaimed a couple of months later, it was Kosovar troops who marched to Vlöre to buttress the government of Ismail Qemal.

However, the Kosovar's written Gheg hardly appealed to Pipa as a praiseworthy expression of shqip[16]:

What Kosovars write today is not "unified literary Albanian", but a language neither Tosk nor Gheg, which is instead a mishmash of Kosovar patterns of speech mixed up with clichés borrowed from official Albanian and also from Serbo–Croatian. Reading Kosovar newspapers, one runs into sentences whose spurious wording does not make sense, their scholarly writing is awkward and verbose, and poems are inferior to the ones previously written in Kosovarçe.

---

16. Ibid., 255. According to Fehime Pipa in *Elementary Albanian, Filltar i Shqipes*, p. VI (Boston, Massachusetts: Vatra, 1968), "A third Gheg literary idiom has lately appeared; it is the idiom of Kosova, "kosovarçe". Although written specimens of that idiom date from the seventeenth century (Pjeter Bogdani, the most important of the old Albanian writers, published his *Cuneus Prophetarum* in 1685), the idiom did not achieve literary status until recently, in the Albanian part of Yugoslavia called Kosmet, an abbreviation of the two words Kosova and Metohija, the two Albanian regions comprising an "autonomous region" within the Yugoslavian federal republic of Serbia. The literary idiom of Kosmet today is basically Middle Gheg: however, it includes enough native elements to make it distinct from the latter. The "kosovarçe" can best be described as intermediate between "shkodrançe" and Middle Gheg'. On the religious element in the Albanian language of Kosova, see Albert B. Lord, "The Battle of Kosovo in Albanian and Serbocroatian oral epic songs", in *Studies on Kosova* (New York: Boulder, 1984).

The Islamic heritage among the Kosovars

The Muslim presentation of the Kosovar cause may be broadly divided into categories:

- The superficially informed, well meaning reports or article, published in the Arab or Muslim Press, or through political journals and newspapers such as *Q News International* or through the radio or television.
- Journals with either professional, academic, or educational pretensions, which attempt to explain the woes that beset Muslim minorities to those who inherit the heart of the Muslim World. One of the best informed in the English language, and we are speaking here of articles of a good academic standard, is the *Journal of Muslim Minority Affairs*, published in the United Kingdom. This has published a series of articles about Muslims in ex-Yugoslavia. At a more popular level is the journal of *al-ʿArabī* (printed in Kuwait), which some years ago published (with photos) one of the best written and informed Arab reports on Muslim life in Kosova.[17] Its author, Dr Fahmi Huwaydi, an ex-journalist of *al-Ahrām*, was helped by the Albano–Syrian academic, Dr Muhammad Mūfākū, formerly of the University of Prishtine, and now in the University of Āl al-Bayt, Mafraq, Jordan. Mūfākū's many articles and books (among them being a *History of Islamic Belgrade*, Kuwait 1407/1987). This may be viewed as a vigorous [unintentional?] riposte to Serbian claims), have done much to make the culture of Kosova better known in the Arab World.

Islamic culture took root and began to flourish at a relatively early date in Kosova. The great Ottoman poet, Mesihi, of the Dukagjin family, born in Prishtine, died at the beginning of the sixteenth century. The Fatih mosque in that city was founded in 1416 by Sultan Muhammad II. The process of Islamization was similar to what took place in adjacent Macedonia. It has been explained and described in detail by John Thirkell.[18] The foundation of mekteb-s (Qu'ānic), libraries and tekke-s (Sufi chapels) was

---

17. Details regarding this Egyptian author, and an English translation of the article, may be found in "Muslim Albanian cultural identity in Modern Kosovo, the personal impressions of a contemporary Arab reporter", *The South Slav Journal* 13(1–2), (47–8), 38–54, 1990. As a minor Middle Eastern factor, one might also mention the emigration of Muslim Circassians from the Caucasus to Kosova (as elsewhere in former Yugoslavia) in 1864. The numbers vary from 6,000 to above 30,000. They settled in Grijilane, Urosevac, Prizren, Gracanica, Prishtine, Vucitru and Kosovska Mitrovica. See Alexandre Popović, "Les Cerkesses dans les territoires Yougoslaves", *Bulletin d'Études Orientales* XXX, 159–71 (esp. 163–4), 1978. He furnishes sources on p. 164, *n*. 18, to two sources (G. Bullemer and N. Zupanic) where maps of Circassian settlement in Kosova are available.
18. John Thirkell, "Islamization in Macedonia as a social process", in *Islam and the Balkans, papers arising from a symposium held to celebrate the World of Islam Festival at the Royal Scottish Museum, Edinburgh, 28–30 July 1976*, Jennifer M. Scarce (ed.), 43–8 (Edinburgh: the Royal Scottish Museum, 1979).

well in progress by the sixteenth century, and Kosova was to become an important centre for sundry Sufi orders.[19]

If Islamic letters developed early, they also continued late. As Dr Mufaku has shown, the continued use of the Arabic script as the sole medium for the literary expression of Albanian, verse and prose, was to continue in Kosova well after the adoption of the Latin alphabet in Albania itself. Hence, Albanian was kept alive when otherwise proscribed, and with it a variety of scholarly descriptions both religious and secular. Nearly all the most noted poets were men of the "cloth", or were the product of Sufi schools; poets such as Shehu Hyseni Halvative of Prizren (1872–1926), Sheh Hilmi Maliqi, also of Prizren (1865–1928), Hafiz Islam Bytyci (b. 1910 and assassinated in 1934), Hafiz Imer Shemsiu of Prishtine (d. 1945), Shaip Zuranxhiu of Rahovec (1884–1951) and Vesel Xhalaludin Guta (born 1905 near Ferizaj).

It is true that all of this long post-dated the mighty works of Serbian art, the churches and the monasteries, but the Albanians in Kosova were to develop their own Islamic culture, provincial Ottoman in its architecture, but essentially individual in its verse and prose, lofty in sentiment and making its own contribution to Albanian literature, which, over a period of time, became wholly distinct from its Turkish models.[20]

The Kosovars formed a part of the Islamic Community in Yugoslavia. Islam was implicitly recognized as a faith in Serbia in 1868, and explicitly from the text of the law in 1878, so likewise in that same year in Montenegro and in Bosnia and Herzegovina. In the latter, the Austro–Hungarian administration created the post of "Supreme religious scholar and authority" (Ra'īs al-ʿUlamā), on the basis of an order issued on the 24 October 1882. This was aimed at regulating "Muhammadan and religious relations". The Muslims in Serbian territories composed a separate administrative unit. This latter community was headed by a mufti after 878. His seat was in Nis. A certain number of imam-s and mufti-s were in charge of the Canonic law of Islam (Sharīʿa), and also of the management of religious endowments (waqf-s). Following the Balkan Wars in 1912 and 1913, and

19. For a comprehensive description of these orders, see A. Popović & G. Veinstein, "Les ordres mystiques musulman du sud-est Européen dans la periode post-Ottomane", in *Les ordres mystique Musulmans*, 63–9 (Paris: EHESS 1986). This is followed by Darko Tanaskovic's "Présentation du conq temoignages sur les ordres mystiques Yougoslaves", 101–04. Kosova figures prominently in this article. Another article by this same author is "La situation actuelle de l'ordre des Naqshabandis au Kosovo et en Macedonie", *Naqshbandis* [Proceedings of the Sèvres Round Table, 2–4 May 1985, *Varia Turcica*, XVIII, 681–90.

20. On some biographical details see my "Twentieth century men of letters among the Albanian Kosovan Sufis" in *Sufi*, London issue, Winter 1990–91, pp.22–24. The whole subject has been discussed in far greater length in my book, *Islam in the Balkans* published by C. Hurst and Company, London 1993. Muhammad Mūfākū al-Arnaut has published the content and the sources for much of his arguments in *al-Thaqafa al-Albaniyya fi'l- Abjadiyya al-ʿArabiyya*, ʿĀlam al-Maʿrifa, Kuwait 1983.

following the subjugation of the Muslim population of the Sanjak of Novi Pazar, Kosova and Metohija and their transfer to Serbia, there was a further development of Muslim religious administration; supreme mufti (baş mufti) was appointed to be the head of the hierarchy. In various regions there were appointed lesser mufti-s together with a corresponding number of imam-s in charge of mosques, and official preachers of Friday sermons (khatib-s). The executive matters that were concerned with the day-to-day functioning of Islamic religious administration had been regulated by the Treaty of Istanbul, between Turkey and Serbia, and made on the 14 March 1914. It had been planned to have the Supreme Head appointed by the King, to be chosen from among the three candidates to be proposed by the mufti-s. Then the Shaykh al-Islam in Istanbul would issue a public declaration (manshura) to the supreme mufti. The latter would then delegate to other mufti-s the specific right of Sharīʿa jurisdiction and the issue of legal rulings (fatwa-s).

The Istanbul Treaty was not to be ratified, owing to the outbreak of the First World War. The proposals that were contained within it affected the interior jurisdiction of the Serbian state in respect of the regulating of Islamic religious affairs.

Once Yugoslavia had come into existence, what had been agreed hitherto was to be incorporated as a part of a united religious administration for the entire country. Among its new rules was that which governed the issue of the manshura. A special council consisting of Muslim dignitaries would give it to the Ra'īs al-ʿUlamā. From the year 1930, this was included within the Statute of the Islamic Religious Community of the Kingdom of Yugoslavia (Article 64). The Statute of the community, which was passed as late as 1990, approved of the committees that were to be found in territories where several congregations (jamāʿat) of Muslims existed. Offices for mufti-s were organized in areas where there were several committees of the Islamic Community. These correspond to the regions in which the entire country was divided.

The Supreme Assembly of the Islamic Community was the highest representative body of Yugoslav Muslims. The executive organ of that body was the Riyasa, which was headed by the Ra'īs al-ʿUlamā. Subject to the Islamic community, and within the jurisdiction of it, were the chief educational establishments, which in Kosova included a secondary Islamic school (madrasa) located in Prishtine. Officials of the Islamic Community, at varied levels, were khatib-s, teachers (muʿallim-s), exhortators in regular sermons (at times a sort of "lay preacher", wāʿiẓ-s), mufti-s, and so on, and teachers attached to mosques, Sufi tekke-s and the like, forming "chapel circuits".

Hence, as the above outline reveals, the Albanian Kosovars, who were Muslim in faith, were part of a system that was dovetailed into that of the Muslim community in Yugoslavia as a whole, including Bosnia and

Herzegovina, which lay at its heart and was supremely centered in Sarajevo. Hence, any policy that affected, indeed afflicted, one region was to affect the other profoundly whatever the differences between the Islam that was practised among Slavs or Albanians.[21]

Conclusions

In the light of the above opinions, and by sifting of sundry and alleged facts that are presented, the following tentative conclusions in regard to Kosova's future are offered:

- An ancient distribution of "ethnic elements" and not only the recent and the current, have significance in Balkan calculations. They clearly figure prominently where a planned shifting of population or a redrawing of boundaries are concerned. These matter enormously to the principal contenders.
- "Religious idealism" driven to extreme length will probably continue to weigh heavily in Serbian policy.[22] Kosova will be one focus, however large or small in number the Serbian element may in time become. No proposed solution (put forward by the West or the UNO) is likely to alter this ingrained position (which parallels in some respects the religious cum nationalist viewpoint, in Russia, à propos Islam and Catholicism). Such an attitude will long prevail. It may even harden and will continue, however disguised, until well into the next century.
- The Albanian case for self-rule and recovery of rights in Kosova is not simply an assertion of cultural identity, strongly felt, or of a national

---

21. For a fuller explanation and outline of the organization of the leadership of the Islamic community in Yugoslavia (and I am greatly indebted to it here), see the publication of the Islamska Zajednica u Jugoslaviji Institutucije i Pripadnici "The Islamic Community in Jugoslavia, its institutions and Muslims", published in *The Herald (Glasnik)*, no. 4 (Sarajevo: Supreme Islamic Authorities in SFR Yugoslavia, 1991). This was in Serbo–Croat, English and Arabic. The English translation is by Zulehja Ridanovic. This publication (see also *n.* 9) is probably most readily available as an offprint (a copy is to be found in the library of the School of Oriental and African Studies, University of London; pp. 16–21).

22. The deliberate targeting of cultural and religious monuments (churches, including Serbian Orthodox churches, Catholic monasteries and libraries, mosques and major collections of Islamic manuscripts) by Serbian artillery pieces and arsonists can hardly be matched in recent times, save perhaps in Cambodia, Tibet and the holy cities of the Shīʿites, by the forces loyal to Saddam Hussein. Contrast this with the situation in Hungary, where great efforts have been made to preserve and restore Ottoman religious monuments. Little is available in print in English (other than "Yugoslav" guide books) on the mosques in Kosova. However, Machiel Kiel has, with Nimetullah Hafiz, contributed an interesting article, entitled "The mosque of Kel Hasan Aga in the village of Rogova: an unknown Ottoman monument of the sixteenth century in the Kosovo district" in *Studies on the Ottoman Architecture of the Balkans*, XI (Aldershot: Variorum Reprints [CS326], 1990; reprinted from *Prilozi za Orijentalnu Filologiju* 28/29, 411–21, Sarajevo, 1980).

pride. It has Islamic aspects (massaged of course for political purposes, and spotlighted by the Serbs) that transcend the existing
boundaries in the Balkans.

- A new policy *vis-à-vis* the Kosovars (as distinct from the position of
Enver Hoxha and pre-democratic Albania) has not yet emerged
clearly in Albania. Some wish to disassociate themselves. It is obviously being shaped in the light of evolving events, not only in Kosova
itself, but also in Bosnia–Herzegovina, in the Sanjak and in Macedonia.

- Since Islam in Kosova was "Sufi-conditioned" and "tekke" (teqeja)
based (see Ch. 6, pp. 84), it displays certain characteristics and offers
survival strategies more akin to those known in the Caucasus
and Central Asia (i.e. "parallel Islam") made familiar in the works of
Alexandre Bennigsen.[23]

- Regrettably, the "pragmatic" approach, apparent in Bulgaria, in
relation to its ethnic Turks, is unlikely to appeal to Serb and Albanian.
Serb ethnocentricity exists to a degree of paranoia that is hardly to be
matched elsewhere in the Balkans.

- Continued repressive military occupation of Kosova and population
expulsion cannot furnish either a short-term, let alone a long-term,
solution. Internationalization could be grave. Unlike the Bosnians,
until recently, the Albanians were, and still are, presumably better
known in the Middle East countries and they still have a voice in Cairo,
Damascus, Kuwait, Algiers and elsewhere. Syria is crucial, because of
its key position as a bridge between Sunni and Shi'ite Islam. Popular
reaction, among so different a public as in Turkey, Pakistan and Iran,
is likely to be fierce in the event of Kosovar or Macedonian crisis
comparable with or worse than in Bosnia–Herzegovina. Its effect on
the dwindling Orthodox and Oriental Christian communities in the
Middle East could be very severe, and possibly lead to a "backlash"
against the Copts in Egypt, although the chief target would be the
West.[24]

---

23. Alexandra Bennigsen & S. Enders Wimbush, *Mystics and commissars: Sufism in the Soviet Union* (London: Hurst, 1985).

24. The best general introduction to the whole subject of the Albanians within the wider world of Islam is to be found in Odile Daniel, "The historical role of the Muslim commu-nity in Albania", *Central Asian Survey* 9(3), 1–28, 1990. Muslim opinion in Britain is increasingly hardening against the West and finds evidence of a "secret agenda" at the Muslim's expense, not only in Bosnia–Herzegovina, but also elsewhere, not excluding Kosova. This can be illustrated by the article, "Distorting Balkan history" in *Q News International Limited* 1(15), 5, 1992 and "Kosovo. The violence intensifies" in *Q News International Limited* 3(9), 5, 1994, quoting Amnesty International. Of course, it echoes many reports in the Western media, such as are quoted in the article, "US promotes Serbian genocide – Washington, London, Paris, all connive at butchery of Bosnians" in *The New Federalist* VL(31), 1 and 4, col. 5, 1992.

CHAPTER THREE
Slovenia in the new geopolitical context
NATASHA MILANOVICH

Introduction

Slovenia is a new independent country since 1991 and a former northwest republic of the Yugoslav Federation. It is situated at the edge of central, western and southeastern Europe covering an area of 20,256 km² and, with the population of 2 million, Slovenia has a strategic location between the southern side of the Alps, the northern Adriatic, and the edge of the central European Pannonian plain. Slovenia shares borders with Italy, Austria, Hungary and Croatia. Traffic from the southwestern European states of Spain, France and Italy crosses Slovenian territory towards the landlocked countries of central Europe: Hungary, the Czech Republic and Slovakia, and the former Soviet Republics. Traditionally, the northern Adriatic ports Venezia and Trieste in Italy, Koper (Capodistria) in Slovenia, and Rijeka (Fiume) in Croatia have served as gateway for landlocked Austria and a German state of Bavaria (see Figs 3.1 and 3.2).

Slovenia is ethnically a homogeneous country. About 90 per cent of population are Slovenes, others are mostly of Croatian, Serbian, Muslim, Hungarian and Italian origin, although only small Italian and Hungarian communities constitute officially recognized minorities. The majority of the population are Roman Catholics, and a small Protestant minority exists in the northeast along the Hungarian border. The capital of Slovenia is Ljubljana, a magnificent baroque city with about 270,000 inhabitants in 1994, and there are also dozens of medium-size and small towns forming a polycentric pattern of urbanization. The official language is Slovenian. Throughout the history, Slovenia has retained its own cultural identity, while also being influenced by such diverse groups as the Celts and Romans to the Habsburgs and South Slavs (see Fig. 3.3).

Throughout history, Slovenia was more a bridge between different nations than the crossroads or an area of co-operation between peoples of different origins and cultures. The strategic location and cultural and economic advantages of Slovenia are becoming more important in European integration processes, and as a sovereign and independent state, Slovenia could become a crossroads and a region of co-operation between western, central and eastern Europe.

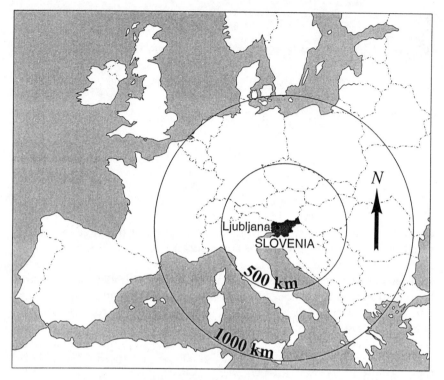

Figure 3.1   Slovenia in Europe.

Slovenes, the Habsburg monarchy and Yugoslavia

Traditionally, Slovenia has an image of a land-locked country between "Prussia and Russia", that is to say, between the Germanic and Slavonic domains and, also of being under the strong influence of Latin traditions. Slovenes lost their independence over a thousand years ago when Prince Kocelj briefly established an independent state of Slovenes in Lower Pannonia (869–74) and was ruled by Bavarian, Frankish, Czech and Habsburg masters. In 1335 it became the hereditary possession of the house of Habsburgs, and between the fourteenth and sixteenth centuries the Habsburg Monarchy was the first to include all of the Slovenian regions until the end of the First World War in 1918, when Slovenia became a constituent country of the Kingdom of Serbs, Croats and Slovenes, known from 1929 as Yugoslavia. Thus, for centuries the institutions governing the Slovenian people were identical with those of Austria, and Germanic influence left important mark on Slovenian life (Vodopivec 1993). From the ninth century, alongside the growing influence of Christianity, Slovenes maintained their Slavic identity, and the Slovene language was increas-

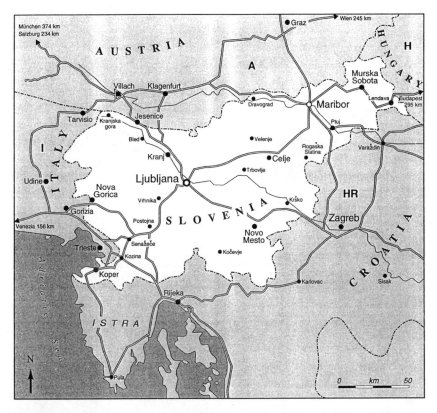

Figure 3.2 Slovenia and its neighbours. *Source:* Zavod RS za statistiko; Republiška geodetska uprava. Slovenia 1993.

ingly used in religious services. The Reformation in the sixteenth century brought a new impetus to Slovene culture and, in spite of the Germanic and Latin influences, the Slovenes maintained a surprisingly high awareness of their own language. The first book, *"Catechismus"*, was published in the Slovenian language by protestant minister Primoz Trubar in 1551, and in 1584 Jurij Dalmatin translated the Bible into Slovene language (Lenček 1984).

The Vienna–Ljubljana railway was built in 1849 and the powerful Habsburg government strengthened the economy of the Empire. Slovenia was providing agricultural produce for the northern part of the monarchy and gave Austria direct access to the Adriatic see. The limited cultural emancipation in the nineteenth century influenced the demands for political autonomy. In 1848, Slovene intellectuals issued the first political programme for a "United Slovenia" for the unification of all Slovene ethnic territories with their own parliament, where Slovenian would be the language of education and local government. In the late nineteenth century

27

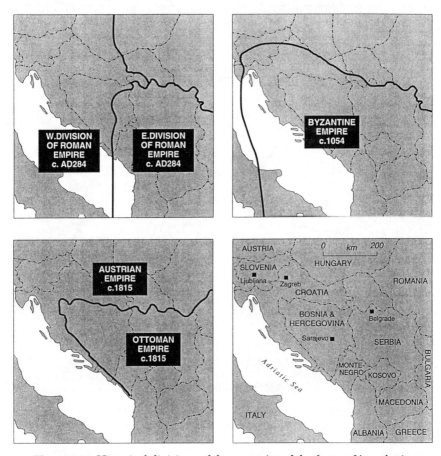

Figure 3.3   Historical divisions of the countries of the former Yugoslavia.

the Slovenes increasingly sought co-operation and partnership with other Slavs in the Habsburg Empire, although few then contemplated a break-away from the Habsburg Monarchy. Slovene intellectuals were still educated in Prague, Vienna or Berlin until the first Slovene university was founded in Ljubljana in the new state of Kingdom of Serbs, Croats and Slovenes in 1919 (Vodopivec 1993).

After the collapse and disintegration of Austria–Hungary in 1918, the Slovenes joined with the neighbouring Croats and the victorious Serbs to form the Kingdom of Serbs, Croats and Slovenes, known as Yugoslavia from 1929. The Slovenes entered the new state with a much reduced terri-tory and about half a million Slovenes were left in Austria, Italy or Hun-gary. In the west of Slovenia, coastal territory was lost to Italy as a reward for changing alliance during the First World War, and in north Carinthia the population voted in a plebiscite to remain in Austria. In the Kingdom of Yugoslavia, Slovenia was a single administrative unit, the province of Drava, where Slovenes enjoyed cultural and linguistic autonomy, but there were no major changes in its political status, as the state administration and decision-making were under the control of Belgrade. Despite the fact that the industrialization process was more advanced and Slovenia was the most developed part of Yugoslavia between the two world wars the Slovenian economy remained mainly agricultural (Svetlik 1992).

In April 1941, at the outbreak of the Second World War in Yugoslavia, Slovenia was divided between Germany and Italy. This lasted until 1945 when Yugoslavia became a communist country and a federation of six republics. The 1950s and 1960s were the years of reconstruction and redevelopment when the processes of industrialization and economic growth were very intensive. In 1948, Slovenia's population was 47 per cent agricultural; however, as a consequence of the industrialization process only 7.6 per cent was agricultural in 1991, and agriculture and fishing accounted for only 4.5 per cent of social product, with manufacturing at about 50 per cent (Vodopivec 1993). During the 1960s and 1970s, new light manufacturing industries were built in order to meet the consumption needs of citizens and to increase exports. These industries were especially dominant in Slovenia, which facilitated intensive economic growth, increased the level of employment and generated a high level of exports (Svetlik 1992). Open borders with Austria and Italy, a degree of public enterprise autonomy and limited market economy, allowed Slovenia to become remarkably prosperous by the early 1970s, when Communist Party leaders in Yugoslavia embarked upon another massive employment similar to the 1950s and, a new investment cycle was initiated, based on foreign loans. These developments brought to Slovenia as a workforce in industry many "guest workers" from the other less developed regions of Yugoslavia, namely Croatia, Bosnia and Herzegovina, and Serbia. The levels of development varied considerably between the six republics; Slovenia was the most highly industrialized and advanced. With 8.2 per cent of the total Yugoslav population, Slovenia was in 1989 responsible for 20.0 per cent of gross national product, 22.2 per cent of exports and 18.5 per cent of imports, and productivity was on average twice as high as in Yugoslavia as a whole (Cvikl et al. 1993).

A distinctive characteristic of the Yugoslav Federation was its multi-ethnic structure and, hence, decentralized method of administration. The level of autonomy of the republics was constantly increasing during 1960s and the stronger demands for the autonomy were weakening the Yugoslav Communist Party. As a result, a new Constitution was passed in 1974, increasing the autonomy of the republics and the articulation of their specific interests, but common policies were increasingly made on a consensus basis. When a consensus was not possible, the Yugoslav Communist Party, known as League of Communists of Yugoslavia, imposed itself

Table 3.1 Basic indicators of Yugoslavia and its republics.

	Year	Yugoslavia	Bosnia and Herzegovina	Monte-negro	Croatia	Macedonia	Slovenia	Serbia
Population (000)	1989	23,690	4,479	639	4,683	2,111	1,948	9,830
Population (%)	1989	100	18.9	2.7	19.8	8.9	8.2	41.5
GNP per capita*	1955	100	80	80	120	60	160	80
	1989	100	65	71	129	65	200	88
Exports (%)	1989	100	16.8	1.8	20.6	5.3	22.2	33.2
Imports (%)	1989	100	12.9	1.1	26.6	6.0	18.5	33.1
Employment (%)	1989	100	15.8	2.5	23.5	7.7	12.4	38.1
Unemployment rate (%)	1989	11.6	16.2	19.2	6.6	17.4	2.8	17.5

Note: * Percentage of national average
Source: Cvikl, M. 1993, Statistical Yearbooks of Yugoslavia, various years.

as an arbiter. Since the League of Communists was also increasingly fed-eralized and losing its power, decision-making on the federal level became more difficult (Svetlik 1992). However, the Yugoslav economic system proved less adaptable to the difficulties posed by the oil crises of the 1970s, and throughout the 1980s economic crisis persisted, characterizing by a falling GNP and real wages, the pressure of foreign debts, hyper-inflation and increasing unemployment. The changes in the political and economic system started in the mid-1980s when the League of Communists started to lose its power and legitimacy because of an increasing economic crisis.

In the northwest part of Yugoslav Federation, Slovenia and Croatia demanded intensified economic and political links with the Economic Community and EFTA countries, the introduction of a market economy and a political democracy, whereas Serbian politicians wanted to centralize power in Belgrade and to continue the policy of non-alignment and sus-taining the existing political and economic system. From 1986 to 1989, despite publishing several documents announcing the elimination of the political monopoly, its separation from the state, pluralization of the polit-ical scene and introduction of the market economy, the Yugoslav Commu-nist Party, rejected the idea of party pluralism until 1990, when the first free party elections since the Second World War were held in all republics of the former Yugoslav Federation.

When in 1989 the liberal group at the Communist Party of Slovenia won political control in the republic, the democratization process started, which led to increasing conflicts with Belgrade. In December 1989, Serbian poli-ticians declared a boycott of Slovene-produced goods because of Slovenia's critical orientation towards Serbia's policies in Kosovo. In January 1990 at the Congress of the League of Communists of Yugoslavia, a Slovenian proposal to restructure the Party and the country as a democratic confederation of sovereign republics, or asymmetric federation, was rejected. In the following months the Slovenian Communist Party changed the name to the Party of Democratic Reforms and in April 1990 the multi-party elections were held, when a right-of-centre non-communist block, Democratic Opposition (DEMOS), won 55 per cent of the votes and formed a government under Lojze Peterle, the leader of the Christian Democratic Party (Svetlik 1992).

As a result of intensive economic development after the Second World War, cross-border co-operation with Austria, Italy and other European countries, cultural identity, political maturity and support of its own people at the end of 1980s, Slovenia became to think of itself as an Alpine and central European nation, different from the Balkans and with prospects in new European integration processes. The question is what would happen if Slovenia left Yugoslav Federation to become a part of another federation, namely the European Union, and what are the costs and benefits of separation from Yugoslavia?

Slovenia: towards a new identity

The political scene

Several civic movements and associations in Slovenia began politically exerting pressure on the Communist Party elite at the end of 1980s. Among the first was a group of journalists of the popular weekly magazine *Mladina* (*Youth*), publishing articles on such topics as privileges of the Yugoslav Communist Party elite and illegal activities of the Yugoslav Army. In 1988 a few Slovenian journalists were arrested by the Yugoslav Army and Slovenian police, despite the opposition from Slovenian representatives in the Federal Parliament and League of Communist of Yugoslavia. The Board for the Defence of Human Rights was formed, which enjoyed massive support by the Slovenian people, and public demonstrations were organized where human rights for the imprisoned journalists and political pluralization were demanded (Simmie 1991, Svetlik 1992).

During the 1989 the following groups and associations were founded in Slovenia: Peace Movement, Group of Amnesty International, Board of Defence of Human Rights, Group of Helsinki Watch, Association of Writers, Sociological Association, Commission for Equity and Peace, and so on. In 1990 the Slovenian National Assembly accepted amendments to the Slovenian Constitution, which facilitated political pluralization and the introduction of the market economy. During 1990 the following political parties were founded: Slovenian Farmers' Alliance (now Slovenian Peoples' Party), Social Democratic Alliance (now Social Democratic Party), Christian Democratic Party, Green Party, and so on. The bases of some of the parties can be recognized in the period before the Second World War. The Slovene Christian Democratic Party is a successor of the pre- Second World War Slovenian People's Party and it is mainly supported by the rural population and religious people in the cities, who over the decades after the Second World War moved into towns during intensive industrialization of the country (Svetlik 1992).

Several of the major opposition political groups established a Centre–Right coalition Democratic Opposition of Slovenia, called DEMOS: the Slovenian Democratic Alliance, the Slovenian Christian Democrats, the Slovenian Farmers' Alliance, the Green Party, the Slovenian Artisans Party and the Social Democratic Alliance of Slovenia (ibid.). DEMOS was headed by Dr Joze Pucnik, a philosophy professor who was living in exile in West Germany for two decades. The common goal uniting DEMOS's diverse parties was defeating of the ruling Communist Party. Outside the DEMOS coalition, at the centre of the political spectrum was the League of Socialist Youth of Slovenia – Liberal Democratic Party and, left-of-centre Party for Democratic Reforms – the reformed Communist Party – led by Milan Kucan, with a social democratic programme advocated the strengthening of Slovenian political autonomy within a reorganized and "confederal" Yugoslav state. Pucnik and Kucan, in addition to being leaders of the two strongest parties, were candidates for the presidency of Slovenia (Broken Bonds 1993).

The First Democratic Elections in Slovenia in 1990

The first democratic elections since the Second World War were held between April and December 1990 in all six republics of the Yugoslav Federation, which exposed their divergent political aspirations and initiated the independence process in Slovenia, Croatia, Macedonia and Bosnia–Herzegovina. Slovenia, Croatia and Macedonia voted overwhelmingly for independence from the Yugoslav Federation in a separate referendum held in December 1990 in Slovenia, in May 1991 in Croatia and in September 1991 in Macedonia. These republics adopted new constitutions (Croatia in December 1990, Macedonia in November 1991 and Slovenia in December 1991) and each republic introduced its own currency (Slovenia in October 1991, Croatia in December 1991 and Macedonia in April 1992; World Bank 1993).

Although 17 parties took part in the first democratic elections in Slovenia in April 1990, it was a centre-right DEMOS coalition victory, obtaining about 55 per cent of the vote: the Christian Democratic Party won 13 per cent of the vote; the Slovenian Democratic Alliance with intellectuals and middle-class people as its electoral base received 9.5 per cent of the vote; the Green Party of Slovenia who based its programme on the preservation of the environment and whose most enthusiastic supporters were young and highly educated people, won 8.8 per cent of the vote; the Slovenian

Farmers' Alliance found members mainly among the rural population and gained 12.6 per cent of votes. Disappointed industrial workers supported by the Social Democratic Party of Slovenia led by Dr Joze Pucnik gained 7.4 per cent of the votes. The Slovenian managers and owners of small companies united in the Slovenian Artisans Party won 3.5 per cent. The former Communist Party for Democratic Reforms got 17 per cent, and the Liberal Democratic Party, which at the beginning represented the communist youth organization in Slovenia and supported by liberally oriented intellectuals and the middle-classes, won 15 per cent of the votes. Therefore, the two strongest single parties in the Parliament became the Party of Democratic Reforms, which although they had lost power were not eliminated from political life, followed by Christian Democrats. The first prime minister became Lojze Peterle, the leader of the Christian Democrats and the strongest party in the DEMOS coalition (Svetlik 1992). However, the president of the former Communist Party of Slovenia, Milan Kucan, won the first democratic presidential elections. His success was a result of his personal popularity, closely related to his strong advocacy of Slovenian interests in the dialogue with the Yugoslav Federal government and military establishment, and defiance of Serbia's communist leader Slobodan Milosevic during the late 1980s.

The results of the first multi-party elections in 1990 showed that the Slovenian people voted against the communist regime, in spite of their losing power, they won enough votes to preserve decision-making in the parliament. In addition to shifting to a parliamentary democracy and a market-orientated economy, Slovenia also became an independent country in 1991.

The emergence of Slovenia: independence and a break up with Yugoslavia
In a referendum in December 1990 the overwhelming majority of the population voted in favour of a sovereign and independent state. Despite of the results of the referendum, the Slovenian government, together with Croatia, still opted for reorganization of the Yugoslav Federation on the basis of a confederation or asymmetric federation. In Spring 1991 Slovenia stopped sending recruits to the Yugoslav Army and founded its own. On 23 June 1991, the members of the European Community unanimously voted not to recognize the independence of Slovenia and Croatia if those republics unilaterally seceded from the Yugoslav Federation. On 25 June, 1991 the Slovenian Assembly accepted a Sovereignty Act for the Independence of Slovenia and proclaimed independence on 26 June 1991 (Ministry of Tourism 1993).

The decision by Slovenia and Croatia to proceed with their plans for independence in June 1991 open an entirely new phase in the Yugoslav crisis. In the case of Slovenia, the republic's assertion of sovereignty from the Yugoslav Federation precipitated a short but fierce war between Slovenian forces and the Yugoslav Army that ended in a debacle for the federal military forces. After ten days of fighting, a cease-fire was arranged by a negotiating team from the European Community, and by October 1991 the Yugoslav Army, which had been considered as a Serbian communist occupation force, had withdrawn its forces entirely from Slovenia. On 8 October 1991, following the expiry of the moratorium, Slovenia became independent country, introduced its own currency and passed the new Constitution on 23 December 1991 (World Bank 1993). Germany was the first European country to recognize Slovenia, followed by Sweden and Iceland and on 15 January 1992 the European Community recognized Slovenia and Croatia as newly independent states. In April 1992 Slovenia was recognized by the USA and became the 176th member of the United Nations in May 1992 (Government of Slovenia 1994). Since then Slovenia has been intensively applying for membership and association agreements to join international organizations and institutions.

The first democratic government of Slovenia, elected in spring 1990, succeeded with the "independence project" in close co-operation with the opposition parties. The declaration of independence in Slovenia was a free political choice resulting from an economic, monetary and communications blockade by Serbia, and after many unsuccessful negotiations within the Yugoslav Federation no other alternative was possible. As the economic situation steadily deteriorated,partly because of the loss of the markets and sources of raw materials in the former Yugoslavia, production in Slovenia declined and unemployment grew, and the DEMOS government was inevitably blamed for failure to implement an effective economic stabilization programme. DEMOS was a coalition of different parties with divergent ideologies and as a consequence they could not agree on domestic policy, most notably the Law on Privatization and the Law on the Election System. Therefore, the government had diminishing support from parliament. At the same time, the DEMOS coalition government faced strong opposition from the Liberal Democrats and the former Communist Party for Democratic Reforms. Completing its historic role, defeating the communists in the first multi-party elections in 1990, DEMOS split in December 1991 and dissolved in February 1992. In May 1992 the prime minister, Lojze Peterle, resigned in favour of Dr Janez Drnovsek, the leader of the Liberal Democratic Party, who became a Slovenian delegate in the Assembly of the Republics and Autonomous Regions of Yugoslav Federation in 1984 and the last President of the Yugoslav Federation in 1989–90. He succeeded in overthrowing Peterle's government by forming a new party coalition consisting of the Liberal Democratic Party, the Christian Democratic Party, the Green Party and the Social Democratic Party of Slovenia. This government was also supported by most of the former communists in the Party of Democratic Reforms. Dr Drnovsek regarded his administration as transitional, involving experts rather than politicians in the run-up to the general elections in December 1992.

The Parliamentary and Presidential Elections in 1992 and a Second Coalition Government

In the second parliamentary elections in December 1992, 22 parties participated in the elections and 8 of them received enough votes to enter the Parliament:

- the Liberal Democratic Party 23.4 per cent
- the Christian Democratic Party 14.5 per cent
- the United List of Social Democrats (composed of several left-wing parties, most notably former communists) 13.6 per cent
- the Slovenian National Party 10.0 per cent
- the Slovenian People's Party 8.7 per cent
- the Democratic Party 5.0 per cent
- the Green Party 3.7 per cent
- the Social Democratic Party of Slovenia 3.3 per cent (Government of Slovenia 1994).

The Parliament now includes the representatives of the right-wing Slovenian National Party, which gained support through their populist ideas. Besides the Slovenian National Party, the Democratic Party of Slovenia is also a new name on the political scene after splitting of the DEMOS coalition.

At the 1992 presidential elections 64 per cent voted again for Milan Kucan. Dr Janez Drnovsek was appointed as a prime minister by the president to form a coalition government in which he specifically defined the relationship between individual ministers and the president of the government, as well as between the ministers and their parties. With the signing of the coalition agreement, the partners should regard the following as the crucial government activities:

- preparation of law on the economic system compatible with systems of the most developed European countries
- privatization of public property
- reorganization of public enterprises and the reform of the banking system
- supporting a stable and convertible national currency
- ensuring stable macroeconomic conditions
- the development of small and medium-size enterprises
- a new tax system and, therefore, a taxation policy that would stimulate and attract new investments, and citizens to saving
- development of all economic activities
- competition policy
- the abolition of surplus of labour in administration
- and ensuring the safety net for all citizens and participation in international organizations and European integration processes (Government of Slovenia 1994).

Dr Janez Drnovsek's coalition government have included the most important political forces in the country, from the former communist to traditional Christian Democrats, the Liberal Democratic Party, Christian Democratic Party, Social Democratic Party and United List of Social Democrats. As a result of ideological and a personal conflicts between the leading members of the coalition parties, Dr Janez Drnovsek first had to form a coalition government with the Christian Democrats and later an agreement with the United List, as Christian Democrats were not prepared to make any agreements with the United List. The Social Democrats joined the coalition made by Liberal Democrats and Christian Democrats after the Liberal Democrats gave them the Ministry of Defence post for their leader Janez Jansa. The desire to hold the office no doubt plays an important part in the coalition government agreements and, despite difficulties, the four major political forces dominating the multi-party system of Slovenia at the end of 1992 were co-operating in order to achieve a relatively stable and competent government.

In accordance with the new Slovenian Constitution, the highest legislative authority is the State Assembly, which has 90 deputies elected for a four-year term according to a complex system that is a combination of the proportional and the majority system. The State Council, with 40 representatives of the social, economic, professional and local interests, performs an advisory role. The State Council may propose laws to the State Assembly, give opinions on all matters within its competence, and may demand that the State Assembly review its decision on a law before its promulgation. The government is the highest executive body, independent within the framework of its competence and responsible to the State Assembly. The President of the Republic represents Slovenia, is the supreme commander of the defence forces, calls elections to the State Assembly, proclaims laws adopted by the State Assembly, proposes a candidate for the prime minister to the State Assembly, and performs other duties defined by the constitution. The President of the Republic is elected for a term of five years and may serve no more than two consecutive terms. The new Constitution of Slovenia derived many of its ideas from western European system, particularly Austria, and the structure and functioning of the State Council have been adopted from the Bavarian example (EIU 1994).

In the spring of 1994, the central parties – Liberal Democratic Party, Green-Ecological Party, Democratic Party, and Slovenian Socialist Party – established a new party, the Liberal Democracy of Slovenia, which, with one-third of the parliament's seats and with coalition partners Christian Democrats with 15 deputies and the left-wing United List with 14 seats, have together a comfortable majority in the 90-deputy State Assembly. In June 1994 the right-wing grouping of the Slovenian People's Party, Social Democratic Party, the Greens and the National Democrats (who split from the Christian Democrats) and Slovenian National Right formed an alliance, called "New DEMOS", against the government they see as being dominated by the old communist establishment to fight the local elections in December 1994 (*Delo* 1994).

In the past two years of Dr Drnovsek's government, several ministers and senior government officials have been removed or have resigned from their positions for various failures and inadequacies. In March 1994 Slovenia experienced what was probably its most serious internal crisis since independence. Janez Jansa, Minister of Defence, was voted out of the office because of the problems between the military and civilian police forces, as well as between both ministries' information services, which was a scandal that followed the departures of Social Democrats from the coalition government. This was a result of a long-brewing conflict between right-wing and centre-left party forces and the political establishment. For many Slovenes, anti-communist Mr Jansa personifies the country's struggle for independence, whereas president Milan Kucan and Prime Minister Dr Drnovsek were once prominent figures in the former communist regime. Further political scandal erupted in September 1994 when foreign minister, Lojze Peterle, resigned, on the grounds that the Liberal Democracy were unjustifiably concentrating all political power in the coalition government and the Parliament. The Christian Democrats leadership has faced increasing problems inside the party as it tries to justify its continued presence in a left-of-centre government in which the Liberal Democrats appear to have the final word in all important matters. Also in October 1994 Mr Peterle's agreement with Italy on changing property and restitution legislation was not accepted and approved by the parliament, and he threatened to withdraw the Christian Democrats from the coalition government after local elections in December 1994 (*Delo*; *Mladina* 1994).

First local elections in Slovenia in December 1994

The results of the local elections in December 1994 for mayors and local councils, and a shift towards right of the centre alliance parties, brought new challenges to the coalition government. Fourteen parties took part at the local elections. Five parties – Liberal Democracy, Christian Democratic Party, United List of Social Democrats, Social Democratic Party and Slovenian People's Party – gained around 70 per cent of the votes and are becoming the most important political actors in Slovenia (Kropivnik & Vehovar 1994). In the new 147 communes, coalition partners won in 57 localities (Liberal Democracy 23, Christian Democratic Party 21 and United List of Social Democrats 13) and opposition alliance parties in 46 localities (Slovenian People's Party 27 and Social Democratic Party 18) (*Delo* 24 December 1994). The results of the elections showed that there is a strong polarization between urban municipalities, where Liberal Democracy and United List of Social Democrats are dominant, whereas Slovenian People's Party is more dominant in rural areas and Christian Democrats have their base in both rural and urban areas among religious population. The Social

Democratic Party gained more popularity and a higher vote as a response to affairs and scandals between the ruling Liberal Democracy and Christian Democrats, and the Slovenian National Party had fewer votes than in the national elections in 1992. Dr Dimitrij Rupel, a university professor and a former foreign minister in the first coalition government (1990–2) as the candidate of Liberal Democracy was elected mayor of the capital city Ljubljana (*Delo* 17 and 24 December 1994).

However, the political transition in the past few years was not without its problems. Independence and democracy were achieved, extreme nationalism is controlled, but the political scene is still immature and unstable, with endless parliamentary disputes between different ministers of the government and various political parties are still dominant. However, a consensus to preserve national sovereignty, political democracy and a market-orientated economy prevails among all political parties.

Cost and benefits of Slovenian independence
In 1990, average per capita income in Yugoslavia as a whole was estimated at US$3060, but income per capita in Slovenia was about twice the national average and seven times the level in Kosovo, the poorest region. The persistence of these income disparities was exacerbated in the 1980s by zero output growth and a sustained fall in total productivity (World Bank 1993). In spite of several proposals for new political arrangements and radical economic structural reform programmes aimed at eliminating the system of self-management, privatization and market economy, no agreements between politicians in different republics have been possible (Verlic 1993).

The military conflict in the former Yugoslavia since 1991 has caused severe economic disruption in terms of casualties and refugees, disruption of trade and capital flows, and the loss of infrastructure and supply linkages. The domestic shocks to the economies of the republics in the former Yugoslavia have been exacerbated by external shocks in the form of the collapse of CMEA trade, the rise in oil prices during the Gulf War, and the loss of markets, tourism and remittance income as a result of the war (World Bank 1993). All republics of the former Yugoslav Federation have experienced a common set of domestic and external shocks to their economies since 1990, but the consequences were different because each republic startedfrom a different initial position and had different policy responses to the changing situation. Slovenia started from the best initial situation, as the most economically developed republic, and with relatively less war damage during the move to independence.

In the former Yugoslavia the Slovenian population (8% of the total) generated 15 per cent of the national income and 25 per cent of exports. The dissolution of the Yugoslav Federation led to a sharp decline in trade between Slovenia and the other republics, from an equivalent of 83 per cent of GDP in 1990 to 30 per cent of GDP in 1992 (ibid.). Slovenia no longer

Table 3.2 Foreign trade (million $US) 1992–3: main trading partners with Slovenia.

Foreign trade	1992			1993		
Country	Exports	Imports	Trade balance	Exports	Imports	Trade balance
Total EU	4462	4115	346	4294	4829	–532
Germany	1805	1394	411	1798	1625	173
Italy	880	839	41	755	1048	–294
France	616	493	123	528	521	6
UK	141	74	67	148	103	45
Austria	341	500	–159	303	552	–249
Croatia	952	852	100	737	591	146
USA	195	167	28	451	188	28
Former Soviet Union	226	251	–26	296	217	80

Source: Statistical Office of Republic of Slovenia 1993.

enjoyed its traditional sources of raw materials or the markets for its products in the former Yugoslavia. Slovenian producers were familiar with the market, and Slovenian products were known to be of higher quality than those of other producers in the former Yugoslavia. The international market is far more difficult to penetrate and profit margins are probably lower than in the old Yugoslav market. Most of the trade is conducted now with western Europe, and external trade is amounting to US$10 billion dollars in 1993, equivalent to about 85 per cent of GDP. In 1992, foreign trade – including trade with the other republics of the former Yugoslavia (mainly Croatia) – shows that the European Union took 55 per cent of Slovenia's exports and supplied 50 per cent of its imports, with Germany, Italy and France being the leading partners (ibid.).

Inflation has been high during the 1980s. The level of inflation in Slovenia was 267 per cent in 1991, about 90.6 per cent in 1992, 26 per cent in 1993 and declined further to 18 per cent in June 1994 (EIU 1994). The former Yugoslav currency, the dinar, was replaced in October 1992 by the tolar, allowing Slovenia to establish monetary control. As a result of political and economic reorientation, and the cost of reconstruction from the brief war with the Yugoslav Army, led to economic depression and a falling standard of living in Slovenia during the second half of 1991 and the first half of 1992. Gross domestic product in Slovenia is estimated to have fallen by 12 per cent in 1991, with the most severe decline in the service sector. Foreign exchange reserves were built up to 1.5 months of imports, mainly through sales of public rented housing for hard currency. The situation started to improve near the end of 1992 as international banks, including the World Bank and IMF, and international markets slowly opened for Slovenia, foreign trade was balanced, and the exchange rate of the tolar was stabilized (Cvikl et al. 1993, World Bank 1993). The foreign currency reserves in Slovenia exceeded US$1.4 billion in July 1994, almost equalling the foreign debt (EIU 1994).

As in other central and eastern European economies, Slovenian jobs are heavily concentrated in industry and services, which account for 33 and 62 per cent respectively of GDP in 1990 (Vodopivec & Hribar-Milic 1993). After manufacturing industry, the most important economic sectors are trade (15.3% of GDP), construction (5.5%), agriculture (5.4%) (World Bank 1993). The key features of the Slovenian labour market are high social sector employment, especially in manufacturing industry and services, an egalitarian wage structure and over-generous employment benefits, a relatively well educated labour force with high female participation, and little geographical mobility. Slovenia has suffered from considerable hidden unemployment, partly because of political pressures to maintain full employment. After stable unemployment of 1.5 per cent in the mid-1980s and a rise in 1988 and 1989, unemployment has exploded since 1990, soaring to 9.7 per cent in December 1991 and 15 per cent in December 1994. Plant closures have also become, for the first time, an important cause of unemployment. Most new labour market policies involve employment redundancy, unemployment insurance legislation, wage-setting policies, and early retirement (Vodopivec & Hribar-Milic 1993).

Slovenia will require significant foreign investment to meet its debt obligations and gradually to build its foreign exchange reserves. Even without membership in the EU, Slovenia has managed greatly to increase the inflow of foreign investments. Direct foreign investments roughly tripled in value between 1989 and 1990, and grew another 40 per cent in 1991 despite the war. Capital investment began to flow into the country, primarily from Germany, Austria and Italy and in 1993 foreign investments were $2143 billion dollars (EIU 1994).

Since 1991 Slovenia has adopted policies that should contribute to economic recovery. The Slovenian economy is now at the crossroads, and prospects will depend on the achievement of fiscal sustainability and the success of structural reforms, especially in the enterprise and financial sector. The foreign exchange system is one of the most important achievements of Slovenia's macroeconomic stabilization and the full convertibility of the tolar is expected in 1995.

The economic reform programme

The Slovenian government introduced economic reforms in 1991 to lower inflation and increase the critically low level of foreign exchange reserves, real devaluation of the exchange rate followed by a managed float, very tight monetary policy, and restriction on nominal wages. The government aims to implement microeconomic reforms that include supportive fiscal and incomes policies, and a social safety net. These reforms include privatization of most publicly owned enterprises, rehabilitating and privatizing banks, and introducing state ownership and control of the very few enterprises that provide public services. The privatization legislation was passed in November 1992 and formally named the Property Transformation Act including the privatization of enterprises. It began to be implemented in May 1993, and the privatization process has been intensive during 1994 despite restitution rights and property claims, which are producing various delays (Cvikl et al. 1993, Economist intelligence Unit 1994).

No less then three privatization proposals were considered by the Parliament of Slovenia in 1992. The two failed proposals represented diverging approaches that favoured internal privatization through worker–manager buyouts, and the other favoured external privatization through distribution of shares to citizens and pension funds, coupled with the establishment of mutual funds. The latter approach is similar to methods used in the Czech and Slovak Republics, Russia and Poland. Internal privatization was denounced by Jeffrey Sacks when he argued that the plan unfairly benefited existing managers, was open to speculation since accurate evaluation without functioning capital markets is impossible, and failed to fit the circumstances of large capital-intensive and expensive enterprises. Defenders of internal privatization argued that Slovenian managers are not typical of managers in communist countries. Many are highly educated and skilled and are quite familiar with management in a market milieu. A compromise was finally passed in November 1992 by Dr Drnovsek's coalition government, combining internal and external approaches. The proposal allows the sale of the whole enterprise, employee purchase, or transfer of shares, and requires 10 per cent of the book value of social capital to be distributed as shares to the Slovenian Pension and Invalid Fund, 10 per cent to the Compensation Fund, 20 per cent to authorized investment companies, 20 per cent to employees, and 40 per cent to the population. The method of privatization is chosen by the individual company, subject to the approval of the Agency for Privatization of the Republic of Slovenia (Cvikl et al. 1993). The privatization of publicly owned enterprises is supported by programmes aiming at reforming enterprises in the public sector, reducing total loss, and developing the institutional and legal framework of a market economy. The most important legislation, enacted in 1994, includes the Competition Law, the Company Law, the Law of Commercial Public Services and the Law of Auditing. At the time of writing (1995), security market legislation and a new bankruptcy law are now awaiting adoption by Parliament. In the 1995–8 period the new investments will be concentrated on the improvement and modernization of capital equipment in the manufacturing sector, and improvement of transport and communication infrastructure (EIU 1994).

The benefits of separation from the former Yugoslavia have proved to be not only political but also economic. As of early 1994, Slovenia appeared to be the most successful of all the former Yugoslav republics in implementing the difficult political and economic transition to manage its own domestic and foreign affairs. Slovenia was historically a more market-orientated country than most other countries of central and eastern Europe, which could make its transition to a market economy and integration with Europe much easier in comparison with some other central and eastern European countries. Much of its trade with the rest of the former Yugoslavia and other countries of central and eastern Europe has been lost, but Slovenia's long-term aim is to straighten its geographical location as a link between the technologically advanced West and markets in central and eastern Europe and CIS countries (World Bank 1993, EIU 1994).

Despite economic success, Slovenia still has an international image of a country between "Brussels and Bosnia" because of its proximity to the war in the former Yugoslavia and conflicts with Italy, which are delaying association agreement with European Union.

International participation and conflicts with neighbours

A strong consensus continues to prevail among most of the political parties in Slovenia on a wide range of essential issues, including commitments to national independence, political democracy and a market economy, and to close co-operation with the West in general and, with the European Union in particular. In May 1992 Slovenia became a member of the UN and now also takes part in international co-operation associations as the European Security Council, the Visegrad co-operation, Partnership for Peace and the Council of Europe. In spring 1994 a free-trade agreement with Poland was negotiated, to follow similar agreements already in place with the Czech Republic, Slovakia and Hungary to become a member of CEFTA (Central-European free Trade Organization) in 1995. Talks on the mutual liberalization of trade continue also with the European Free Trade Association (EFTA). Slovenia became a member of the World Bank and IMF in 1992 and relations with international financial institutions are strengthening further, particularly with the European Bank for Reconstruction and Development (EBRD) and the European Investment Bank (EIB), which are expected to play a major part in the financing of Slovenia's transport and telecommunications networks. In December 1994 Slovenia signed an association agreement to become a member of the new World Trade Organization in 1995. Slovenia's relationship with the European Union, although good, has been developing far more slowly than that of other central European countries because of the conflicts with its neighbours, Italy and Croatia (Delo 1993–4).

Conflict with Italy and Croatia

Since spring 1994 the new Italian government is pressing Slovenia for more concessions to enable Italians, or their descendants, who left their homes after the Second World War, to return the property owned in what is now Slovenia's part of the Istrian peninsula. Slovenia insists that the issue of Italian claims had been settled by the Osim agreement between the Yugoslav and Italian governments in 1975, under the terms of which Yugoslavia, and now Slovenia as a legal successor, promised to pay compensation of US$110 million. Thus, although Slovenia has offered financial compensation, Italy insists on the physical return of property that is in the ownership of Slovenian government, and in cases where the property is owned privately, the Italians should be able to purchase it. Italy's intention is to prevent Slovenia's progress towards associate membership of the European Union and other European institutions and she has already vetoed Slovenia's application to join the other central and eastern European countries in obtaining associate partnership status in the Western European Union. Italian claims for restitution of nationalized property in Slovenia were also recently supported by another neighbour, Austria, for the right of the German-speaking minority who lost their property and citizenship rights in Slovenia as collaborators with the Nazi regime during the Second World War (*Delo* 1994).

Slovenia is seeking closer ties with the West, and more particularly with the European Union, but the government and the parliament are not willing to make such concessions to accommodate Italian demands for restitution of property to the Italian citizens or their descendants. The Slovenian government realizes that existing legislation banning foreigners from owning land and property will eventually have to be revised and changed with corresponding legislation in the European Union to achieve association agreement or actual membership in the future.

The other problem facing the Slovenian government is the relationship with Croatia, which deteriorated during 1992. The subject of controversy between Slovenia and Croatia include Slovenia's access to the Adriatic sea through the Bay of Piran and the demarcation of the frontier in respect of three small villages, the restitution of Croatian hard-currency deposits in Ljubljanska Banka, and Croatia's share of the Krsko nuclear power plant. Since the internal administrative borders between republics of the former Yugoslav Federation were set in 1945 and precisely delineated in the mid-1950s, they have often not followed the historical, natural, or administrative divisions made by the predecessor state (Kingdom of Yugoslavia) or former rulers (Austrian–Hungarian and Ottoman Empire). The constitution of the former Yugoslav Federation foresaw republics as autonomous units with the dominance of a nation, but the administrative borders introduced have usually failed to separate ethnic communities. The borders between the new countries, Slovenia and Croatia, were set up in 1991 along the lines of the administrative divisions in the former Yugoslavia. The crucial aspect for Slovenia is the Bay of Piran in Istria and access to the sea via its own waters. Historically this part of Istria is Slovenian and in 1951 the Slovenian Communist Party gave a strip of northern Istria to the Croats as a friendly gesture (*Delo* 1994). The designation of the state boundaries and improvement of political relations are in the interests of both countries, and border areas should be developed as regions of co-operation, not a conflict.

Immigrations, refugees and citizenship legislation

Throughout history, Slovenia was an emigration country until the Second World War when the situation changed, and the numbers of immigrants coming from the other republics of the former Yugoslavia, as a consequence of increased employment in industry and manufacturing, exceeded the number of Slovenes emigrating both to other republics of the former Yugoslavia and abroad. Most immigrants came from Croatia, Bosnia, Herzegovina and Serbia, although Slovenia remained ethnically the most homogenous of all former Yugoslav republics.

Table 3.3 Ethnic structure of population in Slovenia 1953–91. Total population in thousands (000).

Census (year)	1953		1971		1981		1991	
Ethnic groups	Total	%	Total	%	Total	%	Total	%
Slovenes	1415.4	97.0	1624.0	94.0	1712.4	90.5	1727.0	87.8
Croats	17.9	1.2	42.7	2.5	55.6	3.0	54.3	2.7
Serbs	11.2	0.8	20.5	1.2	42.2	2.2	47.9	2.4
Muslims	1.6	0.1	3.2	0.2	13.4	0.7	26.8	1.4
Montenegrins	1.4	0.1	1.9	0.1	3.2	0.2	4.4	0.2
Macedonians	0.6	0.04	1.6	0.1	3.3	0.2	4.4	0.2
Albanians	0.2	0.01	1.3	0.1	2.0	0.1	3.6	0.2
Hungarians	11.0	0.7	9.8	0.6	9.5	0.5	8.5	0.4
Italians	0.9	0.1	3.0	0.2	2.2	0.1	3.0	0.2
Austrians	0.3	0.02	0.3	0.02	0.2	0.01	0.2	0.01
Germans	1.6	0.1	0.4	0.02	0.4	0.04	0.5	0.03
Yugoslavs	–	–	6.7	0.4	26.2	1.4	12.3	0.6
Others	4.3	2.9	11.7	0.7	21.3	1.1	73.2	3.7
Total	1466.4	100.0	1727.1	100.0	1891.9	100.0	1966.0	100.0

Source: Statistical Office of Republic of Slovenia 1993.

According to the most recent census in 1991 there were as many as 12 per cent of non-Slovenes living in Slovenia, but only Italians who live in the coastal regions and Hungarians in northeastern Slovenia have a status of autochthonous minorities and they enjoy all the privileges of citizenship and special minority rights. Very liberal law on citizenship in Slovenia decreed that immigrants from other republics who had permanent residence and employment in Slovenia at least six months prior to the plebiscite in 1990 could apply for Slovene citizenship. In November 1991, 94 per cent of population had Slovenian citizenship (*Delo* 1994).

During the final years of the former Yugoslavia, migrations were influenced more by economic factors than by political ones. As a consequence of the war a significant number of refugees fled to Slovenia from Croatia in 1991 and Bosnia and Herzegovina since 1992. The official figures range between 40,000 and 70,000 people. The costs of caring for refugees, however, proved burdensome to the Slovenian economy and also added to traces of xenophobia and nationalism at the fringe of the political spectrum. The extreme right-wing voters worried that foreign immigrants to Slovenia, some of whom were granted Slovenian citizenship, would become a financial burden and take away Slovenian jobs. As a consequence, the Slovenian Nationalist Party won 10 per cent of the votes in the elections in December 1992, making it the fourth largest party in the parliament.

Conclusion: a search for a new identity

Slovenia's experience suggests that secession from the former Yugoslavia may have political and economic benefits. Slovenia probably enjoyed the most market- and outward-orientated economy, with a relatively narrow technological gap in relation to many countries in central and eastern Europe. GDP per capita is comparable with Greece and Portugal and two or three times higher than that of more advanced central and eastern European countries. Together with Czech Republic, Slovenia has probably the most developed economy in central and eastern Europe (see Figure 3.4), but its status is not recognized internationally for several reasons (EIU 1994).

Following the end of the one-week war between Slovenian forces and the Yugoslav Army in June 1991, Slovenia has been able to separate itself from the brutality and violence of the Yugoslav conflict. The Yugoslav Army and the Serbian and Montenegrin politicians decided to pull out of Slovenia, as controlling or absorbing Slovenia was never a Serbian goal, unless it could be done with Slovenian acquiescence and thus without a major conflict. Serbs and Montenegrins who came to Slovenia after the Second World War amount to only about 3.8 per cent of the total population of Slovenia (Statistical Office of Republic of Slovenia 1993) and, while creating a vision of Greater Serbia, nationalist politicians in Serbia were primarily concerned with large Serbian minorities in Kosovo, Croatia and Bosnia and Herzegovina.

Because of its proximity to the former Yugoslavia, Slovenia shares much of the political risk associated by foreign investors with Yugoslavia. The violent collapse of the former Yugoslav Federation in 1991 affected Slovenia's economy most adversely. Macroeconomic imbalances, with hyperinflation inherited from the former Yugoslavia, were the key problem that had first to be resolved prior to other reforms, and also implementation of privatization was hindered by political disputes stemming from the process of introducing parliamentary democracy. The only physical

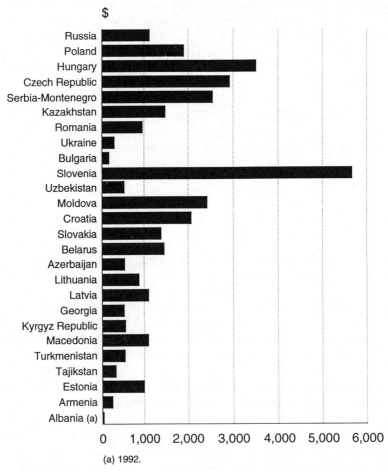

Figure 3.4 Gross domestic product per head in Central and Eastern Europe in 1993. *Source:* Economist Intelligence Unit (1994).

evidence of the closeness to the conflicts in Croatia and Bosnia are the refugees. The greatest worry is that Slovenia seems to be easily forgotten by the rest of the world. For how long Slovenia will have an image of the country between "Brussels and Bosnia" will depend on the success of Slovenian diplomacy in creating a perception that Slovenia is quite different from the rest of the former Yugoslavia, which is ethnically homogenous, culturally and historically compatible with the central Europe, and enjoys proximity to western European markets.

Together with a fear of Balkanization, a related longer term problem is fear of Germanization. Historically, Slovenia has been in the sphere of influence of pan-Germanic imperialism and, until the mid-nineteenth century, German was the language of administration and local cultural institutions.

German nationalism destroyed the pan-Slavic federation in Austrian–Hungarian Empire, which subsequently pushed Slovenia to find another alternative in the Kingdom of Serbs, Croats and Slovenes in 1918, hoping to achieve political and cultural autonomy and hence independence (Bučar 1993). The disputes with Italy incline Slovenian politics increasingly towards Germany and Austria, both of which were allies in the independence process and important trading partners and foreign investors. Given the small size of the Slovenian economy, the impact of a few significant foreign investments could be very important and the first indications of a defensive reaction against foreigners can be seen in the new Slovenian legislation as unwillingness to allow foreigners to buy land and property.

The other difficult area is foreign policy, where Slovenia is not doing well enough in attracting recognition and in gaining membership of the European Union, which could enable Slovenia to develop a normal free-trade economy. Slovenia's relations with Italy can destabilize the country internally and slow down the integration process within the EU, but opens the questions of harmonization of property rights with EU countries. Rather than regarding the property rights question as an act of Italian hostility, the Slovenian government could see it as a move towards full integration and membership of the EU. Slovenia and the European Union are important to each other. Slovenia's move towards independence was motivated by the desire to join the process of integration in Europe and closer association with European Union will mean approval for foreign investments in Slovenia, guaranteed access to European markets and eligibility for funds from the EU's regional programmes (ERDF, ESF), which have proved a major enticement for less developed members such as Ireland, Portugal and Greece (Cvikl et al. 1993). EU acceptance of Slovenia will provide an opportunity to show real commitment to the integration of central and eastern European countries.

Domestic political life still suffers from sectional interests, fragmentation of political parties and confusion of objectives. The turmoil in political life, internal affairs and scandals in Slovenia are signs of the low maturity of the democracy when people still immaturely base their vote on personalities, not policies. However, a fundamental consensus prevails in the government to preserve national sovereignty and political democracy, to maintain progress towards a market-oriented economy and to keep extreme nationalists from gaining significant power.

Slovenia could experience long-term socio-economic benefits through enhanced macroeconomic stability, sovereignty and control over monetary and fiscal policy, active foreign policy, regional co-operation and partnerships with international organizations. Developments in Slovenia will to a larger extent depend on the situation elsewhere in the former Yugoslavia, however much the Slovenes may try to divorce themselves from the Balkans. In order to develop its full trade potential, Slovenia will have to recapture quickly some of the export markets it has lost in the former Yugo-slavia, and especially so in Bosnia–Herzegovina, Serbia and Montenegro. The war, the consequences of which Slovenia feels only indirectly, will even-tually have to end and Slovene companies could play an important role in reconstruction of the areas destroyed. Economic success and international participation will bring political stability and confidence in future and Slovenia may find its identity as a sovereign and independent state at the crossroads of regional co-operation between western, central and south-eastern Europe.

References

Bučar, F. 1993. Slovenia in Europe. *Nationalities Papers* XXI(1), , Association for the Study of the Nationalities of the USSR and eastern Europe.

Cohen, L. 1993. *Broken bonds: the disintegration of Yugoslavia*. Boulder, Colorado: Westview Press.

Cviic, C. 1991. *Remaking the Balkans*. London: Pinter.

Cvikl, M., E. Kraft, M. Vodopivec 1993. *The cost and benefits of Slovenian independence*. Policy Research Working Papers, The World Bank, Washington DC.

Eyal, J. 1993. *Europe and Yugoslavia: lessons from a failure*. London: Royal United Services Insti-tute for Defence Studies.

Gray, C.W. & F. Stiblar 1992. *The evolving legal framework for private sector activity in Slovenia*. Policy Research Working Papers, Socialist Economies Reform, Country Economics Depart-ment, The World Bank, Washington DC.

Harris, P. 1992. *Somebody else's war: frontline reports from the Balkan Wars 1991–92*. Stevenage, Englad: SPA Books.

Kropivnik, S. & U. Vehovar 1994. Geografska porazdelitev volilnih glasov v Sloveniji: Mesto za LDS, vas za SSDS. Sobotna Priloga. *Delo* (26 November).

Kropivnik, S. & U. Vehovar 1994. Pet velicanstvenih: Teritorijalne znailnosti lokalnih volitev "94". *Delo* (17 December).

Lenček, R. L. 1984. A paradigm of Slavic national evaluation: bible–grammar–poet, four hun-dred years of the South Slavic Protestant Reformation (1584–1984). *Slovene Studies* 6(1–2), 57–71.

Lydall, H. 1989. *Yugoslavia in crisis*. Oxford: Oxford University Press.

Rupel, D. Slovenia in Post-Modern Europe. *Nationalities Papers* XXI(1), Association for the Study of the Nationalities of the USSR and eastern Europe.

Simmi J. and Dekleva J. (eds) 1991. *Yugoslavia in turmoil: after self-management*. London: Pinter Publishers.

Socan, L. 1994. Slovenija – Evropska Unija: Biti ali ne biti -zraven [Sobotna Priloga]. *Delo* (19 November).

Svetlik, I. (ed.) 1992. *Social policy in Slovenia: between tradition and innovation*. Aldershot, England: Avebury.

Thomas, C. 1990. Yugoslavia: the enduring dilemmas. *Geography* 75, 265–8.

Verlic-Dekleva, B. 1992. Challenges of urban development in Slovenia. *Netherlands Journal of Housing and the Built Environment* 7(4), 377–89.

Vodopivec, M. & S. Hribar-Milic 1993. *The Slovenian labour market in transition: issues and lessons learned*. Policy Research Working Paper, The World Bank, Washington DC.

Vodopivec, P. 1993. Slovenes in the Habsburg Empire or Monarchy. *Nationalities Papers* XXI(1), Association for the Study of the Nationalities of the USSR and eastern Europe.

REFERENCES

EIU (Economist Intelligence Unit) 1994. *Country reports: Slovenia*. London: EIU.

East European Newsletter, **8**(20), 5 October 1994.

East European Newsletter, **8**(22), 2 November 1994.

Republic of Slovenia, Trends in Developing Economies, vol. 1 Eastern Europe and Central Asia, 1993, p. 76–9, The World Bank, Washington DC.

Yugoslavia – "The Successor states", Social Indicators of Development 1992–1993, The World Bank, John Hopkins University Press, Baltimore and London.

"Slovenia for Everyone", Public Relations and Media Office of Government of Slovenia, Ljubljana, June 1994.

"On the Sunny Side of the Alps", Ministry of Tourism, Ljubljana, Slovenia, 1993.

Statistical Yearbook of Republic of Slovenia, Statistical Office of Republic of Slovenia, Ljubljana, 1993.

Delo, Ljubljana, September 1993–December 1994.

Mladina, July 1991–December 1994.

CHAPTER FOUR

Islam and Bosnia's Muslim nation
C. SORABJI

Introduction

Bosnia–Herzegovina was internationally recognized as a state in April 1992. Through warfare, "ethnic cleansing" and the displacement of people on a scale unrivalled in Europe since the Second World War, the shape of this part of the Balkans has already changed, *de facto* if not *de jure*. Of those Bosnians fighting to re-create its pre-war from the majority are Muslims. According to the Serbian Ministry of information "those behind this unnecessary chaos [i.e. the war] are . . . the Moslem ruling party and Alija Izetbegović who are hiding their great-Moslem and fundamentalist intentions behind the idea of Bosnia and Herzegovina as a sovereign independent state" (Ralić 1992). The spectre of a Sharia-ruled Bosnia–Herzegovina is also, if more discreetly, evoked in Croatia. Here the claim is less that Muslim leaders are bent on Islamic Fundamentalism than that the Muslim population, deprived of its multi-ethnic Bosnia by Serbian aggression, will rapidly, easily and inevitably turn to fundamentalism. In both cases, however, the incompatibility of Islam and Europe is assumed and the Muslims are viewed as a population whose roots and therefore rights in a European tradition are dubious.

Accompanying such portrayals of Muslim society as an alien society is an underlying implication that Muslims are alien through choice, treachery, fickleness and cowardice. Historically, both Serbs and Croats have claimed the Muslims as belonging to their own nation. The argument has various forms, but central to it are the following elements: the Serb/Croat nation existed as a nation long before the arrival of the Ottomans in the fifteenth century; the inhabitants of medieval Bosnia–Herzegovina were either Serbs or Croats. Those who converted to Islam were therefore either Serbs or Croats; the majority of the converts were Serbs (the Serbian view)/Croats (the Croatian view).

Rali (ibid.) re-iterates the Serbian version of this thesis, whereas President Tudjman's work claims that "the majority of the Muslims is in its ethnic character and speech incontrovertibly of Croatian origin" (1981: 114). Such arguments rest on the notion of "nations" having existed in the fifteenth-century Balkans, and on a 500-year cut-off date for the achievement of nationhood – half a millennium of Muslim identity is not considered sufficient to create a Muslim nation. Whatever their theoretical defects, given that Muslims themselves resist Serb and Croat claims on their identity, such views assist in a presentation of them as wily and unreliable turncoats, prepared to adopt an alien religion in the first place and then to side with whomever offers the best deal in the political marketplace.

This chapter considers the role of Islam in Bosnian Muslims' own understanding of their identity, and its implications for their relationships with Europe, the Islamic world, Serbs, Croats and ex-Yugoslavs of the Islamic faith (principally the Albanians).

Pragmatism

Politically these relationships may be characterized as pragmatic. Under Austro–Hungarian rule (1878–1918), Muslim leaders negotiated with the occupiers to protect landowners' rights, the autonomy of the Islamic religious authorities and the safety of Muslims within a Bosnia that no longer forming part of the Ottoman Empire, left them as a potentially vulnerable minority (Bosnia 1981). Between the world wars the Yugoslovenska Muslimanska Organizacion (JMO) was wooed by both Serbian and Croatian political parties, playing one off against the other to its best advantage (see Banac 1984). Under federal socialism the Muslims' position as a foil to Serbian and Croatian ambitions and their relevance to Tito's non-aligned policy gained them the official status first of an ethnic group (1961 census) and then of a full nation (1971 census). In recent years Muslims' perception of Serbia as a common threat has resulted in a rapprochement with the co-religionists, the Kosovan Albanians, who were previously seen as a threat to the stability of Yugoslavia. From 1990 to the outbreak of war, Bosnian President and Muslim party leader Alija Izetbegović attempted to internationalize the Bosnian "problem" and to keep an equal distance from both Serbia and Croatia; only the failure of the international community to intervene propelled him into alliance with Croatia, an alliance that he himself has likened to "a pact with the devil". In their precarious geopolitical position between Serbs and Croats, the Muslims are safest under some wider umbrella, be it Yugoslavia, a united Bosnia or the EC, and their pragmatism has largely been directed at maintaining such an umbrella and enhancing their status within it.

It is pragmatism that, from a Serbian or Croatian perspective, may be equated with opportunism or an uncertain and changeable (and therefore negligible) national identity with the decline of the Ottoman Empire and the arrival of the Austro–Hungarian, there began a long Serb/Croat battle for the national allegiance of Bosnia's Muslims. Certain Muslim intellectuals aligned themselves with either Serbian or with Croatian identity, but the mass of the population resisted any such move. Before 1918 they found refuge in the concept of *Bosnjastvo* favoured by Benjamin von Kallay, the Austro–Hungarian governor of Bosnia 1882–1903, an all-Bosnian identity, which was in fact espoused only by Muslims. Between the wars JMO leaders included active Serbs, Croats and Undeclared, but this assortment did not threaten the unity of the party or dilute its aim of preserving Bosnian autonomy. For the most part Muslims resisted being drawn into either the Serbian or the Croatian camp, one 1927 law student even declaring himself a Slovene in protest (Hadzihajić 1974: 227). The 1961 recognition of "Musliman" as an ethnic description saw 25.69 per cent of Bosnians choosing it and this figure rose to 39.57 per cent in the 1971 census where "Musliman" was accounted a national description. In this context, Serb and Croat hypotheses about the weakness of Muslim identity falter; Bosnia's Muslims did not have a full national name before 1971, but they were aware of a distinctive identity that in the Yugoslav context could only be conceptualized as "national", and increasingly concerned to institutionalize it after their Second World War experience as second-class citizens in a fascist Croatian state, and victims of Serbian Chetnik massacres.

Islam

Opinions commonly expressed on the Islamic ingredient of this national identity tend to fall into one of two camps. Either the Muslims are natural allies of the Middle East and all too likely to want an Islamic state, or they are not really Muslims at all, as evidenced by their consumption of alcohol, Western clothing, and so on. The former view has, in recent years, been disseminated by the Serbian leadership (and to a lesser extent by the Croatian) but also finds resonances in western Europe. The latter was the official view of the communist regime, which always denied that the Muslim (capital "M" for nationality) and muslim (small "m" for religion) bore much relationship to each other, and it finds resonances among liberals both within ex-Yugoslavia and in western Europe, The presumption is either that "they're dangerous because they're Islamic, or that they're not dangerous because they're not Islamic", but in either case it is assumed that an Islamic identity is more or less necessarily incompatible with European identity, democracy, liberalism and so on.

This chapter suggests that Islam *is* central to the popular understanding of Muslim identity, but that its meanings are diverse and differently understood and emphasized at different times, in different contexts and by different sections of the population. Islam is no monolith and it implies no iron-cast and unchanging relationships with the Middle East, with western

Europe, with Serbs, Croats, Albanians or others. Rather it supplies a basis for stronger or weaker relationships, conceptual and political, with these groups. In an equation that may sound odd to west European ears, many Muslims have since the late 1980s identified Islam strongly with European civilization and values. Hand in hand with the equation has gone a widespread belief that Europe would never allow a war in Bosnia but would be sure to intervene.

The mid-1980s

Lockwood (1975) has pointed out the strong relationship between "*nacija*" (nationality) and "*vjera*" (faith) as understood by Muslim villagers. In Sarajevo in 1985 and 1986 this conceptual relationship was also evident in the Muslim neighbourhood from which I pursued my anthropological fieldwork, a neighbourhood peopled by born-and-bred Sarajevans and by long-term and more recent migrants from Bosnian villages and from the Sandzak. It was spelled out to me by one Sarajevo-born housewife in her twenties who wanted to know my "*nacija*". English did not satisfy her and neither did "British"; the answer she was looking for was "Protestant" and only this satisfied her as to my "*nacija*". "Nacija – that means faith", she explained. The line between nationality and religion is slim throughout Bosnia–Herzegovina. Croatian-ness and Catholicism are closely related and, as the proverb says, "Nema Srpstva bez tri prsta" (There's no Serbian-ness without three fingers – a reference to the way Orthodox Serbs cross themselves).

Of course, this did not mean that all Muslims were devout. Levels of religious observance ranged from regular prayer, Ramadan/fasting and so on, through occasional observance to total negligence and heavy alcohol consumption. But as Akinar (1983: 2) has pointed out:

on religion, and least of all Islam, is an army whose strength can be judged by the number of men on active service . . . In fact the only way in which a Muslim can sever himself from his community is by a conscious and voluntary rejection of Islam.

Very few went so far as to outrightly deny the existence of God or the validity of the Prophet. The consumption of alcohol and other behaviours so often used in evidence that the Muslims are not "real" Muslims weighs as little as the thefts committed throughout the Christian world. For example, because a Catholic steals, one would not say that s/he was not a Catholic, but simply that s/he had broken one of the rules of Catholic faith.

This is an important point for, like the other religions of the region, Islam is not simply a set of clearly definable rules of practice and is not so understood by Muslims. Alongside the detailed prescriptions for daily prayer, the annual *Hajj/Hadji/Hajji*, and so on, Islam is also understood as a domain of loose moral imperatives – hospitality, cleanliness, generosity, honesty, kindness, courtesy, industry and so on. The first three are often regarded by Muslims as virtues especially belonging to Islam, but all form part of a general field of morality that can potentially be seen as overlapping with that of non-Islamic ideologies or non-Bosnian Muslim societies. Thus, in socialist Bosnia, many who were both party members and self-confessed believers could easily assert that, after all, Islam and communism said the same things – work hard, don't cheat your neighbours, redistribute your wealth, and so on. These sorts of accommodations between Islam and communism have also been noted in the Soviet Union (for example, Carrere d'Encausse 1979), and accommodations between Islam and secularist nationalism noted in Turkey (Tapper & Tapper 1987). In part they are born of necessity under unsympathetic or openly oppressive political regimes, but they should not be viewed as completely bogus concessions to the authorities, made through guilty self-delusion or with fingers crossed behind the back. As a moral system, Islam is capable of being interpreted as related to other moral systems, and the removal of the one-party regime in Bosnia, although accompanied by religious revival, did not send Muslims running "back" to a rigid Islam of rules and regulations but left them with a moral system, the political implications of which could be re-understood in the new circumstances.

This reliance on Islam as a moral system was very evident in the social circles of mid-1980s white- and blue-collar workers, and particularly in the purely Muslim or Muslim-dominated neighbourhoods of the old town. Here people greeted each other with "Merhaba!" or "Aksam Hajrula!" in place of the Serbo–Croatian "Dobar Dan/Dobar Vecer" used in the town centre. The neighbourhoods were self-consciously Muslim and Islamic, but Islam was seen to lie less in ritual or theology than in life values. To have a dirty home, be mean with guests or gossip too much were signs of the inadequate Muslim, far more than a failure to pray or fast. Rarely did Muslims evaluate each others' actions in religious language. It was not "haram" (Arabic: forbidden by God) to slander someone but "neposteno" or "ne valja" (Serbo–Croatian: dishonest, not good). It was not "sunset" (Arabic: recommended by the Prophet and pleasing to God) to wash your hands before meals but "fino/valja" (Serbo–Croatian: nice or good).

Even the loose Islamic revival movement, largely composed of young people in their teens and twenties, relied heavily on Islam's nature as a system of values. Many of those who could be seen to fall within the domain of the revival were or had been students at Sarajevo's medresas or Islamic Theological Faculty. Of those, some were urbanites and some from rural backgrounds whose secondary or higher education was made possible by the stipends and accommodation that religious academies could offer in a way that secular ones could not. Others were studying at the university or working as professionals – lawyers, doctors, architects, engineers, and so on. All were religiously observant and keen on acquiring or improving their knowledge of the Arabic language, the Quran, the hadiths and the

Islamic world, and some but by no means all of the young women had adopted headscarf and long dresses. But much of what dominated their conversation and behaviour was not religious prescriptions for specific action but broader moral questions of modesty and respect.

A focus on Islam's moral dimensions went hand in hand with a flexible interpretation of the Bosnian Muslims' relationship with non-Bosnian Muslims. Thus, the fairly widespread anti-Albanian feeling was supported by accusations that their Kosovan co-religionists were lazy, ungrateful and undisciplined and therefore somehow not properly Muslim; western Europe was "kulturni" – civilized – and therefore akin to the Muslims. The "revived" Muslims were far more interested in the Middle Eastern Muslim world than others, and in identifying with it and praising it placed great emphasis on its moral qualities. Turkish boys, for example, were adept at reciting the Quran because proper family relations of obedience and respect provided them with an appropriate environment for learning.

The late 1980s and onwards

With the decline and fall of the one-party system and Serbia's increasing self-assertion, particularly over Kosova, these emphases altered. Anti-Albanianism dwindled as Muslims came to see in Kosova not an Albanian threat to the unity of Yugoslavia but a Serbian threat that might redirect itself at them. Images of nobility under oppression rather than idle ingratitude helped to redefine the Albanians as fellow Muslims. At the same time the Muslims' identity as Europeans began to receive stronger stress. The structure and outlook of the Islamic religious establishment, the Islamska Zajednica (IZ), changed at the same time.

In the mid-1980s the IZ had devoted much energy to promoting the socialist brotherhood and unity of Yugoslavia's nations and nationalities while, circumspectly given the famous 1983 trial of Alija Izetbegović and 11 others for Muslim nationalism, trying to strengthen the position of the Muslims *vis-à-vis* Serbs and Croats. The establishment was widely treated as a functional equivalent of the secular authorities. People knew what they had to put into the state – for example, military service – and what they could get out of it, for example medical care. In the same way, when I asked what the IZ was or what it did, the reply was never that it provided guidance on matters of faith or represented Islam in Bosnia. Instead, answers were along the lines: "it organises the payment of *zekat* and *sadakatul-fitr*" (Islamic taxes), or "when someone dies you can arrange the funeral through the IZ". Like the secular authorities the IZ was something out there to benefit from, contributed to and otherwise dealt with. At worst it was treated as an ideological lack of the socialist authorities. The joke was that you had to be Party member to land a good job in the IZ, and particular officials, including the Reis-ul-Ulema (the highest official) and the head of the Bosnian IZ Assembly, were the subject of much criticism (the latter, Ferhat ef. Seta, nicknamed "*Šteta*" – what a pity!).

From the late 1980s the IZ began a process of restructuring, which included the removal of certain officials and the rehabilitation of others who had been demoted or deposed under socialism, and which pointed in three directions (the first and third being more strongly played than the second):

- towards a more "international" and less Bosnian-dominated Islamic community of Yugoslavia (i.e. a community giving more weight and voice to non-Bosnian Islamic organs)
- toward stronger conceptual and material ties with the wider Islamic world
- towards Europe and the associated notion of democracy.

Late 1988 and early 1989 saw protest rallies of imams (priests) calling for the resignation of the Reis-ul-Ulema and Ferhat ef. Seta, and for the IZ to change its constitution. In March 1989 the IZ agreed to the new constitution and also pronounced its condemnation of Albanian nationalism and irredentism. Throughout the summer there were protests over Salman Rushdie's *Satanic verses*. In November Jakub ef. Selimoski was unanimously elected as the new acting Reis-ul-Ulema. A Macedonian, Selimoski was the first ever non-Bosnian to hold the position and this break with the past was accompanied by a changing outlook on the Bosnian Muslims' relationship with others. By spring 1990 the IZ's new Constitution was promulgated (see below) and the highest organs of the IZ were calling for the lifting of emergency measures in Kosova and for democratization and dialogue in the province. Selimoski pronounced the national homogenization of Yugoslavia's Muslims (Bosnian, Albanian, Turkish, Romi, etc.) to be impossible and also unnecessary since Islam rose above national divisions. In October 1990 the Yugoslav IZ announced its intention of remaining united, even if the country itself were to fall apart. In early 1991 the IZ openly condemned the actions of the Serbian government in Kosova and called on all members of the Islamic community to show solidarity with the Kosova Muslims and to understand this both as an Islamic duty and as human solidarity. In August 1991 the IZ issued a document calling on the world's Islamic institutions to pay more attention to the plight of Yugoslav Muslims. In September the Bosnian IZ held a conference on the future of Islam in eastern Europe at the Sarajevo Holiday Inn, inviting representatives from eastern Europe and the Soviet Union.

This period then saw an increasing emphasis on supra-national Islamic identity uniting Yugoslav and east European Muslims. Individual national identities were recognized and supported and before the 1991 census the Bosnian IZ joined with the party of Democratic Action (SDA, the Muslim political party) in calling on Muslims to give their mother tongue as

"Bosnian" rather than the old standard "Serbo–Croatian". But support of national identities was conceived of as the best route to achieving the IZ's primary task: safeguarding the wider Islamic community.

Alongside these developments the role of protecting and advancing Bosnian Muslim national interests had been taken on by the SDA, which was formally established in May 1990. Its President, Alija Izetbegović, personally subscribed to the IZ's view of Islam as more important than national identity and in a July 1990 interview with *Valter* said "I love my Muslim nation but I'm not too much in love with it. For me ideological orientation is more meaningful than national feeling . . . At the end of the day nationality is based on biology, not on the soul".[1] The SDA's campaign emphasized religious freedom, many of its personnel had close links with the IZ, and some had left IZ employment in order to be active within it (and it was with accusations of over-religiosity and Islamic fervour that Vice-President Adil Zulfikarpasić left the SDA to form his own party just weeks before the elections).

In spite of the SDA's religious flavour, however, it is important to point out that it was not a pan-Islamic party but a national one focusing on the Bosnian Muslims' rights and prospects, and thus ran in parallel with the efforts of the Serbian SDS and Croatian HDZ. In doing so it relieved the IZ of this task, leaving it free to concentrate on supra-national Islam in Yugoslavia. In certain respects the two organizations' efforts mirrored each other. Whereas the IZ supported national specificity as a means of protecting Muslim populations and the wider Islamic community, the SDA supported first a united Yugoslavia, then a mixed federal/confederal Yugoslavia and finally a united, multinational independent Bosnia–Herzegovina as a means of protecting Bosnian Muslims, whose safety is best guaranteed under an umbrella including Serbs and Croats.[2]

Links between political and religious activism and activists have a history stretching back to the period of Austro–Hungarian rule and the interwar years when the brother of the JMO's post-1921 president was the 1938–42 Reis-ul-Ulema. Yet such interconnections say little about Muslim desires for religio-political rule. In the early 1990s the SDA's clerical flavour and the increasing energy and vocality of the IZ-fuelled Serbian claims about the Muslims' alleged aim of an Islamic Bosnia. An increased interest in Islamic religious activity on the part of ordinary Muslims (an interest mirrored within the Serbian Orthodox Croatian Catholic populations) provided further ammunition for the attack. Yet rather than a leaning towards the

---

1. Quoted by T. Loza in *Ex-Yugofax*, No.13, August 1992.
2. The sda also campaigned in the Sandzak region of Serbia and Montengro, as did the interwar jmo who called Sandzak Muslims "blood of our blood" (Purivatra 1972). Like Bosnians, Sandzaklian Muslims call themselves "Muslimani", and many have relatives in Bosnia. "Ethnic cleansing" has been reported in parts of the Sandzak in 1992.

Middle East or fundamentalism, the activities of the IZ and SDA, and certainly of ordinary Muslims, were largely aimed at and understood in relation to Europe.

The passing of communism and the 1990 rise of the three national parties left many Sarajevans, and particularly those old enough to remember the Second World War, disturbed at the prospect of revived ethnic tension. A poll conducted in three Bosnian towns in May 1990 (see *Danas* 22 May 1990) saw 73 per cent in favour of the ruling (later overturned) banning nationally based parties.[3] But along with the uneasiness there was also optimism about Yugoslavia's eventual prosperity and entry into the EC. 1990 and 1991 saw Muslim Sarajevans fasting and celebrating Ramadan and participating in religious rituals in greatly increased numbers. The old Islamic revival of the mid-1980s now appeared to be joined by new enthusiasts, and the meeting of the two was sometimes the cause of conflicts and misunderstandings (see Sorabji 1992). What is important is that the majority of those enjoying the new freedom of religious expression saw their activities as intimately related to their new European future. The freedom to worship openly was one strongly associated with the values of the West, and the demise of communism and the one-party regime that had inhibited religious activity was seen as the opening of a door to freedoms and democracy intimately associated with ideas of that West.

The new IZ constitution of April 1990 echoed this feeling. The document redefined the Yugoslav IZ's identity along three lines. First, it adopted Arabic names for various of its restructured organs: *Mesihat* and *Riyaset* replaced the Serbo–Croatian "Staresinstvo" and thus legitimated the IZ in relation to the wider Islamic world. Secondly, the IZ assembly that had previously represented Bosnia–Herzegovina, Croatia and Slovenia was substituted with two separate assemblies, one based in Sarajevo, the other in Zagreb. This restructuring accompanied the IZ's aim of continued unity in the event of Yugoslavia's division. Above all, however, the new constitution emphasized and advertised itself with the concept of democracy and of giving a voice to Muslims at the lower levels of the establishment. Given the popular association of democracy specifically with the new Europe, this move stressed the Islamic community's relationship with the Western rather than the Eastern world.

With the JNA's summer 1991 attack on Slovenia and the later warfare between Serbia and Croatia, many Sarajevan Muslims held fast to the belief that, although Serbs and Croats may fight, Muslims were too civilized for such hostility and would remain calm and reasonable in the face of all. This

---

3. With 1,039 respondents, all of whom had telephones and lived in major towns, this survey cannot represent a scientific sample of Bosnian opinion in general. But it does give some idea of urban views and perhaps casts some light on the later development of a Sarajevan understanding of the war as urban/rural conflict.

rational and peaceful stance was one deemed entirely in keeping with the Europe that they believed would protect them from Serbia and Croatia, as well as with Islam, seen as a religion of justice and tolerance. As the war approached Bosnia itself, the idea of European-style civil values was re-understood by many Sarajevan Muslims as pertaining to Bosnians *en masse* rather than Muslims in particular. At the same time, SDA officials, alongside their contacts in the Islamic world, made increasing and far stronger attempts to gain the support of the EC and UN, and, in doing so, altered their outlook from a Muslim nationalist one to the all-Bosnian stance that has characterized their politics throughout the war. When the shelling of Sarajevo began in April 1992, a third interpretation began to emerge: rather than Muslim civility versus non-Muslim aggression, or Bosnian civility versus non-Bosnian aggression, this was a conflict between urban civility and peasant aggression.

The future

No national identities are cast in stone: all are constructed in relation to other identities and all change in nuance over time. This is as true of Croatian and Serbian as of Muslim identity, but the Bosnian Muslims' extreme vulnerability to political turbulence in the Balkans and their dual and interrelated membership of Europe and Islam makes changes in their political orientation more necessary and change in their self-perception of identity more evident. In the lead up to war in Bosnia, ordinary Muslims emphasized the way in which Islam, seen as a religion of justice and tolerance, identified them with western Europe (as well as with the beleaguered Albanians of Kosova). What precise role Islam and the concept of "Europe" will play in their future self-perception is, at this stage of the war, hard to foresee.

Along with Croatian public opinion, some in western Europe appear to be expecting a full-scale turning towards the Middle East and Jihad. Given that in retrospect their pre-war "reasonableness" and "civility" seems no more than naïvety and blindness, it would be strange were Bosnia's Muslims not to become more politically radicalized. However, the expectation of a rapid and wholesale transformation into Mujahedin probably owes more to European fears (and self-justifications) than to Bosnian reality.

At the end of 1991, Turkey established a consulate in Sarajevo; by July 1992 it had supplied 7,000 tons of relief aid to Bosnia and, without wanting to act unilaterally, it had pressed for more international action on behalf of Bosnia and its Muslims. In June 1992, Saudi Arabia reportedly raised more than £10 million for Bosnia, and most of the supplies donated to the Croatia-based Muslim charity Merhamet come from Saudi Arabia. Iran supplied weapons and in August 1992 Iran pressed for action on the

Muslims' behalf. Small numbers of freelance fighters from various parts of the Muslim world are fighting alongside Bosnian Muslims. Although this is perceived as being too little too late, in comparison with what has been offered by Europe it is at least something. But it is not quite enough to erase the feeling that the whole world has abandoned Bosnia–Herzegovina. And although Bosnian Muslims do not share Christian suspicion of the Middle East simply on the grounds that it is (largely) Muslim, this does not imply that they are at home with the customs and expectations of those Middle Eastern freelance fighters who arrive in Bosnia to aid the war effort. An increasing emphasis on a radical Islam associated with the Middle East is therefore a probable *element* within a general radicalization, but is by no means the whole story.

Europe's failure to intervene does not automatically crush Muslims' understanding of themselves as Europeans. An alternative possibility is an increased sense of self as authentic Europeans (perhaps drawing more heavily than heretofore on their claimed descent from the pre-Ottoman Bosnian Church, a heresy associated with Bogomilism) betrayed by a decadent and "non-European" Europe. Such a stance would have parallels with the Serbian view of Serbs as the misunderstood Europeans, the defenders of Europe against Islam and the East.

The Islamska Zajedica's aim of maintaining and fostering a supranational Islamic community in the region has been shattered by the war and the build-up to it. As early as March 1991, from the heart of an expanding Serbia, Belgrade's Mufti threatened to sever his community from the increasingly pro-Albanian IZ. The sympathy felt in Kosova for Bosnia's Muslims is based only in part on shared Muslim traditions, for the Islam of Kosova has always been a more tekija/dervish based version than that of Bosnia, and the Albanian population anyway includes Catholic and Orthodox members. At any rate, whatever the sympathies, Kosova's energy is primarily directed towards avoiding the aggression of Serbia.[4]

---

4. Much of the chapter stands the test of time. Those wishing to bring the story up to the mid-1990s are advised to refer to the following article by Enes Karic: "Islam in Contemporary Bosnia", Q News, 16 February–1 March, 10, 1996.

References

Akiner, S. 1983. *The Islamic peoples of the Soviet Union*. London: KPI.

Banac, I. 1984. *The national question in Yugoslavia*. Ithaca, New York: Cornell University Press.

Carrere d'Encausse, H. 1979. *Decline of an empire*. New York: Newsweek Books.

Donia, R. 1981. *Islam under the Double Eagle*. New York: Columbia University Press.

Hadzihajić , M. 1974. *Od tradicije do identita*. Sarajevo: Svjetlost.

Lockwood, W. 1975. *European Muslims: economy and ethnicity in western Bosnia*. New York: Academic Press.

Purivatra, A. 1972. *Jugoslovenska Muslimanska Organizacija u Politickom zivotu Karljevine Srba, Harvata i Slovenaca*. Sarajevo: Svjetlost.

Ralić , P. 1992. *Who's who in Bosnia and Herzegovina*. Belgrade.

Sorabji, C. 1992. Mixed motives: Islam, nationalism and mevluds in an unstable Yugoslavia. In *Muslim women's choices: religious belief and social reality*, C. El-Solh & J. Mabro (eds). Oxford: Berg.

Tapper, R. & N. Tapper 1987. Thank God we're secular! Aspects of fundamentalism in a Turkish town. In *Aspects of fundamentalism*, L. Caplan (ed.), 51–78. London: MacMillan.

Tudjman, F. 1981. *Nationalism in contemporary Europe*. New York: Columbia University Press.

CHAPTER FIVE

Borders, states, citizenship: unscrambling Yugoslavia

JOHN B. ALLCOCK

The Socialist Federative Republic of Yugoslavia (SFRY) is no more. The former League of Communists, which gave to the country both its cohesion and its distinctive direction, disintegrated irrecoverably at its aborted XIVth Congress in January 1990; and the fragments that remain within the various republics have reconstituted themselves as distinct parties. Each has its own name and its own constitution; and although each declares itself to be a "modern party in the European tradition of democratic socialism" (or something along those lines), it is plain from their conduct that they each address the struggle for power within an exclusively republican framework.

Beginning with the secession of Slovenia and Croatia, on 26 June 1991, each of the republics of the former federation has declared its own independence, autonomy or "sovereignty", although in several cases their future form is far from certain. At the time of writing, civil war still rages in Bosnia–Hercegovina; somewhere between a third and a quarter of the Croatian republic is controlled by secessionist local Serbs and subject to supervision by the UN Protection Force; an independent republic of "Kosova" strives unsuccessfully to elevate itself above the level of a concept. A "third Yugoslavia" – the so called Federal Republic – uniting Serbia and Montenegro, remains without international recognition.

The story of the second Yugoslavia has drawn to its close as terribly as did the first. For many, this outcome has been only what one should have expected. Stefan Pavlowitch has entitled a perceptive and ironic collection of essays *The improbable survivor* (Pavlowitch 1988), which perhaps conveys the impression that the 46 years of the existence of the SFRY are the fact that really requires explanation, and not its final demise. An intellectually less respectable breed of commentators, the kind of *lumpenintelligentzia* that inevitably provides the core of nationalist movements, writing with that special degree of perceptiveness that hindsight always brings, assure us that the end of socialist Yugoslavia is not only as terrible but also as inevitable as that of royal Yugoslavia.

Everywhere the press writes of "playing the nationalist card" – for so long concealed up the sleeve of history – which has brought the Yugoslav experiment to its necessary end. As the nationalist ideal trumps the cards of all the other players, and states are forced to bow to the inexorable reality of nationhood, the game has terminated and all bluffs have been called. A new deal is called for, in which states will arise in the Balkans, this time constituted upon their natural and necessary basis of nationality. (This metaphor has been discussed critically in Allcock 1992a.)

The trouble with this kind of political folk wisdom is that it leaves too many of the loose ends of history unaccounted for. Certainly, if one tries to write a kind of "Whig interpretation of history" with regard to the Balkans, which sets out to tell the story of an inevitable movement towards the creation of free and democratic nation-states in the region, huge areas of acknowledged fact have been subjected to historical sleight of hand, or at least apologetically bracketed for the time being. Not only is it necessary to set aside movements for South Slav unity dating back to Napoleon's Illyrian Provinces, the search for "Trialist" solutions to the problems of the structure of the Dual Monarchy, or the existence in one form or another of a unified state in the region for most of the time since the First World War, but somehow one must overlook the inconvenient fact that no single nation on the territory that was known as Yugoslavia has ever constituted an independent modern state.[1] It is hard to see what kind of historical necessity can be attributed to the nation-state in this part of the Balkans.

Some definitions

As this chapter is written within the discipline and traditions of sociology, which sets it off from the majority of others in this collection, it is as well to begin with some definitions. Terms taken for granted within one intellectual tradition are often given different emphasis in others. Two key terms in the discussion that follows will be "state" and "nation".

The first of these terms belongs (in Max Weber's phrase) "in the house of power". The central characteristic of a state is that the agencies of government claim to exercise legitimate authority over a given territory. To the notion of statehood is attached that of "citizenship", which links together those claims that the state is able to enforce upon all those who live within that territory (duties), and, reciprocally, the rights that individuals may seek to realize either in relation to their co-citizens or the state itself. These configurations of duties and rights bind, or are available to, all those who are regarded as fully adult participants in the political process in that

---

1. An excellent recent discussion of the different forms and emphases taken by the "Yugoslav idea" is given in Djilas (1992).

territory, regardless of other statuses that they may enjoy. The idea of citizenship has a vital part to play in the legitimation of modern state regimes, and in securing the compliance of all who inhabit their territories.[2]

"Nations" on the other hand, belong in "the house of culture". They have to do with the sense of identity that individuals possess, typically as members of communities that are more inclusive than kin groups. They have emerged in the modern world as the largest and most inclusive reference groups with which individuals typically identify.[3]

Since the French Revolution these two concepts have been linked very often in theory and practice, in that, ideally, the citizens of a state should also share the same national identity. Conversely, it is expected that the members of a nation will possess some continuous piece of territory on which they will live, and where government will be exercised in their interests. (This idea is commonly expressed in terms of a putative "right to self-determination".)

There have been obvious advantages to the construction of this linkage, in terms of the reinforcement of the legitimacy of state regimes. Citizenship and nationality work together to tie individuals into the reproduction of political order through a double moral bond. Their obligation as citizens of the state operate as reinforcement to their commitment to the national community; and their claims to be able to exercise rights are given force by the sense of mutual solidarity as co-nationals. Both the theory and the practice of the modern state have come to rely heavily upon at least an implicit link between the two.[4] The "nation-state" became the characteristic political form in which modernity was expressed.

In fact, however, the link has been less than perfect. There are many examples of the union in a single state of people of more than one nationality. It is not at all unusual for people to change their citizenship (e.g. through migration) while retaining their nationality. Nevertheless, just as economic theorists expect that a modern capitalist economy will function most effectively when there is a "perfect market" for the factors of production, so too the modern state is expected to function best where there is a "perfect polity". Where ascriptive factors such as nationality interfere to give citizens differential access to the political process, so the problems of legitimation are compounded. Where a state is populated by groups with differing nationalities, it is vital for its uncomplicated functioning that these

---

2. The lively current interest in the concept of citizenship is suggested by the recent republication of Marshall's *Citizenship and social class* (1992). An interesting discussion of the links between citizenship, the nation-state and nationalism, which differs in some respects from that presented here, is presented in Giddens (1987).

3. There has been a rapid growth of work on nationality and nationalism in recent years. See especially Hobsbawm (1990) and Kellas (1991).

4. I have to acknowledge that these issues are often conceptualized rather differently in the USA, where the terms "citizenship" and "nationality" tend to be used indiscriminately.

differences are bracketed, and that all participate in politics simply as citizens.

Life is in reality a good deal more complex; and just as one rarely if ever encounters a perfect market in the economic world, so too the "perfect polity" is a theoretical rather than an empirical reality. Nevertheless, the distinction is a useful one in helping us to understand the problems associated with the disintegration of Yugoslavia, which have to do in very large measure with the difficulty (perhaps one should say in relation to the Balkans, the impossibility) of mapping nationality onto territory.

Yugoslavia's external borders

The main concern of this chapter is with the division of the former Yugoslav state, and hence its principal preoccupation is with the change in status of what were previously internal borders. Nevertheless, a few remarks are in order about the international context of this process.

There is an old Yugoslav joke about the country's international borders: *"Jugoslavija je okružena brigama"* (Yugoslavia is surrounded by cares). The word "cares" (*brigama*) is an anagram composed of the initial letters of the names of the seven neighbouring states. The sense of threat implied here has to do in large measure with the way in which no single one of these frontiers corresponds to an uncontested ethnographic boundary; neither are they sanctioned by any great antiquity.

A rapid review of these is appropriate, in the order suggested by the anagram. Somewhere in the region of 30,000 Bulgars still occupy six municipalities along Serbia's eastern frontier. The Macedonian/Bulgarian frontier is still the subject of a substantial Bulgarian question mark. Perhaps 50,000 Romanians are to be found east of Smederevo, and in the Vojvodina, principally around Vršac. Serbian historic claims run as far into Romania as Arad.[5] On the Yugoslav side of the frontiers between Italy and Slovenia/ Croatia there are still about 12,000 Italians and an uncertain number of Slovenes and Croats on the Italian side of the divide. The situation is complicated by the fact that many people in the region still declare themselves to be "Istrians". Macedonia is unhappy about the alleged suppression of

---

5. The map that was presented to the peace conference after the First World War by the Yugoslav Committee conveys graphically these ambitions (a copy of this without attached credit as to its source is in the archives of the Research Unit in South East European Studies at the University of Bradford). This has clearly been adapted as the basis for Boban (1992: *Karta* I, p.15). This more recently published version downplays considerably the extent of former Yugoslav territorial ambitions, especially in Albania, Bulgaria, Greece and Romania. All figures for contemporary ethnic distribution cited in this paper are from *Savezni Zavod za Statistiku*, 1991. Additional information about the distribution of national minorities within the region is given in Poulton (1991).

Slav identity in Greece. The Slovenes remain keenly aware that the referendum in the Klagenfurt Basin after the First World War created a border that they regard as unnatural. The distinctive complexities of the ethnography of the Vojvodina meant that the drafting of any state boundary in that region was bound to be arbitrary. Historic Serb claims in Hungary extend as far north as Baja in Szeged: on the other hand, there are still more than 350,000 Magyars in the Vojvodina. Finally, Albanian settlement extends into Yugoslavia along the length of the international frontier, with an estimated 2.2 million Albanians distributed principally in the former Autonomous Province of Kosovo and western Macedonia.

No international frontier between the former Yugoslav federation and any of its neighbours is older than the end of the Balkan Wars (1911–13); many sections date only to the end of the First World War, and the frontier with Italy was settled on its present line only after the resolution of the Trieste crisis in 1954.[6]

Two criteria (ethnographic distribution and historical association) are generally taken as laying the foundation for stable and legitimate state frontiers. The fact that they are not met with any regularity in the case of the international borders of the former federation transmits a significant measure of uncertainty into much of the discussion about the legitimacy and viability of new states that might be constructed out of the debris of Yugoslavia. The problem is compounded by the fact that these criteria are even less able to provide us with an uncontested basis for the transformation of former internal administrative boundaries into international frontiers.

Yugoslavia's internal borders

The Yugoslav state was composed across one of the major liminal zones of Europe: but the historical accretion of lines of division did not leave a coherent pattern of units that could be disaggregated simply. Each historical era has left different and conflicting traces, none less arbitrary than the others. Although ideologists of each nation make appeal to definite territories as their "traditional", "historical" or "natural" homelands, these are typically to a large extent either fictionalized or at best a montage of pieces chosen from quite different periods in the past. This is true even of those lines of cleavage that are cited as having the greatest antiquity and the most obvious character.

---

6. Actually the question of the Italian border was not determined definitively until the Treaty of Osimo, in 1975. For a more detailed treatment of some of these issues see, Allcock (1992b) and Englefield (1992).

Three of the criteria generally cited as the major focal points for the growth and consolidation of national identity have been important as the bases for typical claims to national territory in Yugoslavia: religion, historical association with territory, and language. In the case of the south Slavs, none of these provides an unambiguous guide to the way in which nation-states may be delineated, and not infrequently they contradict each other.

Religion

Possibly the least contested point of difference in the Balkans is that which separates the Roman Catholic north and west from the Orthodox south and east (Croats and Slovenes from Serbs, Montenegrins and Macedonians). Yet even this is far from clear as a guide to the link between peoples and land. What is meant by the notion of an historical line of division between eastern and western Christianity depends upon whether reference is being made to the patterns of missionary activity responsible for the conversion to Christianity of the local population, the cleavage between the eastern and western Churches of 1054, or the *de facto* boundaries of ecclesiastical organization after the fall of Constantinople in 1453. Furthermore, the notion of an essential historical divide of this kind ignores completely the extensive movements of migration that, whatever the original state of the board, have rearranged the pieces since then. Whichever of these original starting lines one chooses it would divide modern Montenegro, and maroon all Serbs west and north of the Drina, Sava and Danube rivers on the "Roman" side of it.

The principal drawback in using the schismatic division within Christianity as a basis for identifying national territory in this region is the obdurate fact of the existence of many Muslims. Although the rise of a succession of independent states in the Balkans has been used regularly as a pretext for the expulsion of "Turks", it remains the case that the former Yugoslavia was the home to the largest indigenous Islamic population in Europe (Popović 1986, Norris 1993). The census of April 1991 recorded more than 2.3 million ethnic Muslims, to which should be added an unknown number of those who declared their nationality as Serb, Macedonian or "Yugoslav" while adhering to the Islamic faith. In addition to these, the majority of the estimated 2.2 million Albanians and many of the 200,000 Romanies were also Muslims. This means that, given the fact that the reported number of Albanians is almost certainly an underestimate, more than 4.5 million of the 24 million inhabitants of the SFRY, or roughly a fifth of the population, were Muslims.

The selection of religion as a principal focus for national consciousness, and subsequently as the basis for the delineation of states, provides the occasion for one of the most difficult of all of the current problems facing the region. In particular, the relatively recent, but rapid and effective (although incomplete), ethnogenesis of Muslims, has complicated enormously the task of determining the future of the Republic of Bosnia–Hercegovina, where ethnic Muslims constituted about 41 per cent of the population at the time of the census. Substantial numbers of Muslims in the Sandžak are an embarrassment within a Serbian state in which national consciousness is ever more frequently and forcefully identified with Orthodox Christianity. Above all, in spite of the fact that language is by far the most salient factor in the formation of Albanian national consciousness, the fact that the great majority of Albanians are Muslims has become one of the principal features focusing hostility on them in both Serbia and Macedonia.

The structure of religious adherence in Yugoslavia therefore cuts across rather than reinforces several of the other potential lines along which territorial division might take place.

Historical association with territory

A significant complicating fact in any discussion of the proper boundaries for the successor states to Yugoslavia is the long shadow cast by the great empires. Although the memory of Samo (AD 627–58) touches Slovene consciousness only lightly, the medieval states all feature prominently in the definition of the "historical" territories and identities of the other South Slav peoples. Hence, Macedonians base their own sense of antiquity by reference to Samuil (976–1014); the Croats see newly independent Croatia as taking up where Zvonimir (1076–89) left off; Serbs aspire to the reconstitution of the empire of Dušan (1331–55); even the Bosnians are able to legitimate the idea of an historically continuous Bosnian political entity by citing the kingdom of Tvrtko (1353–91). The unavoidable drawback with all of these historical justifications for statehood is that from a territorial point of view they are massively contradictory. Their contribution to contemporary debate, if it extends beyond promoting a diffuse sense of national self-worth, can only be bloodshed.

If any single historical fact can be taken as dominating the contemporary consciousness of the south Slav peoples, however, it is the history of their division between the two great empires – Habsburg and Ottoman. Slovenes and Croats often remind others of the significance of this divide in terms of differences of economic development and "civilization". Any attempt to use their legacy as a guide to the delineation of nation-states on the Balkan Peninsula today, however, is doomed to failure.

The boundary between the spheres of influence of the Austro–Hungarian and Turkish states fluctuated widely before the Treaty of Carlowitz in 1699. Even so, the line determined on that occasion is probably the most stable border in the Balkans. Separating Croatia from Bosnia–Hercegovina, however, it makes no sense ethnographically and is of little help in relating peoples to territory. Centuries of migration, and especially the creation of the Hasbsburg "Military Frontier" during the eighteenth century, have led to the settlement of many Serbs north and west of that line, in lands that Croats have claimed as parts of "historical" Croatia. The attempt to secure the autonomy of Serb areas within Croatia (the so-called Krajina and Banija) is rooted in these population movements (see Rothenberg 1960, 1966, Nouzille 1991). If this line were to be taken as a guide to state draftsmanship, Serbia would be deprived entirely of the Vojvodina. The other side of the coin, of course, is that Ottoman advance overran large areas of Croat settlement that retain their sense of ethnic identity in Hercegovina.

Within the confines of the great empires there were, of course, other historical divisions of sovereignty or administrative responsibility. These too are typically of little help in determining lines along which new states might be demarcated. The post-1945 frontier between Slovenia and Croatia does not correspond completely to the ancient borders of the Habsburg Duchies of Carniola and Styria and the region of Küstenland (Englefield 1992: 10–11). On this basis, negotiations were set in motion during 1993 in order to settle the dispute between the two republics over the precise demarcation of their mutual boundary.

More dramatic is the difficulty of determining the borders of "Croatia". It has been a characteristic of Croatian nationalism since the nineteenth century to refer to the "thousand year" history of a Croatian political community.[7] This idea is more ideological than strictly historical in character. Following the transfer of the Croatian crown to Hungary in 1089, the Croatian lands were battered by historical changes over several centuries, especially by the rise of a Bosnian state under Tvrtko, the expansion of Venice, and in the fifteenth century by the Ottoman invasion. Anything that could meaningfully be called an independent Croatian state was obliterated by the defeat at Mohácz in 1526, following which Turkish suzerainty was extended briefly as far north as Vienna. Turkish power north of the Sava was not finally broken until the War of the Holy League in 1699. Large areas of what is now the Republic of Croatia were then incorporated into the so-called "Military Frontier", which was directly answerable to Vienna rather than Budapest. Venetian power waxed and waned along the Adriatic coast. The existence of an independent Ragusan republic (modern Dubrovnik), until its overthrow by the armies of Napoleon, should not be overlooked. The political history of those regions that have now come to be considered as "Croatia"–Slavonia, central Croatia, Dalmatia and Istria – has been very diverse. The territory that now falls

---

7. This sense of continuity is displayed very well in a lavish collection of old maps recently published in Zagreb amid enormous publicity. See Muzej za Umjetnost i Obrt (1992).

within the Republic of Croatia therefore was never part of a single unified state before the creation of the Kingdom of the Serbs, Croats and Slovenes at the end of the First World War.[8]

Within the former Ottoman lands, the task of finding historical foundations for modern nation-states is no easier. To some extent the border between Bosnia and Serbia, along the Drina river, and between Serbia and Macedonia, is sanctioned in the boundaries of the former Turkish *vilayets*; but the Ottoman view of Montenegro would give little cheer to the contemporary government in Podgorica!

If recent census figures relating to declared ethnicity are taken as the basis for mapping borders, then the boundaries of Montenegro stand out as clear and uncomplicated. Such clarity is almost entirely spurious, however, as successive redraftings of the frontiers of Montenegro took place during the nineteenth century entirely in response to considerations of *realpolitik* – typically according to the principal of "the spoils to the victors".

Language

The criterion that possibly is most often evinced by nation-builders who embark upon the drafting of state boundaries is language. Here too we find ourselves on uncertain ground in redrawing the map of Yugoslavia. Linguists generally acknowledge the standardization of three languages in the former federation: Serbo–Croat, Slovene and Macedonian. The process of standardizing each of these on the foundation of a group of dialects has been in some respects controversial, and in each case under different historical circumstances the linguistic map of the Balkans could have been drawn differently.

This is even true of one of the politically least contested of divisions in this respect. Had the history of the standardization of Slovene or Croatian taken a different course, the small differences between the same dialects of the former and the *kajkavski* dialect of the latter might have permitted a

---

8. The idea of a "thousand year history" has served two quite different ideological purposes over the centuries. At first the insistence upon a presumed continuity with the kingdom of Zvonimir was principally significant as a legal symbol deployed during the late eighteenth and nineteenth centuries in order to defend the rights of the Croatian nobility vis-a-vis the Habsburg crown. The reference is clearly to an entitlement that is of greater antiquity than the union with Hungary. Following the unification of the Croat lands with the Yugoslav state, the entire rhetorical focus of this image of historical continuity has shifted. The Croatian nobility was finished as a political force by this time, but the same rhetoric was taken over by more modern political forces as a defence against other South Slav (and typically Serbian) attempts to control Croatian economic and political destiny. It has survived into our own day, when it has found in the hands of a new nationalistic, anti-communist elite.

mutual assimilation. A key feature in the differentiation of Slovene from Croatian was the standardization of the latter upon the *štokavski* group of dialects. In the early history of Croatian literature, in fact, the use of the *čakavski* speech of the Dalmatian coast provided the basis for written communication.[9] This period, still regarded by some as a literary Golden Age, lasted until the end of the sixteenth century. At this time several important figures began to use *kajkavski* as a vehicle for literary expression, and also *štokavski*. By the end of the seventeenth century, however, *štokavski* had secured a kind of consensus as the dominant form; and although both *čakavski* and *kajkavski* continued to be used a creative media, they remained in effect marginalized. This development confirmed the relative isolation and separate development of Slovene and Croatian, and linked the future development of Slovene and Croatian firmly with that of the Serbs.

It is often thought (quite mistakenly) that the speech of Serbs and Croats is differentiated by the use of the *ekavski* variant by the former, and the *ijekavski* variant by the latter, of the *štokavski* group of dialects. In fact the area of *ijekavski* speech includes most Serbs resident in Croatia and Bosnia, is shared with Montenegrins and (most remarkably) the inhabitants of the heartland of "old Serbia" – Raška and the Sandžak. What is more, when the founder of Serb philology, Vuk Karadžić, looked for a model of "pure" speech upon which to base his standardization of the language in the early nineteenth century, he chose that of eastern Hercegovina – far from Serbia itself, and typically *ijekavski* – thus further cementing the possibilities for standardizing a common Serbo–Croat language.

Vuk's decision was especially significant with respect to another aspect of the standardization of "Serbian" speech, namely the marginalization of the "Timok–Prizren" dialect. The distribution of this cannot be mapped with great precision, but it extends southeastwards of a line running roughly between Zaječar and Prizren, but dipping south of both Priština and Niš. This dialect shares a number of features with Bulgarian (such as its attenuated case structure), and indeed many nineteenth-century ethnographers mapped it as such.[10] Whatever the rights and wrongs of the controversy about the status of Macedonian in relation to Bulgarian, the existence of this dialect certainly complicates the task of distinguishing Serbs unambiguously from Macedonians, and fuels Serbian nationalist claims that Macedonia is really "South Serbia".[11]

---

9. This section on language is based principally upon Magner (1967), Franolić (1984), Lenček (1982), Comrie & Corbett (1993: Chs 6 and 7).

10. A fine collection of such maps is available in Strupp 1929, including sources from Austria, Britain, Czechoslovakia, France, Germany, Italy, the League of Nations, Russia, Serbia and the USA. The degree of agreement between them is remarkable.

11. One possible implication of this line of argument is that it validates the good sense of the proposals of the San Stefano settlement – but that would be to set the cat among the pigeons!

Any sociologically informed scrutiny of the use of language as the basis for the determination of the shape of nation-states in former Yugoslavia must recognize that the process of standardization has been everywhere to some extent arbitrary. Far from it being the case that state borders have been mapped onto linguistic ones, it is more true to say that linguistic-standardization has been used as an instrument of state-building. (This is nowhere clearer than in the case of Macedonian, which has only been standardized in the period since 1945, and quite plainly has been seen as a primary cultural buttress to the existence of the politically distinct Macedonian state and nation (Galpin 1975).

These processes are still at work today, as is witnessed by the efforts currently being made to bring about the linguistic equivalent of "ethnic cleansing". In post-independence Croatia a combination of neologism and linguistic archaeology is being employed to replace "Serbianisms" with "purely" Croatian words or phrases. Equally, within the Serb-controlled areas of Croatia and Bosnia–Hercegovina (and even among more cosmopolitan groups in Serbia itself) there has been a campaign to eliminate the use of the Latin script.[12]

In praise of citizenship

The conclusion of this review is that there is no clear basis for mapping state boundaries onto the distribution "peoples" within the territory that formerly constituted Yugoslavia. The use of terms such as "Serb", "Croat" or "Slovene" as anything like the denominator of a modern nation is a creation of the late nineteenth century, and in the case of terms such as "Montenegrin" or "Macedonian" the phenomenon is even more recent. It is equally important to point out that the process of naming and delineating nations has had its corollary in the elimination of other contenders for use that might be considered to be historically at least as valid.[13]

---

12. The Belgrade news weekly *Intervju* changed from Latin to Cyrillic script at the beginning of 1993 in response to this kind of political pressure.

13. Pre-eminent among these possibilities is a "Bosnian" identity. It is not difficult to make out a case for the historical longevity of a concept of specifically Bosnian identity, although the historical evidence is rather contradictory. Many observers have noted that typically in the past Bosnians would distinguish themselves as "Muslim", "Orthodox" or "Catholic" (i.e. by specifically religious allegiance), rather than as "Muslim", "Serb", or "Croat" (i.e. by ethnic identity). There is some evidence that this pattern was unevenly established with respect to period, region and ethnicity (the Serb–Orthodox link being more common than the Croat–Catholic). The attempt to establish these differences systematically in terms of ethnic labels is largely a post-war creation, and indeed until the outbreak of the civil war was still incomplete in large areas of the republic. (For discussion of aspects of this question, see Ramet 1990.)

Nevertheless, we are now faced with a kind of reality, however irrational its basis may appear, in which history has bequeathed to the Balkans a rich but contradictory vocabulary of "national" identity, together with a pattern of emergent states. There is no possibility of starting with a *tabula rasa*. Marx's dictum that "men make their own history, but not with materials of their own choosing" is no more true than in this region. The collapse of Yugoslavia confronts the peoples of former Yugoslavia with the task of reconstructing the pattern of states in the region. However, it is by no means clear upon what basis political order might be re-established in the Balkan Peninsula, in a way that steers a reasonable course between national mythologies, the undisguised use of force, or the appalling prospect of population movements designed conform ethnicity to state boundaries? One possible answer lies in renewed attention to the concept of "citizenship". Possibly the most urgent problem facing the Balkans is the task of decoupling the notions of nationality and citizenship.

This has, in different senses, been attempted in the past in Yugoslavia, by King Alexander and by Tito. The first tried to create a sense of Yugoslav nationality by decree, and is best symbolized by his division of the country in 1929 into ten *banovine* (governorships).[14] With the exception of the Prefecture of Belgrade, these were named after the principal rivers, and deliberately (for the most part) cut across historical national territories. The intent to undermine specifically national discourse is suggested by the contemporary practice of speaking of Serbs, Croats and Slovenes as three "tribes": by implication these names were characteristic of a pre-modern age, which was to be followed by the creation of a modern nation – Yugoslavia. With the disappearance of these "tribal" identities, it would be possible for all to become equal citizens of the one state. The second such attempt was in some respects highly contradictory, in that, for rhetorical purposes at least, it involved the deliberate creation of new nations – initially Macedonians and Montenegrins, and subsequently Muslims. However, along with this deference to the importance of nationality went a longer-term expectation that the political maturity of Yugoslavia's working class would be accompanied by the withering away of national identity and its replacement by a homogenized Yugoslav identity based specifically upon class.

Whereas in Alexander's "First Yugoslavia", citizenship was tied to the arbitrary attempt to create a new nation, in Tito's "Second Yugoslavia" political identity was deemed to be unproblematic because the state was populated only by a single class – the "working people of Yugoslavia".[15] Both of these endeavours can be regarded as serious attempts at political

---

14. See Boban (1992: Chs IV and V). The borders of the *banovine* were revised in relatively minor respects in 1931. A more serious and extended analysis of the comparisons between these periods is contained in Petranović & Zecević (1991).

modernization, even though they were flawed in fatal respects. Alexander's efforts foundered on the falsity of the belief that one can create a political identity by decree under conditions where the facts of the daily experience of citizens contradict the official version of reality – namely, Serbian hegemony.

The communist vision of a state in which class solidarity replaced the bourgeois concept of nationality was undermined from the outset by the "transitional" arrangements made to secure the legitimacy of the Party. The federal structure that was deemed necessary as a corrective to the "unitarianism" of Royal Yugoslavia from its inception begged the question of the nature of the units of which the state was composed. The public justification given was that "Yugoslavia", was the homeland specifically of the various South Slav peoples, each of which was acknowledged in a republic of its own. *Ad hoc* adjustments were made in order to accommodate Muslims in Bosnia (a "South Slav people" with no republic) and Magyars and Albanians in Serbia (non-Slav peoples nevertheless were given special constitutional status in the Autonomous Provinces). All other ethnic groups were consigned to the status of "nationalities". The distinction between "nations" (*narodi*) and "nationalities" (*narodnosti*) was enshrined within the constitution, and conveyed very clearly the implication that there were differences in the relationship that each had to the state. The principal reason why, in a sense, this did not matter for political purposes (aside from the numerical inferiority of the "nationalities") was the fact that the primary point of attachment of the citizen to the state was through the system of self-management. One's rights and duties were prescribed, first and foremost, in terms of one's status as a member of the "working people of Yugoslavia".

All of this fell apart with the approaching disintegration of the former federation. With the movement towards ever greater independence of the republics during the late 1980s, it became clear that the concept of "national sovereignty" upon which any revised version of Yugoslavia might be founded would replicate *de facto* within the republics this same constitutional distinction. The novel factor under any such new dispensation, however, was that each republic would be identified first and foremost with only one "nation", and that all others living within it could expect to be relegated to the position of "nationalities", regardless of the status they had been able to claim within the post-war federation.[16] Thus, Serbs living in

---

15. The similarities between these attempts merit some comment in the light of the totally different rationales that were advanced. Both schemes largely excluded from discourse some important groups: most notably Macedonians in Alexander's model and Albanians in Tito's. Both attempted to adapt language to their purpose. I have been shown news magazines from the 1930s that printed articles together in Serbo–Croat (using both Latin and Cyrillic scripts) and Slovene, and which captioned pictures in all three. *Borba* adopted a very similar approach in socialist Yugoslavia. Both adopted what was in effect a double standard, using nationality on some occasions and suppressing it on others.

Croatia, for example, or Croats in the Vojvodina, could expect in effect to be deprived of their status as members of a charter group and labelled at least by implication as a kind of *gastarbeiter*. This was, understandably, particularly hurtful to groups that had been resident in these localities for many centuries. It could certainly be represented as threatening by those political leaders (such as Serbia's Slobodan Milošević) who saw that, in the disintegration of the communist system, identification with nationality offered the primary means of relegitimating themselves.

Although the holding of multi-party elections throughout the Yugoslav federation in 1990 was hailed outside Yugoslavia as signalling the arrival of "democracy", for the most part this term remained misplaced. In spite of the novelty of party pluralism, elections hovered uneasily between the established communist plebiscitary form, and a mechanism for producing purely "ethnic" representation. The result has been the creation of what Misha Glenny has called a series of "ethnarchies" (Glenny 1992). In none of the emerging political configurations has there been room for "citizenship" in the sense that we have defined it, a status defined in terms of political rights and duties that attach to individuals regardless of other statuses that they occupy.[17]

Conclusion

The implications of this analysis for the future of the states merging from former Yugoslavia are not encouraging. If the creation of a system of states in this region of which the borders are not open to challenge for one reason or another is impossible, then, for better or worse, the territorial boundaries that have been inherited from the former Yugoslavia may as well be defended. To open the door to particular requests for revision, however apparently reasonable each case might be taken in isolation, would prob-

---

16. I do not have access to constitutional documents relating to Bosnia–Hercegovina at the time of writing: but inspection of the constitutions of all of the other republics shows that in one form or another they perpetuate the distinction of status between a "charter" nation and other "nationalities". See, Republic of Croatia, 1991, Chap. I and Chap. II, Articles 12 and 15; Republic of Macedonia, 1992, Preamble; Republic of Serbia, 1990, Preamble, and Chap. I, Article 8; Republic of Slovenia, 1992, Preamble, and Part I, Articles 5 and 11. Compare the language of these "post-communist" documents with that of Socijalistička Federativna Republika Jugoslavije, 1988, Introduction and Part I.

17. This remains true even in Slovenia, where the relative ethnic homogeneity of the population has permitted a tacit marginalization of the issue of nationality in politics. In effect the "symbolic violence" involved can be considered more blatant in this case, where specific constitutional privileges attach to the "autochthonous minorities" (namely the 2,000 Italians and 9,000 Magyars), whereas the 19,000 Muslims, 52,000 Serbs and 63,000 Croats recorded in the last census are reduced to complete constitutional anonymity (Savezni Zavod za Statistiku 1991).

ably trigger an infinite succession of such requests that, taken as a whole, would not be amenable to reasonable solution. For all their faults the post-war borders are probably the best that are pragmatically available.

Those who entertain the notion that the creation of ethnically homoge-neous states upon the rubble of Yugoslavia is still desirable (or at least the best that can practically be hoped for) ought to consider the following facts. The international community has attempted to broker two different but closely related "solutions" to the problems of Bosnia–Hercegovina. The "Vance–Owen" initiative, which occupied the centre-stage of the UN–EC sponsored negotiations throughout the second half of 1992 and first of 1993, projected the division of the area into ten "cantons" – three identified with each of the principal ethnic groups, together with a mixed prefecture of Sarajevo. Following the demise of this as a realistic prospect, after its rejection by the Bosnian Serb Assembly in April 1993, a second scheme (the "Owen–Stoltenberg" initiative) was proposed, which canvassed the divi-sion of Bosnia–Hercegovina into three quasi-republics, linked into some kind of federation. The lifetime of this project was even shorter than that of its predecessor. By the end of 1993 it had become apparent that none of the three contending parties (for quite different reasons) would sign such an agreement unless they did so under considerable duress. By the end of the year, international attention had switched, in effect, to the achievement of lower-level goals, particularly the securing of Sarajevo as a "safe-haven".

The fate of these schemes, even when supported by very substantial international diplomatic pressure, is indicative of the difficulty of the pros-pect that will face any attempt to map states onto ethnicity in the central Balkans. If two such attempts have failed ignominiously in Bosnia, in spite of the deployment of massive diplomatic pressure from both the UN and the EC, there seems to be little reason for assuming that similarly conceived approaches could prove effective as responses to the remaining problems of state-building in the Balkans.

Even more intractable difficulties are evidently in view, as the skein of problems necessitated by the end of Yugoslavia unravels. In their pursuit of ethnically "pure" and "self-determining" states, the principal parties to the conflict have all intimated ambitions that are mutually contradictory. Serbian demands for a high degree of self-government for the Serbs of the Krajina would seem to imply that (logically) they ought to be prepared to offer the same privileges, based upon the same political theory, to Albani-ans living in Kosovo. Suggestions of this kind invariably meet with a hostile response, and the insistence that at some other level the two cases are not comparable. Croatian active military intervention in support the succes-sion of the mainly Croat "Herceg–Bosna" (western Hercegovina) from Bos-nia–Hercegovina, and its eventual incorporation into a unified Croatian state, are founded upon a commitment to ethnic self-determination, which evaporates the moment one mentions that the same arguments might be applied in the case of Serbs living in the Krajina. The creation of a "Muslim" state in central Bosnia is frequently canvassed as the solution to the problem of finding a future home for "Muslims". However, this proposal is typically considered solely within the context of the search for a negotiated solution to the constitutional structure of Bosnia–Hercegovina. It leaves aside entirely the implications of any such development for the future of the 200,000 Muslims of the Sandžak, the 70,000 Muslims of Kosovo, or the 50,000 Muslims of Macedonia. In short, what may appear as a part of a tidy solution to Bosnia's problems could turn out to be an open invitation to massive "ethnic cleansing" elsewhere.

The "reasonableness" of an outcome, however, has never been a guarantee of its probability. In the middle of a civil war it would be a very rash social scientist who would care to predict its end-state, on these grounds or any other. In particular, it is impossible to foresee the course of the struggle for Bosnia–Hercegovina, the resolution of the problem of Macedonia, and the future disposition of the borders of an Albanian state.

The purpose of this chapter is not to risk predictions of this kind. What certainly follows from the foregoing analysis, however, is that no stable pattern of state boundaries can be constructed in the space formerly occupied by Yugoslavia without there having taken place quite profound cultural changes. The kind of changes envisaged, associated with the development of the concept of citizenship, took a very long time to mature in the countries of western Europe. Although various forms of intervention or assistance by outside powers could conceivably assist that process, a political culture that gives adequate space to citizenship can really be created only out of the political experience of the peoples of former Yugoslavia themselves. Consequently, we may anticipate that the current turmoil in the region will continue in one form or another, in more or less serious measure, for many years to come.

References

Allcock, John B. 1992a. Nationalism and politics in Yugoslavia. In *Europe regional surveys of the world, eastern Europe and the Commonwealth of Independent States*, 290–97. London: Europa Publications.

— 1992b. Yugoslavia. In *Border and territorial disputes*, 3rd edn, 196–217. London: Longman.

Boban, Ljubo 1992. *Hrvatske granice: 1918–1922*, 2nd edn. Zagreb: Hrvatska Akademija Znanosti i Umjetnosti Školksa Knjiga.

Comrie, B. & G. G. Corbett (eds) 1993. *The Slavonic languages*, London Routledge.

Djilas, A. 1992. *The contested country: Yugoslav unity and communist revolution, 1919–1953*. Cambridge, Mass.: Harvard University Press.

Englefield, G. 1992. *Yugoslavia, Croatia, Slovenia: re-emerging boundaries*. Territory Briefing 3, International Boundaries Research Unit, University of Durham.

Franolić, B. 1984. *An historical survey of literary Croatian*. Paris: Nouvelles Editions Latines.

REFERENCES

Galpin, W. 1975. *The introduction of the Macedonian literary language in the Socialist Republic of Macedonia.* MA dissertation, University of Bradford.

Giddens, A. 1987. *Social theory and modern sociology.* Cambridge: Polity.

Glenny, M. 1992. *The fall of Yugoslavia: the Third Balkan War.* London: Penguin.

Hobsbawm, E. J. 1990. *Nations and nationalism since 1790: programme, myth, reality.* Cambridge: Cambridge University Press.

Kellas, J. G 1991. *The politics of nationalism and ethnicity.* London: Macmillan.

Lenček, R. L. 1982. *The structure and history of the Slovene language.* Columbus, Ohio: Slavica.

Magner, T. F. 1967. Language and nationalism in Yugoslavia. *Canadian Slavic Studies* I(3), 333–47.

Marshall T. H. 1992. *Citizenship and social class,* revised edn [with a new preface by Tom Bottomore]. London: Pluto Press.

Muzej za Umjetnost i Obrt 1992. *Granice Hrvatske na Zemljovidima od XII do XX stoljeća.* Zaghreb.

Norris, H. T. 1993. *Islam in the Balkans: religion and society between Europe and the Arab World.* London: Hurst.

Nouzille, Jean 1991. *Histoire des frontières: l'Autriche et l'Empire Ottoman.* Paris: Berg.

Pavlowitch, S. K. 1988. *The improbable survivor: Yugoslavia and its problems, 1918–1988.* London: Hurst.

Petranović , B., & M. Zecević 1991. *Agonija Dve Jugoslavije.* Beograd: Edicija Svedočanstve.

Popović , A. 1986. *L'Islam balkanique.* Berlin: Osteuropa-Institut an der Freien Universität Berlin.

Poulton, H. 1991 (revised edn 1993). *The Balkans: minorities and states in conflict.* London: Minority Rights Publications.

Ramet, S. P. 1990. Primordial ethnicity or modern nationalism: the case of Yugoslavia's Muslims reconsidered. *South Slav Journal* 13(1–2), 1–20.

Republic of Croatia 1991. *The Constitution of the Republic of Croatia.* Zagreb: Sabor Republike Hrvatske.

Republic of Macedonia 1992. The Constitution of the Republic of Macedonia. *Macedonian Review* XXII(1), 95–126.

Republic of Serbia 1990. *The Constitution of the Republic of Serbia.* Belgrade: Kultura.

Republic of Slovenia 1992. *The Constitution of the Republic of Slovenia.* Ljubljana: Uradni list Republike Slovenije.

Rothenherg, G. E. 1960. *The Austrian military border in Croatia, 1522–1747.* Urbana: University of Illinois Press.

— 1966. *The military border in Croatia, 1740–1881: a study of an imperial institution.* Chicago: University of Chicago Press.

Savezni Zavod za Statistiku 1991. *Procene Stanovništva prema Narodnosti za SFR Jujoslaviju, Socijalističke Autonomne Pokrajine, 31.03.91g.* Beograd: SZS.

Socijalistička Federativna Republika Jugoslavije 1988. *Ustav SFRJ i Amandmani na Ustav SFRJ.* Beograd: Privredni Pregled.

Strupp, K. 1929. *La situation juridique des Macedoniens en Yougoslavie.* Paris: Presses Universitaires de France.

CHAPTER SIX
Muslims in the Balkans
GEORGE JOFFÉ

The Muslim presence in eastern Europe derives from the historical experience of the Ottoman empire in the region. There are significant Muslim populations in four of the six southeastern European states – Albania, Bulgaria, Romania and Yugoslavia – which, before the advent of communist control, were recognized as distinct religious entities.

Table 6.1 Muslim communities in southeastern Europe (% of total population).

Country	%	Census year	%	Estimate year
Albania	68.0	1930	70.0	1967
Bulgaria	13.4	1946	13.0	1991
Romania	1.0	1948	*	1991
Yugoslavia	12.3	1953	8.5**	1991

Notes: * No specific figure given. ** This excludes Albanians (14.3%).
Sources: D. Turnock, *Eastern Europe, a political and economic geography,* 120 (London: Routledge, 1989) (census figures); Hellenic Foundation for Defence and Foreign Policy, *The southeastern European yearbook 1991* (Athens: Eliamep, 1992); 313–51 (estimated figures).

The picture is complicated, however, because some Muslim communities are normally defined in ethnic terms. In Poland, for example, the Tartar community – 7,000-strong in pre-war times and 3,000-strong in Poland's postwar borders – contains a sub-community of Muslims estimated to number 1,800 (Turnock 1989: 137). They are concentrated around the northern port city of Gdansk, where a mosque and cultural centre was constructed for them with Libyan funds in the late 1980s. In Bulgaria, the situation is complicated by the classification of Muslims as Pomaks (Muslims of Bulgarian Slavic ethnic origin) and Turks. In 1987, there were 761,664 Turks (2.6%) out of Bulgaria's 8,960,749-strong population and 160,000 Pomaks (1.8%). Some 200,000 Turks are believed to have emigrated during 1988 (Staar 1988: 54). Similar complications exist in Yugoslavia, where the Muslim Torbeskians are classified as Serbs – which is their ethnic identity – whereas Muslim Bosniaks are classified as "Muslims" (Balić 1979: 29). There is also a small Muslim minority in northern Greece, concentrated in Thrace and forming 1.3 per cent of the estimated total Greek population of 10,174 million in 1991 (Eliamep 1992: 325–6).

The Islamization of the Balkans

The concentration of the Muslim populations of eastern Europe into the southern part of the region reflects the differential longevity of Ottoman occupation in different areas. During the latter part of the fourteenth century (1361–93), Ottoman forces moved into the area of modern Bulgaria and Thrace and, after the Battle of Kosovo Polje in 1389, Serbia was forced into vassalship with the Ottoman empire (Mellor 1975: 49). In the latter part of the fifteenth century, Ottoman power was extended into Albania, southern Croatia, Serbia and southern Romania. Albania was finally occupied after the defeat of the Albanian patriot Georg Castrioti Skanderbeg in 1468, in the wake of a 30 year-long resistance to Ottoman forces (Staar 1988: 1). In the sixteenth century the remainder of Yugoslavia and Romania, together with southern Hungary, fell under Ottoman control (Mellor 1975: 49).

After the Ottoman failure to capture Vienna in 1683, however, the tide turned against the Ottoman empire in the Balkans, as the Habsburgs began a slow but steady advance southwards. Hungary and the northern part of Romania was conquered by the Habsburgs during the seventeenth and eighteenth centuries. Austria then penetrated into Croatia, creating an ethnic barrier to any future Ottoman attempt at recovery of control by its policy of border settlement by Catholic Croats. The Ottomans, in their turn, used their Orthodox Serbian subjects in a similar way in the Krajina regions, thus protecting the significant Muslim populations of Bosnia–Herzegovina. The result was to create the ethnic divides that have now destroyed the modern state of Yugoslavia.

Ottoman control of the central and southern Balkans was seriously weakened, however, only after Serbia and associated regions – including Bosnia–Herzegovina, with its significant Bosniak Muslim population – broke away in 1878. Bulgaria, too, obtained independence from the Ottoman empire after Russian intervention between 1876 and 1878, although the territorial extent of the new autonomous state, defined originally by the Treaty of San Stefano and including much of Macedonia and access to the Aegean, was curtailed at British and Austro–Hungarian insistence under the terms of the Treaty of Berlin negotiated later in the same year. Bulgaria did recover some more territory from the Ottoman empire in 1885 and 1912 (Staar 1988: 32–3), but the question of control of Macedonia still causes difficulties even today. For Albania and Macedonia, Ottoman control lasted until the outbreak of the First World War. Albania broke away in 1912 and Macedonia in 1913 (Mellor 1975: 50).

The actual geographical location of Muslim communities inside eastern Europe is also related to the pattern of Islamization that actually occurred there. In fact, Muslim communities, certainly in southern Hungary and the Balkans, pre-dated the Ottoman presence. There are reports of scattered, peaceful communities from the tenth to the twelve centuries, which were then repressed in the thirteenth century (Balić 1979: 29). Even when Otto-manization began in the mid-fourteenth century, there was little evidence of coercion – as conventional European views claim (viz: Mellor 1975: 49–52). The repression usually considered to typify the Ottoman period in the Balkans was, in fact, a feature of the decline of Ottoman control, not of its original imposition.

In fact, conversion appears to have been voluntary in many southern areas and in Bosnia. To a large extent this was because the Ottoman inva-sions coincided with the collapse of the indigenous seigniorial society, divided as it was ethnically, religiously and in terms of wealth. The peas-antry was the most enthusiastic element for change and conversion because of its subjugated state and exploited economic circumstances (Braudel 1975: 663). Indeed, it has been suggested by one commentator that Islam was used by some communities to safeguard its national character-istics, particularly in the case of Albania, where it was eventually used to resist Hellenization and Slavization (Balić 1979: 29).

The taxation system initially imposed by the Ottomans, collected through a system of tax-farming – the *timar*-s – was much less oppressive than its Byzantine predecessor. The *timar* system began to collapse over time, however, as Ottoman financial need increased and tax demands became more oppressive. This combined with active discouragement of conversion by the Ottoman authorities (because it reduced the tax base) to render Ottoman rule increasingly oppressive, and indigenous resistance began to increase as a result. Once again, however, conventional views of this part of the Ottoman period over-emphasize the consequences of the increasing Ottoman repression by suggesting that it resulted in wide-spread depopulation and at Ottoman attempts at genocide, as with the Balkan massacres in Bulgaria in 1876. This was, however, very much more the exception than the rule and, although many communities did retreat to the mountainous areas, the real depopulations of the Balkans occurred only with the introduction of intensive modernized farming methods in the seventeenth century – the *ciftlik*-s (Braudel 1975: 724). As Braudel remarks, "The price of progress, here as elsewhere, was clearly social oppression." (Braudel 1975: 725).

One important aspect of Islamization, however, was the partial integra-tion of the Christian populations of the Balkans into the administration of the Ottoman empire. This was performed through the *devshirme* – an annual levy of adolescent Christian males, mainly from the Balkans. The recruits were then educated in Ottoman Turkish and in Islam within the families of the rural Ottoman gentry, before being sent to Istanbul. There they were divided into groups recruited into the Ottoman civil service or into the Janissaries (*yeni cheri*), the elite regiments of the Ottoman army. The system, which came to maturity in the fifteenth century, had been devel-oped by Murad I to provide an alternative to the Christian levies previously used by the Ottoman empire for its military campaigns (Hodgson 1974: 102).

The Janissary system led to a degree of integration of Christian Balkan populations into the administration of the empire. Indeed, the *devshirme* levy was not actively opposed and conversion was often accepted willingly because of the increase in social status it implied. In addition, it also integrated Islam into indigenous society and, in this respect, was particularly successful in Albania and in Bosnia, where it was powerfully aided by the Bektashiyya order.

The Bektashiyya was a *sufi* order that had been founded by Hajji Bektash Wali in Khurasan in the thirteenth century. Its focus moved towards Anatolia and, on the way, acquired a heterodox *"ithna-ʿashara* Shiʿa character. In its final form it absorbed pre-Islamic and hermetical elements and integrated Christian elements as well. These involved a mass-type reception ceremony for new members, a system of confession, and participation by unveiled women in its ceremonies. An inner group also practised celibacy.

Its importance lay in the fact that it was adopted by the Janissaries, thereby giving the core military arm of the Ottoman empire the character of a unique religious corporation – a typical Ottoman administrative structure. From the fifteenth century onwards, the order acquired exclusive authority over the Janissaries, not least because of its similarity to Christian practice. Indeed, in Albania, where it took particular root, it was described as a "mixed religion" (Gibb & Kramers 1974: 61).

The Bektashiyya order took direct part in Janissary rebellions and, in consequence, was severely affected when Murad II destroyed the Janissaries in 1826. Many of its *tekkes* (*zawiya*-s) were destroyed and its practitioners retired to the periphery of the empire. Despite a revival in the mid-nineteenth century, it was dissolved in Turkey – along with all other religious orders – by the Kemalist state in 1925. Thereafter, until the Second World War, its major focus was in Tirana, the modern Albanian capital. After 1967, however, it was suppressed and a small outpost still remains in Cairo. It is not clear whether or not it will re-emerge in Albania in the wake of the collapse of the communist system there. The order, before its dissolution, played a significant part in establishing Islam in Albania and to a lesser degree Bosnia (Gibb & Kramers 1974: 62).

By the end of the nineteenth and the start of the twentieth century, therefore, Islam had become a stable element within the complex ethnic and religious mix of Balkan society. In all the successor states to the Ottoman empire, except Albania, Muslims were in a minority. However, the picture had been complicated by migration patterns, particularly from Albania, From the late eighteenth century, Albanians had begun to migrate northeastwards to Peć s and Priština in Serbia and, after 1878, they also moved northwards into Kosovo, Metohija and Novi Pazar – areas then under Habsburg control or part of independent Serbia (Mellor 1975: 76).

Even in Albania, however, independent government was dominated by the minority Christian community. Socially, feudal and clan relationships persisted and large landowners (the *bey*-s) dominated a large peasant farming community. There was a small urban proto-middle class based on artisans, civil servants and teachers. Within the village, patronage–clientage relationships dominated the traditional village councils and these patterns of social hierarchy were further atomized by religious and geographical divides (Staar 1988: 11). The northern Gheg tribes contained Christian elements – Roman Catholics looking towards Italy as a patron. The southern Tosk confederations were predominantly Muslim, but their Eastern Orthodox Christian minorities looked towards Greece (Turnock 1989: 48).

In Yugoslavia, between the wars, the religious picture was complicated by the migrations of the late nineteenth century. This meant that the Muslim peasantry of Bosnia–Herzegovina (82% of the two million Muslims in Yugoslavia by the start of the 1980s; Turnock 1989: 138) – officially defined as Muslims – were joined by the ethnic Albanians of the Kosovo region, who were predominantly Muslim (by 1981, for example, 85% of the 1.29 Albanians in Kosovo were nominally Muslim; Turnock 1989: 95, 138). It also meant that growth of considerable tensions between the two independent states.

With the advent of the Second World War, Albania, which had already been occupied by fascist Italy, acquired control of Kosovo from German-occupied Yugoslavia, thereby laying the basis for future problems. The territory was handed back to Yugoslavia after the end of the war, although the Albanian presence in the population had significantly increased, on the grounds that the original annexation had been a result of Nazi–fascist collaboration and the new communist regimes in both countries were anxious to correct these injustices. In reality, the Enver Hoxha regime's dependence on Titoist support during the war made such a move on its part inevitable.

Muslims in the Balkans under socialism

Since the end of the Second World War, it has become far more difficult to identify the developments in Muslim communities in eastern Europe. This is partly because the authorities tend to conceal the role of Islam in daily life. It has been compounded, however, by very rapid changes that have been taking place in the Balkans as a result of economic development. In any case, in Albania, religious differences have been subsumed since 1967 under the single rubric of Albanian nationalism, which was never related to religious affiliation. Until the communist system ended in 1989–90, the government continually trumpeted that "Our religion is Albanianism" (Turnock 1989: 29). In Yugoslavia, the nationalist issue has come to dominate political life and, as a result, shrouds the role of Islam in political development. This was particularly in the case of the Kosovo region where major disturbances took place during the 1980s. In Bosnia–Herzegovina, of course, nationalist exclusiveness, mainly by Serbs but also by Croats, has become the justification for the ethnic cleansing of Muslims there since ethnic conflict erupted in 1991–2. Yet, quite apart from this crisis, it has been the case that, as one commentator has pointed out, "In Yugoslavia all political problems are intimately linked with the issue of nationalism" (Holmes 1986: 331). Indeed, the problem of identification has been further obscured by the complicated ethnic definitions adopted by the Yugoslav authorities.

> . . . all nationalities that are sovereign in the sense of territorial sover-
> eignty and all other aspects of sovereignty (secession and separation)
> have been called *nations*, *nationalities* are all those national groups that
> have their sovereign country somewhere else, whereas *other national-*
> *ities* and *ethnic groups* are less numerous nationalities with sover-
> eignty in another country or ethnic groups without state sovereignty.
> (Sterc 1991: 147)

The situation in Bulgaria was not dissimilar, although it was not complicated by the same type of definition. All religious denominations were obliged by a 1949 statute to register with the Committee for Religious Affairs, which was linked to the Council of Ministers. The Committee effectively controlled their activities by controlling their representatives – in the case of the Muslim community, the Grand Mufti. The Muslim community was, moreover, largely Turkish in origin and was therefore treated as coterminous with the Turkish ethnic minority in the country.

The demographic situation

The demographic situation in 1994 is very difficult to determine because only in Yugoslavia were Muslims a demographic category. Even here, the picture is complex because Albanians in Yugoslavia were *not* classified in terms of religion. The result is that, generally, only estimates of the number of Muslims are available. This is particularly the case in Albania since, in 1967, the country was declared to be the world's first atheist state, and religious organizations and practice were suppressed.

The closest estimates were made in the pre-war period, after the first Albanian census in 1921 and similar censuses in Yugoslavia in 1953. These showed that, in 1930, 68 per cent of the Albanian population was categorized as Muslim, compared with 11 per cent Roman Catholics and 21 per cent Eastern Orthodox. In Yugoslavia, the comparative estimates were made in 1953, when Muslims were shown to be 12.3 per cent of the total, Roman Catholics 31.8 per cent, Orthodox 41.5 per cent and "other" 14.4 per cent (Turnock 1989: 120).

Other estimates show considerable variations from these figures, however. Holmes (1986: 332), for example, consistently estimates the Muslim population of Yugoslavia to have been below that proposed by Turnock above. However, it is not clear whether Turnock includes ethnic Albanians in his estimates. However, Holmes does base his figures on the official census figures, as the breakdown given by republic makes clear.

Table 6.2   Muslim and Albanian populations in Yugoslavia, 1948–81.

	Percentages		
	1948	1971	1981
Muslims	5.1	8.4	8.9
Albanians	4.8	6.4	7.7
Total (millions)	15.8	20.5	22.4

Source: Holmes 1986: 332.

Indeed, the breakdown of Muslim and Albanian population figures by republic shows quite clearly that Muslims are almost exclusively concentrated in Bosnia–Herzegovina, as might be expected, with a significant presence by 1981 otherwise only in Macedonia. As far as Albanians are concerned, they are significant only in Macedonia, once again, and in Montenegro. They are, of course, present in Serbia, because of the Albanian population of Kosovo. However, in terms of the overall population, Albanians are not particularly significant even here, partly because of the concentration in Kosovo, leaving Serbia itself with relatively few Muslims and Albanians.

Table 6.3   Population of Muslims and Albanians by republic and province, 1948–81 (%).

	Muslims		Albanians	
Republic	1948	1981	1948	1981
Bosnia–Herzegovina	30.7	39.5	0.0	0.1
Montenegro	0.1	13.4	5.2	6.5
Croatia	0.0	0.5	0.0	0.1
Macedonia	0.1	2.1	17.1	19.8
Slovenia	0.0	0.7	0.0	0.1
Serbia	0.3	2.3	8.2	14.0
TOTAL	5.1	8.9	4.8	7.7

Source: Sterc (1991: 149).

In the case of Albania, Starr suggests slightly higher proportional estimates for 1987 than was the case in the 1930 figures quoted above, with Muslims set at 70 per cent, Roman Catholics at 10 per cent and Orthodox at 20 per cent (Staar 1988: 12). Ironically enough, the Muslim proportion should be higher, given the higher birthrates conventionally assigned to Muslim communities. For Yugoslavia, Staar suggests that ethnic Muslims totalled 1,999,957 (8.6 per cent of the total population of 23.4 million) in 1987, whereas Albanians in Yugoslavia totalled 1,730,364 (7.4%) (Staar 1988: 222).

Perhaps the most useful figures are provided by Balić (1979: 29), who suggests that in 1971 there were 1,580,000 Muslims in Albania and 3,537,000 Muslims in Yugoslavia, out of an eastern European total of 6,592,000 – 24 per cent and 54 per cent of the total respectively. Balić also points out that ethnic Albanian Muslims totalled 2,831,904, whereas ethnic Muslim Slavs totalled 2,094,932, thereby suggesting that in 1971 there were 1,252,000 Albanian Muslims living abroad, mainly in the Kosovo region of Yugoslavia.

Bulgarian demographic statistics are difficult to interpret accurately because of the way in which they have been classified, particularly since 1980. As a result, most figures quoted are extrapolations from that period and cannot accurately allow for population changes as a result of migration as well as birthrate. Nonetheless, the overall figure of around 700,000 to 720,000 seems to be a reasonable approximation. Furthermore, the collapse of the communist regime there may well have unpredictable effects on the size of the Muslim population, especially if Bulgarian Turks who fled in the 1984–8 period return in significant numbers.

Table 6.4 Ethnic identity in Bulgaria: 1987.

Nationality	Numbers (million)	Percentage of total
Bulgarian	7.644	85.3
Turks	0.762	8.5
Gypsies	0.233	2.6
Macedonians	0.224	2.5
Armenians	0.027	0.3
Russians	0.018	0.2
Others	0.054	0.6

Notes: The total Muslim population of Bulgaria corresponds to the Turkish population (762,000) and the Pomaks (160,000), less around 200,000 emigrés: a total of some 722,000 persons.
Source: Staar 1988: 54 (estimates).

Political developments in Yugoslavia up to 1990

The awareness of nationalist tensions in Yugoslavia has characterized the behaviour of the Yugoslav government ever since its inception in the wake of the German defeat at the end of the Second World War. The federal structure was designed to distinguish between two different types of nationalist entity: nations, which were defined as ethnic groups with territory solely inside the boundaries of Yugoslavia; and nationalities or national minorities, which were part of large national entities, most of which were located outside the boundaries of the federal republic (Holmes 1986: 332). Thus, the Bosniaks in Bosnia–Herzegovina were a "nation", whereas the Albanians in Kosovo were a "nationality".

The result was that Bosnia–Herzegovina became a republic (the sixth after Slovenia, Serbia, Croatia, Montenegro and Macedonia), and in 1963 Kosovo became an autonomous region along with the Vojvodina, which became an autonomous province for the Hungarian minority. Although the major nationalist tensions up to the 1980s involved Serbs and Croats, there were outbursts by Muslims as well in the mid-1970s and nationalist outbreaks in Kosovo in 1968, 1975 and 1980 (Holmes 1986: 332–3).

During the 1980s, the central Yugoslav authorities feared that what they called "Pan-Islamism" would erupt in Bosnia–Herzegovina, as a result of visits by Muslim activists to the Middle East, particularly to Cairo and Mecca, and as a result of the Iranian revolution. They also feared that demands might be raised for a Muslim republic inside Yugoslavia. Such fears were rejected by the Muslim intelligentsia there, who argued that the recrudescence of interest in Islam was merely a sign of Muslim self-awareness, not an attempt to upset the delicate ethnic and nationalist balance inside Yugoslavia (Turnock 1989: 138).

In any case, Muslims in Yugoslavia had seen their conditions gradually improve during the 1970s. Although *waqf* property was confiscated in two stages – *waqf* lands being taken immediately after the liberation in 1945 and *waqf* buildings not used for specifically religious purposes being nationalized ten years later (Balić 1979: 36) – educational facilities began to improve towards the end of the decade. A faculty of Islamic studies was opened in Sarajevo, the capital of Bosnia–Herzegovina, in 1978, in the former Gazi Husrewbeg *madrassah*, a 441 year old foundation. This event marked the revival of a college that had been opened in 1937 but was suppressed again in 1941.

Two *madrassah*-s were also opened in Bosnia, one of which taught in Albanian – a recognition of the role played by Albanians in Yugoslav Islam. Islamic *shari͑a* law was not a major subject, however, since it was suppressed in the legal system after 1946 (Balić 1979: 33). Two other *madrassah*-s were also opened in Kosovo and in Metohija (Serbia), and it was estimated that between 25 and 30 new mosques had been opened every year during the 1970s. There was also a flourishing Muslim press, with three journals in Serbo–Croat being published in Sarajevo, one in Albanian being published in Priština (the capital of Kosovo autonomous region) and one being published elsewhere in Turkish (Balić 1979: 34).

The most serious factor in Yugoslavia affecting Muslims, however, was the collapse of the ethnic dispensation created in the federal republic by

Josip Tito after the Second World War. Tito's death ushered in an amendment to the Yugoslav federal constitution that was designed to defuse
secessionist tensions by creating a rotating presidency. However, the
growth of nationalist aspirations in Croatia and Slovenia during the 1980s,
coupled with the explosion of virulent Serbian irredentism as a result of the
exploitation of the tensions created by an Albanian majority in Kosovo by
Slobodan Milošović, the president of Serbia, made the break-up of the
federation virtually inevitable. Given the complex ethnic mix of Bosnia–
Herzegovina and the territorial location of Croat and Serbian majority populations along its border regions with neighbouring republics, the ultimate
collapse of Bosnia–Herzegovina as a viable political entity was almost
equally inevitable.

The political situation in Bulgaria up to 1990

The habit of the Bulgarian authorities of treating Muslims as if they were
all ethnically Turkish has introduced complications in demographic and
political terms, since special arrangements have on occasion been made to
allow Turks or persons of Turkish origin to emigrate. Between 1950 and
1951 around 150,000 persons were allowed to leave for Turkey, leaving
behind 1,000 communities of Muslims of Turkish origin, involving 700,000
persons in all. However, this did not represent the totality of Muslims
in Bulgaria, for it did not include 160,000 Bulgarian Pomaks who were
Bulgarian converts to Islam. Furthermore, under a repatriation agreement
drawn up between Bulgaria and Turkey in 1968, a further 35,000 persons
acquired the right to emigrate to Turkey. By no means of all those entitled
to leave actually did so.

However, the imprecision in the actual size of the Muslim community
resides really in the fact that, after 1980, ethnic breakdowns of census data
were not published. Furthermore, the requirement that ethnic origin be
noted on personal identity documents was abandoned. This situation was
further complicated by the fact that, between 1984 and 1985, the Bulgarian
authorities insisted that Bulgarian citizens of Turkish origin be obliged to
adopt Slavic personal names. Many resisted and, after 100 deaths and 250
arrests, the attempt was abandoned in the face of furious protests from
Ankara. Clandestine pressure continued up to 1988, however, resulting in
many of those affected leaving for Turkey. A formal protocol between Sofia
and Ankara closed the issue in 1988, but many emigrants then returned to
Bulgaria because of harsh economic conditions in Turkey (Staar 1988: 50).

The Muslim situation in Albania up to 1990

The situation of the Muslim community in Albania is intimately tied up with the growth of the Albanian Communist Party. The communist movement began in the 1920s, but the actual party was only created with Yugoslav aid in 1941, when Enver Hoxha, a schoolteacher from the Tosk regions, sought help from Tito. His National Liberation Front, which led the struggle against Italian occupation, eventually eliminated its rivals – the Balli Kombetar, the Nationalist Front and the Legality Front – by 1944 and was thus able to set up a provisional government in November 1944 (Staar 1988: 2–3). Continuing Yugoslav help enabled Hoxha to subdue the powerful Gheg tribes and strip their traditional leaders, the *bajraktar*-s, of their power but the new republic had to repay Yugoslavia by ceding the Kosovo region, which its predecessor had controlled during the Second World War (Turnock 1989: 46).

Thereafter, Albania, which Stalin had recommended Tito to swallow up as part of socialist Yugoslavia, moved steadily towards isolationism. In 1948, it broke with Yugoslavia, as traditional Albania/Yugoslavia hostility replaced the former cordial relations in the wake of the Yugoslav/Soviet split. In 1961, it broke with the USSR as a result of Krushchev's condemnation of Stalin – ironically enough, in view of Stalin's attitude towards it – and in 1978 it broke with China because of the leadership's disavowal of the principles of Maoism.

Domestically, the Tosk tribal leadership enforced its control of the security apparatus and the military, while taking over from the traditional leadership. The *bey*-s and *bajraktar*-s were replaced by communist party officials who, as the *nomenklatura*, allied with the proto middle class of pre-communist times. As the bureaucracy expanded, so did this "New Class", as the Yugoslav dissident, Milovan Djilas, dubbed them.

Even by 1985, 63 per cent of the population was still rural and thus easily controlled along traditional lines, in which the Party official replaced the old patron and the village soviet replaced the original council of elders. The hierarchy of power remained substantially untouched however, even if its nomenclature had changed. Furthermore, the Tosk hegemony removed one element of tribal conflict that had led to the characteristic blood feuds of pre-war Albania – now they became party purges instead (Staar 1988: 11–12).

As far as religious observance was concerned, the party moved rapidly against the Christian churches because of their international links. However, Islam was more sympathetically treated, although from 1950 the Sunni and Bektashi communities were classified as separate religious entities. Nonetheless, the Sunni and Bektashi *hoxha*-s were seen as nationalists and therefore as no threat to the security of the state (Staar 1988: 12; Turnock 1989: 48). It was only in 1967 that this situation changed radically.

All religious denominations were suppressed, over 2,200 mosques, and churches were destroyed and a general attack was launched on religious attitudes (Turnock 1989: 49).

These moves formed part of Albania's own "cultural revolution", declared in a mammoth nine-hour speech by Party Secretary Enver Hoxha. However, his hidden agenda was to destroy traditional attitudes inside Albania, particularly over bureaucratic inertia and the role of women in the labour force. Traditional Muslim attitudes had ensured that women should be subject to arranged marriages and dowry payments and should not participate in public life. All this was now banned, in order to free female labour for the labour force, and Albania was declared an atheist state.

That situation still obtained up to the collapse of the communist system in Albania in 1989–90, even though Enver Hoxha died in 1985 and his chosen successor, Ramiz Alia, was a member of the Gheg tribal confederation and wished to improve relations with the outside world. Albanian nationalism became the glue for the state structure, however, and has been revitalized by the continuing crisis in Kosovo since 1981. Nonetheless, there are still regionalist and religious separatist tendencies. The Gheg region around its capital, Shköder, is ethnically and socially closer to Kosovo in Yugoslavia than it is to Tirana, whereas the fringe southern Tosk populations around Lake Prespa and Gjirokaster tend to be isolationist. Islamic festivals are still observed in the Greek border areas. No doubt, the new political system in Albania will allow these tendencies to develop further, although the harsh economic and political crisis that faces Albania will relegate such developments to the background for some time to come.

The Kosovo crisis

The crisis in Kosovo in March–April 1981 underlined the explosive ethnic situation there, created by the mixture of Serbian irredentism and Albania demographic predominance. Riots broke out over poor conditions in Priština university, originally designed for 15,000 students but, by 1981 with 47,000 students, the third largest in Yugoslavia. The demonstrations soon broadened their demands into claims that Kosovo should become the seventh Yugoslav republic or that the region should be reintegrated with Albania. By the time the riots were ended, local factory workers had become involved.

There were at least three clandestine groups involved – the "Voice of Kosovo", the "communist–Marxist–Leninist Party of Albanians in Yugoslavia" and the "Group of Marxist–Leninists in Kosovo". Albanian television and radio had also stirred the revolutionary pot. Eight demonstrators had been killed, together with one policeman, and 257 persons, including 133 policemen, had been injured. A further 506 persons were sent to prison, and more trials followed in summer 1982 and autumn 1983, after new demonstrations (Holmes 1986: 335–6).

The official response was harsh and, in May 1981, the Party chief, Mahmut Bakali, was dismissed for having advocated ties with Albania. He was replaced by his predecessor of a decade earlier, Veli Deva. The security chief, Mustafa Sefedini, was dismissed in September 1981, as were 12 presidency members. A further five Albanians were also arrested in Macedonia in May 1981 for demanding that half of Macedonia should be ceded to Albania.

The harshness of the official response was a recognition of the fact that Kosovo could not have its constitutional status changed at all. The major reason for this was its status within Serbian nationalist mythology, for it is seen as the heartland of the Serbian nation, from which its members were expelled by the Ottomans (Turnock 1989: 97). Indeed, the Serbian leader, Slobodan Milošović , has inflamed the situation again since 1990 by underlining his determination that Serbs will not tolerate any change in the constitutional status of Kosovo – thereby underlining the degree to which Yugoslavia's constitutional dispensation until the secession of Croatia and Slovenia was dominated by the issue of Serbian nationalism (*Financial Times* 13 March 1990).

Yet the demographic reality has run directly counter to this attitude, as Albanians have increasingly become the dominant element within Kosovo. In the 1981 census the 1,585,000 population of Kosovo was made up from 77.4 per cent Albanians, 3.7 per cent ethnic Muslims (Bosniaks), 0.8 per cent Turk, 13.2 per cent Serb, 1.7 per cent Montenegrin and 0.1 per cent other (Staar 1988: 231). The situation has worsened over time, for, since 1966, when Ranovitch was purged, Serbs and Montegrins in Kosovo have seen their demographic position worsen.

Table 6.5   Kosovo: population distribution (% of total population).

	1961	1971	1981
Serb	27.2	20.5	14.4
Albanian/Muslim	67.4	74.1	78.3

Source: Turnock 1989: 95.

However, it would also be a mistake to assume that the dominant factor in the disturbances was Islam. In fact, most observers considered that the rioters were non-practising Muslims, atheists and Marxist–Leninists, all of whom shared Albanian nationalism in common, rather than any other creed. There is little doubt that the problems would have erupted again, given the continuing antagonisms between Albanian and Serb in Kosovo, had it not been for the collapse of the Yugoslav federation in 1991–2, not least because the Serbian presence in the province has declined to around 2 per cent of the total population.

Since 1991 the Serbian authorities have made it clear that they will not tolerate any new change in the political status of Kosovo, despite the growth of a local Albanian nationalist movement, the Democratic League of Kosovo under Ibrahim Rugova, with tacit support from Albania. Kosovo's special constitution, which allowed for a degree of cultural autonomy for Albanians, has been suspended. In October 1992, Serbian police brutally repressed demonstrations in Priština demanding educational facilities in Albanian, whereas Belgrade made it clear that it would not tolerate any expression of Albanian separatism.

Behind this political repression stands a harsh economic reality. Kosovo, quite apart from its ethnic ambiguity between Yugoslavia and Albania, suffers from severe economic disadvantage. It is potentially one of the richest regions of Yugoslavia, with 50 per cent of the coal deposits and 60 per cent of the lead and zinc deposits. However, it is economically far behind the rest of the country. Only 11.5 per cent of the population was in regular employment at the end of the 1980s, compared with 26 per cent elsewhere in Yugoslavia. Average incomes are only a third of the national level and only one sixth of the level in Slovenia, formerly the richest republic in Yugoslavia (Turnock 1989: 97). Its contribution to Yugoslavia's Social Product in 1989 was only 2 per cent, although it contains 8 per cent of the former Yugoslav national population (*The Guardian*, 19 March 1990).

The future

It is clear that Islam, as a normative element of social and political life in the republics of the former Yugoslavia, and in Bulgaria and Albania, has today only a minor role to play and that this will continue to be the case in the future. However, it permeates much of the structure of society, particularly in Albania. There, as economic pressures grow and as nationalist and liberal aspirations come once again to the fore with the collapse of the old communist system, it may well be that Islam will become, once again, a vehicle through which such frustrations will be articulated. However, its role is bound to be circumscribed by the profound changes wrought by the communist experience over the past half decade.

In former Yugoslavia, particularly in Bosnia, the appalling war has transformed the situation from one in which Muslims formed part of a complex social mix into one where Islam itself has become an ethnic identifier. In that respect, Islam has been forced to accept the normative values of its opponents among the Serb and Croat Christians who have played such a large part in destroying the old multi-ethnic and multi-confessional republic. That, in the context of post- Cold War Europe is the ultimate tragedy, for it will legitimize similar patterns of destruction in other states and may force Europe and the Islamic world onto a path of further confrontation.

Elsewhere, the outlook is more clouded. In Bulgaria it is difficult to avoid the conclusion that the collapse of the communist system will further marginalize the Islamic community, given its predominantly Turkish ethnic character and the overpowering Bulgarian demographic domination within the population. In what used to be Yugoslavia, it is difficult to avoid the conclusion that ethnic cleansing will profoundly change and isolate the Muslim community itself, vitiating any hope of confessional pluralism in the successor political entities that eventually emerge. It is also difficult to avoid the conclusion that, even if this outcome would have been inevitable in the long run, it was powerfully abetted by European political incompetence and disinterest as the Yugoslav crisis unfolded. Isolation, marginalization and dissolution now seem to be the tragic but inevitable ends to the 500-year long Muslim experience in the Balkans.

References

Balić, S. 1979. Eastern Europe, the Islamic dimension. *Journal of the Institute of Muslim Minority Affairs* 1, 1.

Braudel F. 1975. *The Mediterranean and the Mediterranean world in the reign of Philip II*. London: Fontana.

Eliamep 1992. *The southeast European year book 1991*. Athens: Hellenic Foundation for Defense and Foreign Policy.

Gibb H. A. R. & Kramers J. H. 1974. *Shorter Encyclopaedia of Islam*. Leiden: Brill.

Hodgson M. G. S. 1974. *The venture of Islam*, vol. III: *Gunpowder empire and modern times*. Chicago: University of Chicago Press.

Holmes L. 1986. *Politics in the communist world*. Oxford: Oxford University Press.

Mellor E. H. 1975. *Eastern Europe, a geography of the COMECON countries*. London: Macmillan.

Staar R. F. 1988. *Communist regimes in Eastern Europe*. Stanford: Hoover.

Sterc S. 1991. The ethnic origin of "Yugoslavs" in Croatia. In *Geopolitical and demographical issues of Croatia*, I. Crkvencic (1991). Geographical Papers 8, University of Zagreb.

Turnock D. 1989. *Eastern Europe: an economic and political geography*. London: Routledge.

CHAPTER SEVEN

Croatia rediviva
MLADEN KLEMENCIĆ

Introduction

In 1700 the Croatian scholar Pavao Ritter Vitezović (1652–1713) published in Zagreb his work *Croatia rediviva* (*Resurrected Croatia*). He was encouraged by a recent anti-Ottoman campaign at the end of the seventeenth century, when large areas were liberated from the Turks and reincorporated into Croatia. The title of his study expressed then his vision of the integrity of the Croatian lands, but it can also be applied symbolically to present-day Croatia. In 1992 Croatia reappeared on the political map of Europe as a sovereign state; before that it existed as a country but not as a state. Throughout many centuries it survived always in a semi-independent status within larger empires, unions or states, but Croatian memories have to reach far back in history for the country's real independence. *"Croatia rediviva"* is therefore an illustrative phrase for the new position and status of Croatia.

What makes the reappearance of Croatia more interesting from the perspective of political geography is the current problem of the country's integrity. Starting in 1991, certain areas of Croatia became "de facto" beyond the control of legal authority. This came as a consequence of the aggression that followed the break-up of Yugoslavia. Moreover, UN peace forces have had to be deployed in those areas since 1992 in order to encourage the peace process, but after two and a half years there are still no signs of progress.

Historical foundations

The Croats are one of the Slavonic nations, who established themselves in the region between the Kupa, Sutla, Mura, Drava, Danube and Drina rivers and the Adriatic Sea during the complex ethnogenetic process lasting from the Middle Ages up to modern national integration in the nineteenth and twentieth centuries (Macan & Šentija 1992). The area inhabited by the Croats occupies a favourable communication position as a contact zone between the central Danubian basin and the Mediterranean. But from the perspective of stability, the location of Croatian territory within a zone of confrontation between central European Catholicism, East European

Orthodoxy and Near East Islam appeared to be more important. Too often the area was a stage of confrontation and rivalry between neighbouring powers. Because of this, the Croats did not enjoy favourable conditions for the creation of their own state. Limited sovereignty or autonomy, as well as territorial disunity, are therefore frequent and frustrating elements of Croatian history.

The Croatian name was initially associated with territory in the hinterland of the Byzantine thema of Dalmatia. The region began to be called Regnum Chroatorum ("the state of the Croats") in the mid-ninth century. It became strong, expanded its territory and even gained papal recognition. Its core area was the triangle formed by the towns of Knin, Šibenik and Nin. Since it was formed on the territory of the former Roman province of Dalmatia, it is usually known under the name of Dalmatian Croatia. The geographic borders of Dalmatian Croatia were on the Raša and Cetina rivers in the coastal area, whereas inland the border followed the Sava and Una rivers towards the mouth of the Sana river and from there to the source of the Kupa river. North of it, on the territory of the former Roman province of Panonnia Savia, a northern Croatian principality was established. It was originally called Slovinje and later Slavonia. In the tenth centuries, with the unification of both principalities, a united Kingdom of Croatia was established. Under its native dynasty until the end of the eleventh century, Croatia became an influential maritime power. According to monuments preserved from that time, it appeared to be a flourishing period of Croatian culture and history. Generally, it was also a rather stable period from a territorial viewpoint. Only the eastern border of the Croatian Kingdom was changeable, depending on its power. During favourable times, Croatian rulers controlled the area up to the Drina river in the east, which also encompassed the original territory of Bosnia around the spring of the river of the same name, so the surface area of Croatia totalled around 100,000 km². The Principality of Zahumlje in the southeast, which together with Travunia and Dukla (Doclea) was known under the name of Red Croatia, from time to time also acknowledged Croatian authority. The Principality of Neretva or Pagania had even closer ties with Croatia. At the time, the Byzantine thema of Dalmatia encompassed only a few islands and towns along the coast, which, from time to time, recognized Croatian authority and were annexed to the country in the twelfth century.

After the last king from the Trpimirović dynasty died, the nobility recognized the Arpad dynasty as their rulers in 1102 and entered a personal union with Hungary. Croatia did not lose its state individuality by this union. The unity of the Croatian lands was manifested in the person of a *ban* (viceroy), as the king's governor, and in a separate diet (*sabor*). But personal union with Hungary was the beginning of a long-lasting period in which Croatia was tied with either Hungary or later Austria. The constant struggle to keep sovereignty or at least certain autonomy throughout that period was an essential trait of Croatian history and a source of national awareness. One can argue about the degree of Croatian "de facto" individuality at certain stages of history, but cannot deny that Croatia always existed *de jure*. Real Croatian sovereignty was certainly as high and wide as the balance of power allowed, but the Croats have always been specially keen on the juridical foundation of their statehood.

The territory gradually became smaller after personal union with Hungary was established in 1102. Some parts came under the influence of foreign authorities to a lesser or greater degree (battles with Venice for Dalmatia, Hungarian royal rule in Slavonia), thus breaking Croatia's administrative integrity. From the twelfth to the fourteenth century, Bosnia became independent and extended to the former Croatian territory. Along the coast, Venetian authority and influence became stronger, whereas from 1358 in the southernmost part Dubrovnik started to develop as an independent republic.

Threatened by the Ottomans from the east, the Croatian diet elected the Habsburgs as Croatian rulers in 1527 in order to strengthen the country's defence. On the one hand, that election ensured a powerful ally for Croatia, but on the other hand it faced Vienna's tendencies for centralization. After the Ottoman Empire laid siege to the Balkan peninsula at the end of the sixteenth century, Croatia was reduced to its smallest territory in history (around 16,800 km^2). Apart from *Reliquiae religuiarum* ("remnants of the remnants") of Croatia, only the Republic of Dubrovnik and some Venetian-controlled Adriatic islands and towns remained outside Ottoman authority. The whole of Bosnia and all other parts of Croatia fell under Ottoman rule. The Turks organized that territory in 1580 as the Bosnian *pashalic*.[1] From that period the name of *Croatia Turcica* (Turkish Croatia) was preserved for the last conquered part of Croatia between the rivers Vrbas and Una (today part of Bosnia–Herzegovina).[2]

The liberation of Croatian lands started at the end of the seventeenth century and was carried out gradually. By the Treaty of Karlowitz (*Srijemski Karlovci*) in 1699, the northern state territory, that is, the Kingdom of Croatia and Slavonia, regained regions of Baniya, larger parts of Lika and Slavonia as well as part of Srijem. The rest of Srijem was annexed to Croatia after the Treaty of Pozarevac in 1718 and the remaining part of Lika once again became part of Croatia after the Treaty of Svishtov in 1791.

Along the boundary with the Ottoman Empire, Austrian authorities in the sixteenth century organized a defence system known as the *Militärgrenze* or *Vojna krajina* (Military Frontier). Although the authority in the

---

1. The only Ottoman province solely of countries populated with south Slavonic nations. Smaller units were sanjaks.
2. For simplicity, the formal title "Republic of Bosnia and Herzegovina" is reduced to "Bosnia–Herzegovina" or sometimes simply "Bosnia" throughout the text.

Military Frontier gradually came into the hands of the military command in Vienna, it was never formally accepted by the Croatian state. The far-reaching consequences of the new Military Frontier led to demographic changes (Kocsis 1993/94). The area was devastated and deserted. Many Croats were forced to leave it because of the instability and destruction of war, so that the military authorities settled a new population from the Balkan interior there, among whom were significant numbers of Vlachs of Orthodox religion. Later, in the ethnogenetic process under the influence of the Serbian Orthodox Church and propaganda, they became a part of the Serbian nation. On the basis of their existence within Croatia, and in fact manipulated by them, Serbia started in the nineteenth century to develop Greater Serbian pretensions on Croatian lands deep to the west.

Venetian Dalmatia to the south also started to extend gradually during the anti-Ottoman wars. With the territorial changes of the seventeenth and eighteenth centuries, the characteristic shape of the Croatian lands was formed. Boundaries established then were later used as a basis for all future delineations. The area around the Bay of Kotor and Budva (today part of Montenegro) was also under the Venetian Republic. At that time it was known as *Albania Veneta* (Venetian Albania).

National revival in the nineteenth century strengthened the awareness of Croatian togetherness and instigated a tendency towards the territorial unification of Croatian lands and independence. This is the origin of the name for the Triune Kingdom of Dalmatia, Croatia and Slavonia. In 1848 Josip Jelacić was *ban* of Croatia and Slavonia. He was also nominated governor of Dalmatia and Rijeka, as well as commander of the Military Frontier, and he regained Medimurje from the Hungarians. In this way, during his rule he gathered the Croatian lands formally together for a short time. But the problem of disintegration was still actual until the break-up of the Habsburg Empire. The Kingdom of Croatia and Slavonia remained divided into civilian and military parts. In the mid-eighteenth century the Military Frontier was reorganized into regiments, whereas Civil Croatia was organized into *zupanijas* (counties). Finally, in 1881 the Military Frontier was completely reincorporated within Civil Croatia.

After the fall of the Venetian Republic (1797) and the Republic of Dubrovnik (1808), southern Croatia came into the possession of the Habsburgs. Austria united former Venetian Dalmatia, the Dubrovnik area and the former Venetian Albania into the Kingdom of Dalmatia in 1815. After the Berlin Congress in 1878, Dalmatia was extended to include the narrow coastal strip southeast of the Bay of Kotor. Istria and the Kvarner Islands, also predominantly Croatian areas in ethnic terms, were under Austrian rule too, but organized as an independently governed province. Therefore, during the nineteenth century all Croatian lands were under Habsburg rule, but administratively separated. Division was especially stressed after the reorganization of the Monarchy in 1867 and its division into Austrian and Hungarian parts. On the basis of the 1868 Compromise, the Kingdom of Croatia and Slavonia had special status within the Hungarian half, but Dalmatia and Istria remained in the Austrian part.

After the demise of Austria–Hungary in the First World War, the South Slavonic provinces of the former monarchy proclaimed the independent state of the Slovenes, Croats and Serbs on 29 October 1918. Representatives of the Triune Kingdom, along with representatives from Istria, the Slovene lands, Bosnia and Herzegovina and Vojvodina, participated in the National Council in Zagreb, which represented supreme state authority. This state entered into association with the Kingdom of Serbia, which had been joined earlier by the Kingdom of Montenegro as well as Vojvodina. Thus, establishment of a common state – the Kingdom of Serbs, Croats and Slovenes – was proclaimed on 1 December 1918 and confirmed during the Paris Peace Conference. In 1929 it was renamed the Kingdom of Yugoslavia.

For the Croats at that time Yugoslavia seemed a reasonable solution. They were happy to quit their long-lasting association with Hungary and Austria. Moreover, union with Serbia seemed promising as protection against Italian claims on the Adriatic coast (in 1915, by the secret Treaty of London, Italy was promised large parts of the Croatian coast if they entered the war on the Entente's side).

For the first time in history a common Yugoslav state was formed, encompassing constituent parts that underwent completely separate politogenetic development. The nations that formed a common state had already been established as separate political and territorial entities, and therefore the union could exist only under tolerant government that would recognize the autonomy of its constituent parts. Serbian politicians were opposed to that conception and they attempted to enforce the idea of a unitarian state. From the very beginning they considered Yugoslavia as a Serbian war gain, that is, a Greater Serbia. Therefore, Yugoslavia was a great disappointment for the Croats, as well as for other non-Serbs.[3] Instead of creating a federal state, Croatia lost its autonomous status, which it had enjoyed up to 1918.

Nevertheless, on the eve of the Second World War an autonomous Croatian unit, the Banate (Banovina) of Croatia, was established in 1939 (Boban 1993). It was composed of two former banates: the Sava and Primorje banates, and Croat-dominated districts from neighbouring banates. The Banate of Croatia had an area of 65,465 km^2. It included former Croatia–Slavonia (excluding eastern Srijem) and Dalmatia (without the Bay of Kotor area) and also some parts of Bosnia–Herzegovina. The idea and intention was to reorganize the state into three federal units: Croatian, Slovenian and Serbian (other nations were not then recognized!). The Banate of Croatia was seen as the beginning of a process that was soon to be stopped by German aggression and the break-up of Yugoslavia. But even before the

---

3. An excellent insight into the first few years of Yugoslavia is provided by I. Banac (1984).

war broke out, Croatian autonomy was rejected by a vociferous and strong Serbian opposition; also it was not welcomed by Croatian Serbs.

After the fall of the Kingdom of Yugoslavia in 1941, the Ustasha[4] regime, under the tutorship of the Axis Forces, established an Independent State of Croatia, which apart from the Croatian lands also included Bosnia and Herzegovina. Territorial concessions were the price the regime was forced to pay. Since 1920 Italy already had the Istrian peninsula, some islands and the town of Zadar. Additionally, it annexed large parts of the Croatian coast. However, a strong anti-fascist movement developed within the territory of the Independent State of Croatia, which after capitulation to Italy in 1943 proclaimed annexation to all parts of Croatia that came under Italian occupation after the First World War and during the Second World War. After the fall of the Independent State of Croatia, two republics were established in its area: Croatia and Bosnia–Herzegovina, both as federal units of the re-established Yugoslavia.

Delimitation between Yugoslav republics was carried out in 1945. Only a few details were discussed afterwards. The Croatian boundaries were mostly defined according to its historical lines, established during the anti-Ottoman wars. After the Trieste crises had been solved in 1954, Croatia was awarded an additional district in Istria, after which the surface area of the Croatian Republic within Yugoslavia totalled 56,538 km^2. Within the same territory, the Republic of Croatia declared its independence in 1991 and became an internationally recognized state and member of the UN in 1992.

Boundaries

The historical basis

The present-day boundaries of Croatia are for the most part defined by the lines of division established long before the formation of the Yugoslav state in 1918 (Klemencić 1991, Englefield 1992). Croatia's boundaries have a long historical continuity that is the consequence of the fact that Croatia managed to maintain elements of statehood throughout its history. Only some 250 km out of the total length of Croatia's land boundaries, extending for 2,028 km, were boundaries delimited for the first time within Yugoslavia.

For most of its length the Croatia/Hungary boundary is one of the oldest in Europe. This is particularly true of the sections marked by the Drava river, which has always separated the Croatian and Hungarian

---

4. *Ustaša* – the Croatian Revolutionary Movement – founded in 1929 after dictatorship was introduced in Yugoslavia by the Serbian monarch. In 1941 the movement's leader Ante Pavelić was sponsored by Italy and Germany to take a leading position in Croatia. The 1941–5 activity of the Ustasha regime compromised an idea of future Croatian independence, including the 1991 declaration of independence.

states. In the Medimurje region only, where it is defined naturally by the Mura river, the boundary is in a sense more recent. It was finally defined after the First World War, when Medimurje was transferred from Hungary to the State of the Slovenes, Croats and Serbs. Hungary's possession of Medimurje was questionable, since the region formerly belonged to Croatia and was always settled by the Croats. The Baranya boundary is the most recent section of the Croatia/Hungary boundary. It was first established in 1920 without reference to any earlier line. In this way, the southern part of the former Hungarian province of Baranya was joined to the Kingdom of the Serbs, Croats and Slovenes. Ethnically it was a highly mixed area in which Hungarians lived side by side with considerable numbers of Croats, Germans and, to a lesser extent, Serbs, but functionally depended on the town of Osijek (Bognar 1991).

The Croatia/Slovenia boundary is also a very old one. Its sections are part of an historical line that had for centuries separated Croatia from the Slovene lands of Carniola (Kranjska) and Styria (Štajerska). The Medimurje boundary also largely coincides with the earlier boundary of that part of the Croatian region, except for a few villages in the Štrigova municipality, which were joined to Slovenia in the twentieth century. In contrast to the greater long-established section, the western part of the Croatia/Slovenia boundary is recent. The Istrian boundary was drawn after the Second World War, and after the temporary Free Zone of Trieste was divided between Italy and Yugoslavia. The delimitation between Croatia and Slovenia was carried out along ethnic lines.

The boundary with Bosnia–Herzegovina is the longest. Its present-day course is the result of centuries of Ottoman rule over Bosnia. The boundary section marked by the rivers Sava and Una reflects the historical boundary of Croatia towards the Ottoman Empire. Sections of the Sava and the lower course of the Una river were fixed by the Treaty of Karlowitz in 1699. The Treaty of Pozarevac in 1718 altered it by extending Croatian territory farther east, thus bringing the whole of Srijem under Croatian authority. The same line was confirmed by the Treaty of Svishtov in 1791, which was particularly important for establishing the boundary along the upper Una river. Having won back the greater part of the Lika region in 1699, Croatia then extended its sovereignty over Kordun and the rest of Lika. Thus, in 1791 that boundary section was fixed almost completely as it is today. The same line was confirmed as a boundary between Croatia and Bosnia after the Second World War, except for a couple of former Croatian villages near Bihać, which were transferred to Bosnia. The southern section of the boundary towards Bosnia–Herzegovina is inherited from delimitations between Venetian-controlled Dalmatia and the Ottoman Empire, carried out in the seventeenth and eighteenth centuries. The present-day boundary is the same as the so-called Linea Mocenigo, which gave Venetian Dalmatia its final shape in 1718. In the extreme southeast, the frontier coincides with the boundary of the Republic of Dubrovnik. There, Croatian territory is interrupted at Neum, giving Bosnia–Herzegovina an outlet to the sea. That was part of a diplomatic scheme by Dubrovnik in 1700, which gave the Ottomans a small stretch of coast in order to avoid direct territorial contact with Venice's Dalmatia territory. This historical boundary was respected by delimitation between the Yugoslav republics after the Second World War.

The short Croatia/Montenegro boundary corresponds to the boundary of the Republic of Dubrovnik, but not that of Austrian Dalmatia. The former Dalmatian coastal strip comprises the Bay of Kotor, Budva and Spic and was given to Montenegro after the Second World War, although it had never been part of it before. The former Bosnia–Herzegovinia exit to the sea in the Bay of Kotor, known as Sutorina, was also allocated to Montenegro. The origin of that outlet is the same as that of Neum. It was another buffer that separated the Republic of Dubrovnik from Venetian possessions, but contrary to Neum was not given to Bosnia–Herzegovina after the Second World War.

The oldest section of the Croatia/Serbia boundary is the central one on the river Danube, down stream of the Drava river mouth. This has been Croatia's boundary since 1699, when the Ottomans were driven out of Slavonia. The northern section, also on the Danube, was defined in 1945 after a special boundary commission decided that Baranja should be part of Croatia. The southern section was also defined for the first time in 1945, splitting the historical Croatian province of Srijem. Eastern Srijem, with a predominantly Serbian population, was transferred to Serbia, whereas the western part, with its predominantly Croat population, stayed within Croatia.

Thus, it can be concluded that the greatest part of Croatia's current boundaries is the legacy of earlier periods. Recent historical boundary revisions, carried out within Yugoslavia, are rather rare, but they were carried out at the expense of Croatia. Such revisions are to be found on the Croatia/Montenegro and Croatia/Serbia boundaries. Generally, the northern and western boundaries are old and more stable. The eastern boundaries are the result of continuing contraction and loss of territory generating from Ottoman conquest in the Balkans, and ending with the interrepublican delimitation within Yugoslavia.

Legal basis

As was known in the late 1980s, the existing boundaries of the Yugoslav republics were questioned by Serbia. For Serbia, only the international Yugoslav boundaries were legitimate, whereas republican boundaries were referred to as "administrative" and "invented by the communist regime" and as such were subject to change. When Croatia and Slovenia proclaimed independence on the basis of referenda in which all citizens of the respective republics were invited to participate, Serbia accused the two republics of "secession". Since "secession" was illegal, the boundaries of "secessionist" republics should have been proposed by the rest of Yugoslavia. As the basis for a "new" delimitation, the principle of self-determination of peoples who wished to remain in Yugoslavia had to be applied. Since the Serbs were the only people advocating the preservation of Yugoslavia, this meant in reality that they would fix all other boundaries.

The Croatian counter-thesis considered that boundaries were based on both the historical background and constitutional provisions. Croatia pointed out, calling on the historical background of delimitations, that boundaries had deep and long-standing roots. Moreover, according to provisions of the 1974 Federal Constitution, the republic boundaries were inviolable and since republics were defined as states in themselves, Croatia called for their international protection. Boundaries were the subject of Article 5 of the Federal Constitution: "The territory of a republic cannot be changed without the agreement of the republic, and the territory of an autonomous province without the agreement of the autonomous province ... The boundary between republics can only be changed on the basis of their mutual agreement . . ." Similar provisions were included in the constitutions of all republics, including Serbia.

As boundary issues were not solved by negotiation, the international community tried to mediate in the conflict (Cvrtila 1993). At the peace conference on (former) Yugoslavia, which began in the autumn of 1991 under the auspices of the European Community (EC), a special arbitration commission of experts from EC countries was formed. On the basis of presented requests and documentation from all the republics, the appointed commissioners answered all questions through several (Degan 1992). Opinion 1 stated that "Yugoslavia is in the process of dissolution" because four out of its six republics expressed their desire for independence. The main principles for delimitation before the former republics were explained in Opinion 3. Four main principles were to be followed:

- all external boundaries of former Yugoslavia "must be respected"
- boundaries between republics "can only be changed on the basis of free and mutual agreement"
- in the absence of such an agreement "the former boundaries become boundaries protected by international law", following the principle of *uti possidetis iuris*;
- the "alteration of existing boundaries by force is not capable of producing legal effects".

Opinion 2 is also of importance, in which the arbitration commission answered the question put forward by Serbia about the status of the Serbian ethnic community in Croatia and Bosnia–Herzegovina. The right to self-determination for Serbs outside Serbia "must not involve changes to existing boundaries". Serbian communities in the two republics were therefore given directions on how to regulate their rights within them. In

January 1992 as a result of the views and opinions made by the arbitration commission, all EC members, as well as other countries, recognized the republics of Slovenia and Croatia, and later Bosnia–Herzegovina and Macedonia "within the boundaries that existed before the beginning of confrontation in June last year".

National identity

Throughout history the Croats did not have many chances to establish their own state, but their national identity has deep and longstanding roots (Fernandez-Armesto 1994). Memories of their medieval kingdom were kept alive among Croats for centuries long after its fall, but an even stronger source of national self-awareness was the continuity of unbroken statehood that Croatia enjoyed within its unions with Hungary and Austria. Indeed, in both unions Croatia was nominally recognized as a separate unit. The Croatian diet (and parliament since 1848) always persistently insisted on that fact. The struggle put up by the Croats for their state and national individuality is therefore essential if one wants to understand Croatian identity (Macan & Šentija 1992). On the basis of that juridical tradition, one of the two strongest political parties formed by the Croats in the nineteenth century was significantly called the Party of (Croat State) Right. It stood firmly on the position of Croatian individuality and sovereignty. Even Croatian politicians who aspired to wider (South) Slavonic integration, saw an eventual common state as a union in which Croats would be able to keep their national and historic particularities. Therefore, when Croatia finally entered the South Slavonic common state in 1918, it was far too late to change or deny Croatian national identity. Moreover, Serbian attempts to impose the concept of "one nation consisting of three tribes" were too crude and violent to attract the Croats. Somewhat different was the concept promoted by the Yugoslav communist regime after the Second World War. Tito's regime promoted "Yugoslavism", but was also repressive towards the Croats. Croatian national expression was considered as a direct threat to "brotherhood and unity". Steady persecution of Croats in both royalist and communist Yugoslavia caused deep distrust towards a South Slavonic union among Croats, strengthened Croatian national sentiments and deepened their desire to establish an independent state. Resurrection of Serbian imperialism in the late 1980s and aggression in the early 1990s were therefore only final impulses for Croatia's striving for independence.

One of the most complex questions in the former Yugoslavia was a linguistic one.[5] There are certainly close linguistic ties between Croats

---

5. More about language can be found in Banac (1990).

and Serbs as well as Montenegrins and Bosnian Muslims. Very often, the standard variants they speak are considered to be one language. However, reality is much more complex. Traditionally, Croats used dialects belonging to three distinct dialect groups (*A concise atlas . . .* 1993). The so-called Kajkavian and Cakavian dialects have always been used exceptionally by the Croats and there is a rich vernacular literature written in those dialects. Only dialects belonging to the third dialect group are spoken by both Croats and Serbs. In the nineteenth century a dialect belonging to that (Štokavian) group was accepted as the standard language variant, partly in order to bring Croats and Serbs closer together. Soon afterwards, the Serbs developed a theory by which all speakers of Štokavian were Serbs. That falsified theory became one of the footholds of Greater Serbian policy and territorial claims. On the other side it forced Croatian linguistic scholars into an arduous struggle for Croatian language individuality (Banac 1990). Now, as the Croats and Serbs have their own separate states, the language issue is no more. Each side will develop its own variant language freely and independently, and will be able to name it in accordance with national sentiment or any other heart's desire.

Differences are greater concerning writing. Although the Serbs traditionally use the Cyrillic script, the Croats exclusively use the Latin alphabet (twenty-five consonants and five vowels). In the past the Croats also used the Glagolitic script and the Bosancica script, which had been a Croatian form of the Cyrillic script.

Catholicism is also an important element of Croatian national identity. It has played a significant role in Croatian history because of the outlying position of Croatia within a Catholic-dominated part of Europe. This position more often appears to have been a hindrance than fruitful, since contacts with Eastern Orthodoxy and Islam were often conflicting. Catholicism is therefore highly positioned in the national consciousness of the Croats as a mode of their defence, and can be compared with the Irish and the Polish experiences. The feelings of Croats towards the Holy See were transparently manifested during the visit of John Paul II to Croatia in September 1994. Almost a million Croatian citizens, and Croats from the diaspora, gathered in Zagreb and took part in public worship led by the Pope in the Croatian language.

Naturally, there are also Croats who are not Catholics. Some of them are protestants too, and there are also Muslims by religion who consider themselves as Croats in both Croatia and Bosnia, although that combination of ethnic and religious identity was more frequent in the past (Banac 1984).

Since Croatia experienced all its trouble coming from the position on or beside historical dividing lines, the Croats are especially keen to consider themselves part of what is usually called the "West". Most of them see themselves as "defenders of the eastern frontier of Western culture and values". When Croatia claimed its independence from Yugoslavia, "return to Europe" was among its main slogans. Unfortunately for the Croats, they are rarely recognized by the West as such. Croatia is more often considered to be part of the Balkans, whereas Croats tend to see their own country as a part of central Europe or the Mediterranean. In the mental map of most Croats, the Balkans is an everlasting source of threats for Croatia's bare existence. Deep frustration is the only consequence that can come out of that misunderstanding.

Croatia is quite often considered to be an old-fashioned and conservative country by the West. There is not much understanding of Croatia's openly expressed national feelings and historicism, the Catholicism of substantial numbers of Croats, their insistence on language purity and other expressions of national feeling. All that is, in the eyes of Westerners, really old-fashioned, because the national state is not a favourite model in Europe any more. It must also be stressed that the poor image of Croats has been steadily mediated for the international public by the Serb-dominated diplomacy of former Yugoslavia. Quite often the Croats really appear to be living in the past, whereas modern Europe is orientated to the future. The problem is in the late politogenetic process. The fact that Croatia reached international recognition as late as the 1990s is not the fault of the Croats. They wanted a state in the nineteenth century and after both world wars when the map was changing, but at that time there was no understanding for a small Croatian nation among the Great Powers. Croatia now needs more understanding and patience. As soon as the problem of the country's integrity is solved, national feelings will not be important any more, and Croats will turn from history to the present and the future.

In spite of the fact that present-day Croatia consists of several historic provinces that had been separated for a long time, national integration is not questioned. Regionalist tendencies are not strong, although there are many typical characteristics particularly for Dalmatia, Slavonia or other regions; most Croats, regardless of their regional origin, sincerely feel Croatia has a main political–territorial framework. The only exception is Istria, where regionalism surfaced in recent times on the basis of the region's position, history and cultural heritage. Yet, even Istrian regionalism cannot be considered as a threat to the country's integrity and national togetherness.

Ethnic structure[6]

The ethnic structural pattern of Croatia is similar to the patterns of the majority of states lying in the central European belt between the Baltic and the Adriatic. One ethnic group, in particular the Croats, represents the majority, whereas the rest of the population consists of ethnic communities or minorities that are represented on a much smaller scale. According to the 1991 census, which was carried out on the eve of the war and of the break-up of the former Yugoslavia, the total population was 4,784,265 inhabitants, of whom 3,736,356 (78.1% were Croats. Among the republics of former Yugoslavia, Croatia was second according to the share of its titular nation to total population. Only Slovenia was ethnically more homogenous.[7]

The second largest ethnic community in Croatia are the Serbs. There were 581,663 Serbs (12.2%) registered in the 1991 census. Approximately one third of the Serbs lived within the regions of Baniya, Kordun, eastern Lika and around Knin in northern Dalmatia, and were a majority there. The Serbs in the eastern and western parts of Slavonia constituted an additional sixth of their total, whereas the rest of them (i.e. roughly a half of the total number) were dispersed throughout other parts of Croatia, mostly in large towns. In the context of the recent Croat/Serb conflict, it is important to stress that Serb-dominated areas lie along the Croatia/Bosnia boundary, hundreds of kilometres away from Serbia. Eastern Slavonia, or more precisely the regions of Baranya and Srijem, which since the 1991 war have been occupied by the Serbs, was not a Serb-dominated area due to its pre-war situation.

As a consequence of migration waves during Habsburg rule, there are several other ethnic communities that have been living within Croatia for at least a century or more. The most homogenous Hungarian community is in Baranya, the majority of Czechs live in western Slavonia, the majority of Italians inhabit the western part of Istria and Rijeka, whereas Slovaks and Ruthenians are concentrated in several villages in Slavonia. The Jews, who were more numerous before the Second World War, live mostly in Zagreb. All ethnic communities mentioned are small, but they are a very important part of society because they give Croatia a specific flavour of central European mixture.

---

6. A collection of more detailed studies on the ethnic structure of Croatia, and particularly of Serb-dominated areas, is provided by Croatian geographers in *Geopolitical and demographical issues of Croatia* (1991).
7. In 1991, according to respected censuses, the percentage of Slovenians in Slovenia was 87.8, Serbs in Serbia, 65.8, Macedonians in Macedonia, 64.6, and Montenegrins in Montenegro, 61.8. The participation of ethnic communities within Bosnia–Herzegovina was: Muslims 43.7 per cent, Serbs 31.3 per cent and Croats 17.3 per cent.

Bosnian Muslims (43,469 or 0.9%) were the third largest community according to the 1991 census, but their relatively large number is a result of recent economic immigration from Bosnia–Herzegovina.

Generally, all non-Croat communities do accept Croatia as their homeland. They supported Croatia's independence in 1991 and many their members were even part of the Croatian Army and fought for freedom together with Croats. Only the Serbs, and then not all of them, are either ambivalent or hostile towards Croatia.

Croat/Serb conflict

War between Croatia and the former Yugoslav Army ended more or less at the beginning of January 1992. During some five months of war operations the Yugoslav army together with volunteers from Serbia backed local Serb irregulars and they seized about one quarter of Croatian territory (Klemenćić 1993). On that territory the so-called "Republic of Serbian Krajina" was self-proclaimed by rebelling Serbs (Vego 1993).

The occupied area of Croatia comprises the regions of Baranya, the eastern part of Slavonia including the Croatian part of Srijem, parts of western Slavonia, Baniya, Kordun, eastern Lika and part of northern Dalmatia. Before the hostilities, according to the 1991 census, 549,083 inhabitants lived within the presently occupied areas, among them 287,830 Serbs (52.4%), 203,656 Croats (37.1%) and 57,597 (10.5% of citizens) declaring other ethnic affiliation (Šterc & Pokos 1993). As a consequence of hostilities, the ethnic composition of those areas has changed drastically. Almost all the Croats were killed or have been forced to leave, and no one has returned.[8] The same happened to most of the other non-Serbs living in the area. In March 1992, UN Protection Forces (UNPROFOR) were deployed in the occupied areas of Croatia in accordance with a plan usually known as the "Vance plan" after Cyrus Vance, the personal envoy of the UN Secretary General, who mediated in the conflict (Baletić 1993). After more than three years of UNPROFOR's presence it can be said that the peace-keeping forces have effectively guaranteed Serbian gains, since the situation on the ground has not changed and no political resolution of the conflict has been reached.

The rebellion of the Serbs in Croatia effectively started in August 1990 with the so-called "tree-trunk revolution", but it was part of a wider scenario conducted from Belgrade, in order to destabilize former Yugoslavia and to reorganize it according to Serbia's desire. Moreover, the whole

---

8. In December 1993 there were in Croatia 250,396 displaced persons from occupied areas registered by the government office for displaced persons and refugees, and 59,959 refugees from Croatia in other countries. Also, Croatia provided accommodation for 282,728 refugees from Bosnia–Herzegovina.

scenario was just one more attempt to realize the two-centuries old Greater Serbian expansionist program and territorial claims (Brandt et al. 1991; Klemencić 1993/4b).

The Serbs living in Croatia, or Croatian Serbs, protested against Croatia as early as 1988, when the communist regime was still in power. At that time there was no excuse for their anti-Croat feelings since the Croatian communist regime was more than generous towards Serbs and it enabled them to have privileged status (Cviic 1991: 73). After the free elections held in spring 1990, Croatian Serbs openly rejected the more independent status of Croatia and totally alienated themselves from the rest of Croatian society. They did not even try to accommodate themselves to a new multi-party situation. Under the influence of Greater Serbian propaganda from Belgrade they equated the newly elected Croatian government with the Ustasha regime. It is true that a Ustasha regime during the Second World War committed war crimes against the Serbs, but historical memories and fears could not be a reason for justifying Serbian armed rebellion and a move towards secession in the 1990s.

After heavy and brutal fighting and several years of total separation, there is an extremely deep division between "Krajina"[9] [10] and the rest of Croatia. Formally, integrity of Croatia is guaranteed by the UN, and its international boundaries should be protected by international law. Because of this the Serbs are not allowed to secede and join Serbia, which is their final aim. On the other hand, the situation on the ground is actually favourable for the Serbs. As long as they keep the territorial "status quo", they consider themselves to be beyond the legal Croatian framework. Negotiations between the two sides have been started several times under the auspices of international mediators, but so far there has not been a single accord acceptable as a starting point for both sides. The only wish for peace can be pointed out as a joint one, but Croatia wants to reach peaceful reintegration and the Serbs want peaceful secession.

---

9. The term "Krajina" or "Serbian Krajina" has recently been used to determine the self-proclaimed Serbian "statelet" in Croatia. The word "Krajina" in the Croatian language has the same meaning as the word "frontier" in English. It used to be a general term, written with a lower case initial letter, usually to denote smaller regions that were historically borderlands. The Austrian defensive belt known as the Military Frontier (or *Vojna krajina* in Croatian) did not correspond fully to the territory of so-called Serbian Krajina. For example, the town of Knin was not within the Military Frontier. It is also important that the Military Frontier did not have special status because of the Serbs living there (totalling 40 per cent of the population), but for completely different reasons. The inhabitants of the Military Frontier enjoyed immunity from feudal obligations in return for military service guarding the frontier against the Turks, irrespective of their ethnic origin or religious affiliation. The continuity between the historic Military Frontier and present-day "Krajina", which the Serbs claim, simply does not exist (Szajkovski 1993).

10. Since this chapter was written, Krajina has been re-incorporated within Croatia, and few of its Serb population are in residence there.

111

From the Croatian viewpoint a resolution of the "Serbian question" should be reached within the framework of the Constitutional Law on Human Rights and Liberties and the Rights of Ethnic and National Communities or Minorities, which was voted in the Croatian Parliament in 1991. A high degree of cultural autonomy for the Serbs is provided by the Constitutional Law, including territorial autonomy in two districts (Glina and Knin) covering most of the area that was Serb-dominated according to the 1991 and previous censuses. Due to personal judgment, it seems that the Croatian government would be ready to give more concessions to the Serbs. Effective partition of the country has caused deep divisions in society. The problem of displaced persons is getting deeper daily. There is steady international suspicion about Croatia's stability and credibility. The most important transportation corridors are out of use and alternative routes do not satisfy needs. Without resolution of the country's integrity, the chances for economic recovery are poor. Therefore, resolution of the Serbian question appears to be of vital interest for Croatia, and that fact forces the Croatian side to open more doors to Serbian claims. The only thing that Croatia certainly could not negotiate is the secession of "Krajina".

The Serbs are expected to recognize the sovereignty and integrity of Croatia and to abolish secessionis tic claims. Within that framework they can probably negotiate more autonomy that they have been offered so far, especially if they get international backing for such a status.

Apart from Baranya and eastern Slavonia, other Serb-occupied areas are traditionally underdeveloped and sparsely populated. Functionally, they depend on Croatia. They have always been economically integrated into Croatia. Moreover, being supplied directly from Serbia proper, self-proclaimed Krajina is not economically viable at all. A direct link is at present possible only across another Serbian "statelet" in Bosnia–Herzegovina. That fact explains why the Serbs so desperately need a land corridor in northern Bosnia. On the other hand, especially from a military viewpoint, the most effective impact on the Greater Serbian project would be to break that corridor.

The are two ways to resolve the Croat/Serb conflict. A military solution means a new war between Croats and Serbs, or more realistically between Croatia and Serbia. Croatia's victory would resolve the question of the country's integrity, but it would probably cause a huge emigration of the Serbs from presently occupied parts of Croatia. However, the military balance is not favourable for Croatia, since Serbia controls most of former Federal Army potential and still has an advantage, especially when considering aircraft and heavy artillery. Moreover, Croatia has been steadily warned by the international community that there would be no sympathy for eventual Croatian military actions. Eventual defeat of the Croatian army would probably mean a final loss of territory. It might also open the door for legalizing boundary changes at the expense of Croatia. The resolution of conflict without a new war is also possible, no matter how deep the conflict seems to be. But the political key for that resolution is not within Croatia. It is held by Serbia. If Serbia abolishes its expansionistic claims and recognizes Croatia within international boundaries, the rebelling Croatian Serbs have to negotiate its future status with the Croatian government. In spite of weaknesses demonstrated so far, international mediators can certainly influence that solution profoundly.

Relations with Bosnia–Herzegovina

Relations between Croatia and Serbia can be characterized as conflicting, but the most complex is the relationship between Croatia and Bosnia–Herzegovina. There is a special and outstanding interaction between the two countries concerning geographical complementarity (Klemencić 1993/4a). There are also many elements of mutually considering economic, historical and ethnic relations (Klemencić & Topalovi 1993).

Bosnia has traditionally been considered as one of the historic Croatian lands. An important part of that viewpoint has been a theory that Bosnian Muslims were of Croat ethnic origin. On the other hand, the Serbs from their perspective viewpoint claim the predominantly Serbian origin of Bosnian Muslims and they consider Bosnia to be one of Serbia's lands. But there has always been an essential difference between Croatian and Serbian claims. The Croatian side was always likely to respect Islamic culture and be ready to accept Bosnian Muslims within its Croatian circle as "Croats of Muslim religion". On the contrary, the Serbian approach has always been extremely exclusive. There was no understanding and no respect for the Islamic tradition of Bosnian Muslims. They have always been contemptuously considered as once Islamized Serbs who should be either re-Serbianized by whatever means or simply exterminated. Such a Serbian attitude has been widely demonstrated during the current war in Bosnia.

On the grounds of recent events in Bosnia–Herzegovina, Croatian policy needs new approaches and attitudes. It has become obvious that Bosnian Muslims should be treated as a separate cultural and political entity.[11] Consequently, Bosnia–Herzegovina can no longer be treated as "Croatian land". An old slogan of the Croatian nationalists, "Croatian boundary on the Drina river" has changed into "Serbian boundary must not extend over the Drina river". That means support for a sovereign and integral Bosnia–Herzegovina, which should be a buffer state between Croatia and Serbia.

---

11. In order to stress their identity, Bosnian Muslims in 1994 started to call themselves "Bosniaks", which is a traditional term for citizens of Bosnia–Herzegovina, especially those spread among Muslims and Croats.

Naturally, Croatia will carry on its care for the Croatian community within Bosnia–Herzegovina but only to help them to ensure a satisfactory status. Such an approach provides fertile grounds for close relations between the two countries in future, not on the basis of nostalgic historical or consanguinic links but on the more promising basis of real interests. As soon as Croatia accepts that approach completely and integrates it into its strategy, it will also be better treated and more widely accepted on the international stage.

However, a much more complicated situation will develop if Bosnia–Herzegovina does not survive as an integral state. Eventual secession of the Serbs and partition of Bosnia are a real threat for Croatia because of a possible merger of Serb-dominated areas in both Croatia and Bosnia into one unit (so-called Western Serbia). When the spatial integrity of Bosnia is ever violated by the Serbs, it automatically lays claims for revision of the Croatian boundaries. Thus, Croatia will always be very much dependent on the situation in Bosnia, even without wishing that on its own. What is important for Croatia is to be unequivocal towards Bosnian integrity. Fortunately, the Washington agreement[12] signed by the Croatian and Bosnian governments (in the latter case, this is more or less a euphemism for "leadership of the Bosnian Muslims") in March 1994 has made the Croatian position towards Bosnia clearer.

Relations towards other neighbouring states

Apart from Serbia and Bosnia–Herzegovina, Croatia's other neighbouring states are Slovenia and Hungary, as well as Italy on the Adriatic Sea. Since the break-up of Yugoslavia there has been a demarcation dispute between Croatia and Slovenia. The two countries proclaimed mutual recognition "within existing boundaries" in 1991, but they have to demarcate the boundary line. A mutual state commission was formed. Several disputed points emerged, but any problems are small and they should be treated as technical. The greatest dispute is maritime delimitation in the Bay of Piran, where there was no dividing line during the Yugoslav period. In contrast with land boundaries, there are no maritime boundaries between republics in former Yugoslavia. Since Croatia is fortunate in terms of the length of its coastline,[13] Slovenia is probably a more interested partner in that maritime delimitation.

---

12. Agreement between Croats and Bosnian Muslims, which proposed a Croat–Bosnian federation in Bosnia–Herzegovina. In addition, a confederation between the Bosnian federation and Republic of Croatia is proposed for the future, but it is not a realistic project, at least until both countries have overcome problems of integrity.
13. Excluding the islands the coastline of Croatia is 1778 km long, and that of Slovenia, 32 km long.

Apart from the 1982 Law of the Sea Convention, a median line should be adopted as a fair solution, but Slovenia seems to be more ambitious in order to secure broader territorial waters and probably direct access to international waters. The problem is that such a claim encompasses changes of the land boundary at the expense of Croatia, which is advocated openly by some marginal groups in Slovenia. Moreover, the dispute over the Bay of Piran is sometimes overestimated by the media on both sides. Yet, it is a dispute likely to become more sever. Two young countries should finally manage to find a mutually acceptable solution.

With regard to its maritime boundary, Croatia is likely to continue to apply the delimitation agreements reached by Italy and the former Yugoslavia (Blake 1993/94). The way Italy and Yugoslavia settled their straight baselines, territorial sea limits and delimitation of the continental shelf in the Adriatic was widely accepted as reasonable, modest and mutually satisfactory. As a successor state of the former Yugoslavia, Croatia sees no reason to change already-existing solutions.

Apart from the dispute between Croatia and Slovenia, another maritime dispute is the delimitation of the Bay of Kotor between Croatia and Montenegro. First, it should be made clear who is Croatia's partner: Montenegro or the so-called Federal Republic of Yugoslavia, proclaimed by Serbia and Montenegro after the break-up of former Yugoslavia. Secondly, that case is clear since the Prevlaka peninsula on the western side of the bay's mouth belongs to Croatia and the rest of the bay is part of Montenegro. The dispute exists only because Montenegro (or FR Yugoslavia) claims a boundary revision in order to gain the whole bay. Apart from that unilateral claim, the maritime delimitation should be easy because the equidistant line provides a fair and only logical solution (Blake 1993/94).

There are no disputes at all concerning boundary lines between Hungary and Croatia. The old international boundary seems to be satisfactory for both sides, so they can renew their historic links under new circumstances and without boundary disputes.

Conclusion

Although Croatia finally reappeared on the political map of Europe, creation of the state has not yet been completed. The aspirations of the Croats over centuries became a reality, but the new state needs to consolidate its integrity and stability. Without the reintegration of currently Serb-controlled areas, Croatia's unique shape would be seriously handicapped. Under the present circumstances of partial occupation, the country's economic viability is endangered too. Croatia's primary course of action is therefore to find a way to its integrity.

Theoretically, the approach Croatia had towards a territorial resolution of the post-Yugoslav crises was confirmed as a right and legitimate one. Former republican boundaries were recognized as international, which was exactly what Croatia advocated. Unfortunately, the country was faced with aggression and it was forced to defend its legal rights with arms. Since military imbalance was more than obvious, Croatia succeeded only partially. Now, there is a gap between the legal rights and effective occupation in reality. To resolve that frustrating situation, Croatia looks for efficient international support and help.

Once integrated within internationally recognized boundaries, Croatia will have to find a solution for the status of its Serbian minority in order to strengthen the country's internal stability. Certainly, a solution, or *modus vivendi* as once interpreted by EC representatives, will not be easily reached, because Croat/Serb relations in Croatia and in general have reached their lowest level in history.

On attaining its current aims it can be concluded that Croatia's territorial aspirations will be satisfied and it can soon become a place of stability and progress in a transitional part of the continent where central Europe, the Mediterranean and the Balkans are in contact. *Croatia rediviva* is therefore still a challenging project for the present generation of the Croats.

References

A concise atlas of the Republic of Croatia (and of the Republic of Bosnia and Hercegovina) 1993. Zagreb: Miroslav Krle a Lexicographic Institute.

Baletić , Z. 1993. UNPROFOR in Croatia. *Politicka Misao (Croatian Political Science Review)* xxx(2), 44–54.

Banac, I. 1990. Main trends in the Croatian language question. In *Most/The Bridge*, Collection of Croatian Literature, vol. I. Zagreb: Croatian Writers' Association.

— 1984. *The national question in Yugoslavia*. Ithaca, New York: Cornell University Press.

Blake, G. 1993/4. Croatia's maritime boundaries. In *Croatia – a new European state*. Department for Geography and Spatial Planning.

Boban, L. J. 1993. *Croatian borders 1918–1993*, Zagreb: kolska knjiga / Croatian Academy of Sciences and Arts.

Bognar, A. 1991. Changes in ethnic composition in Baranja. In *Geopolitical and demographic issues of Croatia*. Department of Geography, University of Zagreb.

Brandt, M. et al. 1991. *Izvori velikosrpske agresije*, Zagreb: kolska knjiga / August Cesarec.

Cviic, C. 1991. *Remaking the Balkans*. London: Royal Institute of International Affairs.

Crkvencić , I. & M. Klemencić 1993. *Aggression against Croatia*. Zagreb: Central Bureau of Statistics.

Cvrtila, V. 1993. The boundaries of the Republic of Croatia. *Politicka Misao (Croatian Political Science Review)* xxx(2), 35–43.

Degan, V. D. 1992. Samoodre enje naroda i teritorijalna cjelovitost drzava u uvjetima raspada Jugoslavije. *Zakonitost* xLvi(4), 543–69.

Englefield, G. 1992. *Yugoslavia, Croatia, Slovenia: re-emerging boundaries*. Territory Briefing 3, International Boundaries Research Unit, University of Durham.

Fernandez-Armesto, F. (ed.) 1994. The Times *guide to the peoples of Europe*. London: Times Books.

Klemencić, M. 1991. A recent historico-geographical basis of the Yugoslav outer and inner borders with special to Croatian borders. In *Geopolitical and demographical issues of Croatia*. Department of Geography, University of Zagreb.

— 1993. Causes and dynamics of the war in Croatia. *Acta Geographica Croatica* XXVIII, 187–94.

— 1993/4a. Four theses about Croatia and Bosnia. In *Croatia – a new European state*. Department for Geography and Spatial Planning, University of Zagreb.

— 1993/4b. Greater Serbian territorial claims. In *Croatia – a new European state*. Department for Geography and Spatial Planning, University of Zagreb.

— 1994. *Territorial proposals for the settlement of the war in Bosnia–Hercegovina*. Boundary and Territory Briefing (vol. I) 3, International Boundaries Research Unit, University of Durham.

Klemencić, M. & D. Topalović 1993. Geopolitische Verflechtungen von Kroatien und Bosnien–Hercegowina. *Sudosteuropa Mitteilungen* XXXIII(1), 50–60.

Kocsis, K. 1993/4. The changing of the Croatian ethnic territory during the last half of the millennium. In *Croatia – a new European state*. Department for Geography and Spatial Planning, University of Zagreb.

Macan, T. & J. Šentija 1992. *A short history of Croatia* [*The Bridge*, special edition]. Zagreb: Croatian Writers' Association.

Szajkovski, B. (ed.) 1993. *Encyclopedia of conflicts, disputes and flashpoints in eastern Europe, Russia and the successor states*. Harlow, England: Longman.

Šterc, S. & N. Pokos 1993. Demografski uzroci i posljedice rata protiv Hrvatske. *Društvena Istrazivanja* 4–5, 305–34.

Vego, M. 1992. The army of Serbian Krajina. *Jane's Intelligence Review*, vol. V(10), 438–45. Coulsdon: Jane's Information Group.

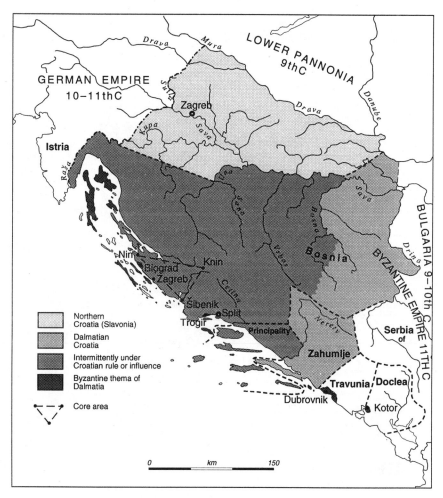

Croatian Kingdom in the tenth and eleventh century.

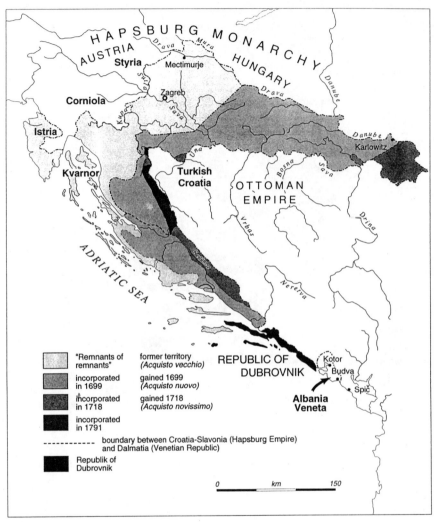

Croatian lands: territorial changes in the seventeenth and eighteenth centuries.
Source: A concise atlas 1993.

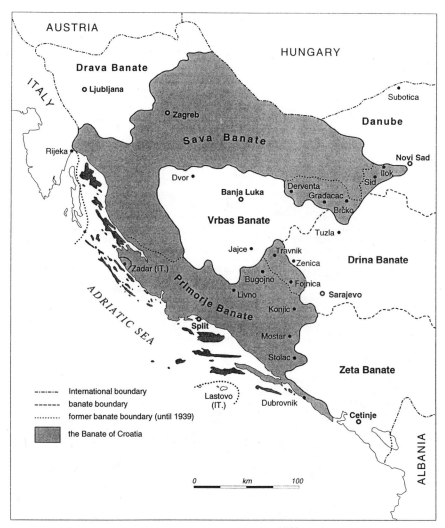

The Banate of Croatia in 1939.

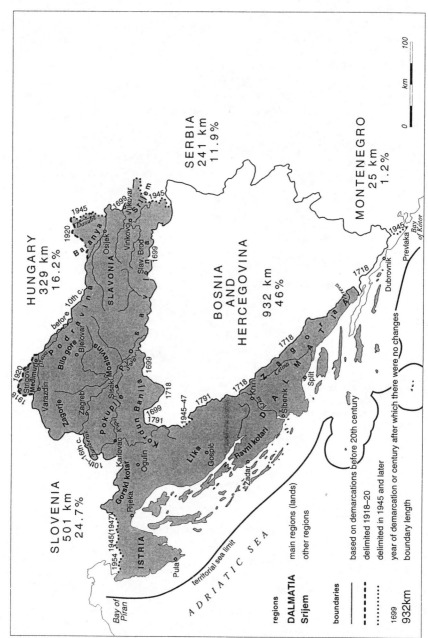

Boundaries and regions of Croatia. *Source: A concise atlas* 1993.

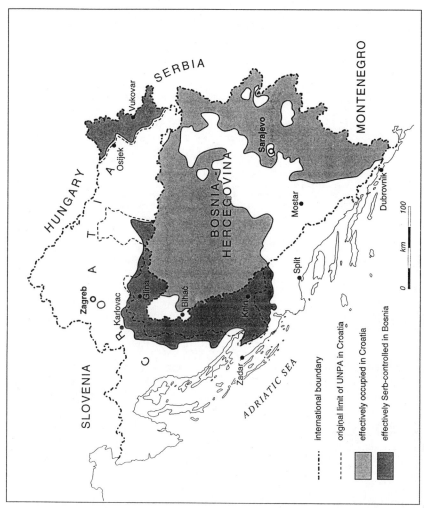

UN Protected Areas and occupied areas in Croatia and Bosnia–Herzegovina (summer 1994).
Source: Miklemencic.

CHAPTER EIGHT
Western Europe and the Balkans
MICHEL FOUCHER

The first thing I wish to comment upon is the title of this chapter. The geo-graphical concepts involved here – as well as the title chosen – bring to mind the historical aspect more than current geographical reality. Do the organizers feel that history is repeating itself in this part of Europe, what with civil wars and rivalry with western European countries? For myself, I would like to deal more specifically with the present situation, particu-larly in the light of the excellent talks we have heard today.

For the moment, the political and military crisis in the Balkan region is limited to Yugoslavia, and the main outside actor is still the European Com-munity (EC). The EC does not include exactly the same territories as western Europe: Greece, a Balkan state, is also a member of the EC, thus giving rise to a relatively new situation. Nor should it be forgotten that the geopolitical status of Greece is historically largely indebted to Canning, and that its geostrategic status is the result of a decision by Churchill, and its NATO membership is one of the consequences thereof.

Yet another EC country is directly involved in Balkan affairs, this time because of its neighbours: Italy. The Italy/Slovenia border was the last to be established inside Europe in 1954. Both Italian and Slovenic minority groups live in Istria. Italy's Adriatic coast is the destination of choice for Albanians fleeing from their homeland. And finally, through the Hex-agonale, Italy has associated states of central and southeast Europe in a regional co-operation structure.

Because of Greece and Italy, the EC is present in the Balkans, or southeast Europe (Mittel-Ost Europa) as they are more often called nowadays, no doubt to avoid re-awakening memories of the past, and the region's sad and dramatic history.

It is, moreover, obvious that Austria, which has applied for EC member-ship, sees the Yugoslavian crisis as both a reason for concern and a chance to exert influence. And it is well known that, in Germany, public opinion, particularly in the Catholic Länder of the South, was convinced from the outset of the need for self-direction of government for the Slovenes and Croatians. Recognition of both people's independence is, as I see it, merely a matter of weeks, perhaps even days, for several states, including Ger-many, Italy, Denmark and Austria. This will inevitably pose some serious problems; indeed, up to the beginning of December, the EC had avoided taking sides, and explicitly designating an aggressor.

Both the EC and western Europe, because of Austria, are therefore playing a part in the crisis, especially from an expressly geopolitical point of view. With this in mind, I would like to limit my observations to the four points that follow.

European countries and the future of Yugoslavia

The birth of Yugoslavia is largely attributable to the intervention of European powers at the end of the First World War. Likewise, the second Yugoslavia, headed by Tito, was strongly supported from the outside, with the result that the Iron Curtain never reached the Adriatic coast.

The recent step taken by Lord Carrington, (President of the Hague Peace Conference) is noteworthy, who, on 20 November last, brought a very official seisin before the Arbitration Commission, which includes five constitutional court presidents. His question was: "Does the Federative Republic of Yugoslavia still exist in accordance with the criteria of national law?" In fact, there are two ways of looking at this:

- according to Belgrade, the republics declaring, or wishing to declare, themselves independent or sovereign does not affect the existence of the Federative Republic of Yugoslavia, nor does withdrawal from the Union, or an intention to do so;
- according to others, we are not witnessing a withdrawal, but rather a breaking-up of Yugoslavia.

Lord Carrington quotes these sources as deeming the six republics worthy of being considered separate successors to Yugoslavia.

Were the Commission to decide in Belgrade's favour, the Serbs will legitimately control:

- the seat at the United Nations
- international representation
- embassies and consulates
- federal infrastructures
- military bases
- money divested, or banked, abroad.

If the Commission decides otherwise, we will be faced with questions of the "succession of states". This is an unheard-of situation in which a west European arbitrational organization finds itself forced to decide the legal, and consequently political, future of a European state that is falling to bits. In other words, each time there has been a major crisis in the history of Yugoslavia, other European countries make the decisions. What criteria are taken into account? And what general European geopolitical context comes into consideration? Going back a few decades, the big task in hand was the dismembering of the Austro–Hungarian Empire in accordance with a project thought up by the Croatian elite, who wanted to group all southern Slavs within the same state by means of a realistic alliance with Serbia, which had already been independent since 1878. The borders of the new country were established in three treaties, all drawn up in the suburbs of Paris (Neuilly, Saint Germain and Trianon). Those who had won the war did their utmost to create Yugoslavia, with Lloyd George and Clememceau at the helm, backed by geographers such as Cvijić to draw the borders.

The Serbs had one major preoccupation when they pulled the borders back to Voïvodine: they wanted to put an end to a geostrategic situation in which Belgrade was a vulnerable border capital. This very preoccupation explains without a doubt the current strategy of conquering key cities located along the Danube in Slovenia and in western Srjem.

More recently, the Allies' final choice in favour of Tito, rather than the *chetniks* led by General Mikaïlovitch, favoured the creation of a second Yugoslavia. A look at the Anglo–Russian conference held in Moscow in October 1944 reveals that the participants were endeavouring to exert leverage "to provide a solution to their country's internal difficulties through a union made up of the Royal Yugoslavian Government, and the national liberation movement'.

These internal characteristics were, however, the result of decisions made by Tito and Djilas, as Yugoslavia was the only country to free its territory with its own forces alone. The constitution, dated 31 January 1946, took its inspiration from the 1936 Soviet constitution. It made Yugoslavia a federation of six republics designed to be autonomous from a linguistic and administrative standpoint, but functioning within a framework of highly centralized power, which itself originated in a national communist movement – which, as I hasten to add, was not imported with the Red Army, as is commonly thought. This caused the rift between Tito and Stalin in 1948. The division of the country into six republics was imagined as early as 1942 in Bihać and in 1943 in Jajce; I shall deal with decisions regarding the borders in a few moments.

In 1974, in response to the "Croatian Spring" of 1971, a new constitution defined Yugoslavia as a federal state with six republics and two autonomous regions.

Is there a third legal path between a break-up into six successor states and the concept of the withdrawal, or maintenance of an international Yugoslavian entity made up of only four republics? Perhaps the Commission will not decide on either of the possibilities. It may instead observe a break-up into three parts corresponding to present reality: Slovenia, Croatia and the four "Serbian block" republics. However, grouping in this way has few constitutional bases. Furthermore, in this case, Macedonia would probably also stake its claim towards independence, whereas Bosnia and Montenegro might be the victims of increased Serbian hegemony, and do likewise.

It is clear, then, that much depends on the choice made by these little republics, namely Bosnia and Montenegro, both of which, I might add, accepted the EC plan put forward on 18 October. The third version of this plan suggests the setting-up of a loose association of sovereign states, in their present borders.

Whatever decisions are made, the European judges will be "cursed" as Robert Badinter declared in *Le Monde* on 28 November 1991. However, much also depends on the more global options open to EC members. And yet, the geopolitical context in which the new political system of Yugoslavia must be defined is very different from that of yesteryear. There hasn't been a world war, but the collapse of communism. The fact that Serbian government officials have been classified as survivors of the communist pattern could easily lead to a temptation for the two supposedly democratic northern republics to withdraw from the Union.

I do feel, however, that what is taking place is different in that the dimension of global security, as in 1945, or of the sanctions taken against vanquished empires, as in 1919, is entirely absent. What is at stake in Yugoslavia in fact concerns the geopolitical scheme that west Europeans would like to see spread all over the continent, supposing, that is, that their ideas are clear, and shared by all.

EC *action within the Yugoslavian crisis*

What effects have the EC's action, analyzed at a given moment, had on a rapidly changing situation?

Let us outline the major steps in the EC's mediation. The EC's troika began mediating after the following three events:
- the independence referendum on 19 May 1991 in Croatia
- the proclamation of independence and the "dissociation" of Yugoslavia by Slovenia and Croatia on 25 June
- the intervention of the Federal Army in Slovenia.

A compromise was reached on 30 June, calling for a ceasefire in Slovenia, and a three-month moratorium on declaring independence. At the beginning of July the CSCE asked the EC to send a mission of observers to check the state of the cease-fire. On 7 July, the Brioni agreement called for an immediate cease-fire and the return of all soldiers to their barracks. A three-month moratorium was also called for, to allow negotiations on the future of Yugoslavia to be taken up once more. Towards the end of July, the observer's mission was extended to Croatia. At the end of August the EC ministers of foreign affairs declared a cease-fire deadline for 1 September at the latest. They also recommended that a peace conference should be organized, and an arbitration commission set up. At the beginning of September the EC presented a peace plan, which was duly accepted by the six republics. The peace conference met for the first time on 7 September in the Hague. On 19 September, Kohl and Mitterand made a declaration suggesting that a European peace-keeping force be sent in. On 25 September, the UN Security Council voted in Resolution 713 decreeing an embargo on arms shipments. On 8 October Croatia and Slovenia confirmed their wish to be independent. On 18 October EC mediators presented a 12-point plan for a political solution, suggesting that the Yugoslavian Federation be replaced by "a loose association of sovereign and independent republics". This was rejected by Serbia. On 9 November, economic sanctions were taken by the EC. On 12 November, the EC requested that the Security Council should "urgently examine the implications of recent demands made by Yugoslavian parties" in which peace-keeping forces are involved. On 14 November, the Yugoslavian parties agreed that the UN could send in a peace-keeping force. On 20 November, the Croatians were beaten at Vukovar while the Federal Army continued its offensive against Osijek and Dubrovnik. Lord Carrington submitted to the Arbitration Commission his question concerning the international status of Yugoslavia. On 23 November, the fourteenth cease-fire was signed in Geneva by Tudjman and Milosevic. On 8 and 9 December, European Summit Meeting was held in Maastricht. On 10 December, yet another "final" cease-fire deadline fixed by the EC.

December will see several European countries including Germany, Denmark, Italy, the Netherlands and Austria recognizing that Croatia and Slovenia are independent.

The UN debate on military intervention will continue. Will there be a Cyprus-type solution, or intervention through a naval blockade (which is rumoured to be the British solution . . .)?

The EC is apparently recognizing that it is relatively helpless, relying as it has since mid-November on the UN, which has sent in Blue Berets to conflict zones, that have then become neutral zones? The EC is also relying on the UN to apply a petroleum embargo. Non-European members, however, look askance at this embargo, seeing in it a possible precedent for interference that might some day turn against them.

As I see it, the intervention of the EC as such, and because it represents influential countries, has in fact created a double issue: an interior issue on the one hand, and a Serbo–Croatian issue on the other. From this point of view, the EC has applied a sort of diplomatic containment strategy with an eye to avoiding a general crisis affecting all of the Balkans, starting with Greece. Likewise, the sending in of observers may have helped to stop the spread of a conflict that, within the territory, does not appear to be a united front. Furthermore, the EC's humanitarian diplomacy gives sustenance to the idea of "the right to interfere".

This type of intervening does, however, have its limits; it happens after the crisis is over; it can only be effective and lasting if it backed up by force;

and it is not accepted by some Third World countries belonging to the UN Security Council ("minimalist" states, including India, and even Romania).

To conclude, then: an agreement as to the role of the United Nations has not been found, for one obvious reason: Croatia and Serbia continue to disagree on where any UN peace-keeping troops should be deployed. Croatia wants them to be sent to areas where fighting is taking place, whereas Serbia wants them to go to areas already seized by the Serb-dominated Federal Army and Serb paramilitary units.

Domestic and external elements leading to the crisis

I shall deal with just four territorial aspects of the present crisis, as follows.

The border problem

In 1946 Tito and Djilas endeavoured to elaborate a constitution in which the external opposition between the two main peoples, Serbs and Croats, would no longer pose any difficulties. This resulted in the creation of new republics (more or less justified by national criteria) designed to tone down nationalism. In Jajce, at the 2nd session of the Anti-fascist Association for the liberty of Yugoslavia, historic limits dating from before the creation of Yugoslavia were reviewed. Examples can be found in Serbia (1912) and in Bosnia (1878), or between Croatia and Slovenia (the former interior boundary with the Austro–Hungarian Empire). The only exceptions involved the dyade of Macedonia and Serbia, and the segment located between Croatia and northern Serbia.

We know that as far as the Serb officials are concerned, these boundaries existing between republics are by no means "borders", as Serbia does not encompass the half-dozen regions with Serb majorities. (These include Krajina in Knin and the self-proclaimed autonomous region of Slavonia, as well as four enclaves in Bosnia). According to Belgrade then, these boundaries cannot be used as the basis for state borders within the present process of decomposition.

The two national questions

At the same time, the historical heritage of the "Militärgrenze" provides an explanation for the extreme overlapping of populations. From this point of view, it can be said that Yugoslavia has already been invented twice to provide an answer to the two-fold national question, that is, the dispersion of Serbian and Croatian populations throughout this area, which is so historically rich in contacts, wars and borders.

To say that there is no national Yugoslavian feeling is a euphemism. In 1919, the grouping of southern Slavs was brought about, from within, by a will to escape. The Slovenes fled from Germanization and the Croatians from Hungarianization. This resulted in a strategy to unite Croatians and Serbs in a single front of resistance, thereby forming a voluntarily independent national entity. Twenty-five years later, Tito rallied the Yugoslavian peoples around a project aimed at toning down nationalism. And today, this same desire for emancipation from Serbian guardianship is growing stronger. Pushed on by the death of Tito and the attraction of the EC, these two northern republics have withdrawn.

Dobritsa Tchossitsh, a Serbian writer thrown out of the Communist Party for bringing up the Kosovo problem, is right when he states that "the sin of Serbian intellectuals" and dissidents is that they did not attempt to take over from the communist leaders. He also feels that two opposed tendencies have always existed among Croatians and Slovenians. The first aimed at Yugoslavian integration. The other hoped to found an autonomous nation-state. This ambiguity in the national way of thinking dates from the nineteenth century. And between these two currents, the winner was always the one who had backing from outside. This was the case for Croatia in 1918: despite being beaten, Croatia took sides with the victors through an association with Yugoslavia in order not to lose Dalmatia and the islands. And as soon as the danger was over, Croatia tried to undermine the new state shared by southern Slavs (interview in the *Journal de Genève*, 27–28 April 1991). This explains the constant importance of outside alliances where the strategies and options of the Yugoslavian peoples are concerned, at least for the northern republics.

In terms of numbers and demographic maps, the last census, taken in March 1991, shows up the following facts. Before the present crisis, 22 per cent of Croatians still lived outside of Croatia, with three-quarters of them in Bosnia; the proportion of Serbs living outside the republic was 25 per cent. Even if a Yugoslavia limited to a "Serboslavia" were created, the Serbs would not even account for 50 per cent of the total population. However, Belgrade feels that this relative demographic weakness does seem to be compensated for by the hegemonic political position, and the constant reference to historical rights.

We must remember that the beginning of the political crisis is linked to a new takeover of Kosovo, starting in 1987, which was considered as a national Serbian cradle, even though it had long had a 90 per cent Albanian population. The January 1977 manifesto published by Serbian intellectuals denouncing an anti-Serbian "genocide" in Kosovo marked the beginning of a strategy of the "Greater Serbian" type. This is why the current crisis is only one aspect of the internal geopolitical contradictions inside Yugoslavia.

Present and possible future phases of the crisis

The Serbs objectives are the following, and have scarcely changed. Indeed, they have been seeking a solution to their national question for a whole century now.

- To bring the Serbs together once again, in spite of their great diversity and their wide dispersion to form a single state structure: not so long ago, this was the invention of Yugoslavia; tomorrow the creation of a "Serboslavia", which will still be multi-ethnic as the "Great Serbia" including the four southern republics, would have fewer than 50 per cent of Serbs.
- Consequently, to extend Belgrade's control to mixed areas in which Serbs are either in the majority or in the minority (the threshold of 25–30% is a minimum objective for the so-called "federal" army) and to link them to one another.
- To chop up Croatia into four or five parts so that Croatia, itself a heterogeneous entity with its Italians and Dalmatians, would be reduced to its initial historic centre, the two Zagorjé, north of Zagreb, the rest being open to negotiation (and consequently security for the Serbs living in Croatian towns).
- To surround Bosnia with its Muslim majority, while cutting off contiguous Serbian regions such as Krajina Bosanska.
- To ensure good sea access.

Beyond this, there is certainly a desire to seek revenge against Croatia, whose past deeds (1941–5) have not been forgiven by the Serbs, no doubt for lack of an initiative by Belgrade to recognize its responsibilities. Hence, the maximum demand lodged by the Serbs: the area under Serbian control should, according to Belgrade (in particular, historians from the Academy of Sciences and government officials), be extended to those regions in which the Serbs were in the majority before 1941. Secret discussions between Tudjman and Milosević did, of course, take place in May. Their aim was to protect future borders, at Bosnia's expense. However, they broke up largely because of the Slovenian precedent, that is, provocations against the Federal Army justifying a precipitated withdrawal, which Zagreb unsuccessfully wanted to repeat.

Other fronts may still be opened, particularly in the mixed areas of Bosnia (Sarajevo first, with 49% Muslims, 30% Serbs, 7% Croatians and 11% Yugoslavians from mixed marriages all living together). This would add a "Muslim" factor. The Muslims have voiced their preference for either a federal Yugoslavian option, or an association of sovereign states. Should the country continue to break up, they may choose either a difficult alliance with the Croatians, who are less threatening than the Serbs, or an impossible independence (see the very recent declaration of sovereignty made by the Parliament of Sarajevo, and the decision for self-determination by Bosnia's four Serbian regions).

Furthermore, Macedonia, also withdrawing, appears to be supported both by Turkey and by Bulgaria (which recognizes a state but not a nation). Greece, however, is against it, because:

- she will not allow a state to bear this ancient name, and
- her national interests converge with those of Belgrade.

The result would be a fatal internationalization of the crisis. And independence-seeking movements, such as Ilinden, are already recruiting troops.

And last, but by no means least, the situation in Kosovo, a province with 90 per cent Albanians belonging to the Republic of Serbia, and considered by Belgrade (all parties included) as the historical hub of the Serb nation. Milosevic, backed by the orthodox circles, built his nationalistic strategy on the theme of the threat to Serbian survival in the Kosovo. The Serbian intellectuals' January 1986 manifesto, in which they denounced the demographic "de-Serbization" of Kosovo, was the starting-point of the current general crisis. The term "genocide" is explicitly used in this manifesto. The Serbs are still acutely aware of the high demographic price they paid to be independent and then to keep Yugoslavia together (one Serb out of five died during the Balkan wars). As Belgrade sees it, the Kosovans and the Albanians of the Kosovo have only one option: to leave, to emigrate. As things stand, they have lost the autonomy Tito granted them in 1974; teachers and doctors have found themselves without a job. It is said that a policy is being forced whereby Serbs coming from Croatia are being moved to other areas.

All in all, it can already be seen that a crisis in Bosnia would then spread into the Sandjak of Novi Pazar (in Serbia), then into Kosovo and into the west of Macedonia, also populated by Albanians, thereby introducing a "Muslim factor" into the crisis. In turn, the powers that be in Croatia should ally themselves to the Bosnian Muslims, who are in favour of such an alliance with relation to Serbia, and to her four "annexes", that is, those Serbian regions that have just unilaterally declared themselves autonomous.

If ethnic logic continues to prevail, a second phase of the crisis may therefore begin, including forced population transfers, and all the danger of civil massacres as was seen between 1941 and 1945, or in 1947, when India and Pakistan were divided: a situation in which each party holds as hostage the dispersed local populations (Serbs from Zagreb versus Croatians from Bosnia, for example in the region of Banja Luka; and Slovenia).

External aspects

The case of Kosovo is obviously the most serious, and for the first time a writer and Albanian national, Ismael Kadarë, spoke out on 14 November 1991 to focus on the 1987 Serbian annexation of a territory in which the third largest population of Yugoslavia lives. He fears the Serbian obsession with Kosovo, whose Albanian population is considered to be heirs to the higher civil servants of the Ottoman Empire. He feels that the Serbs still feel resentful and have a plan for revenge.

We know that the serious incidents in Kosovo could lead to a retaliation by the Federal Army in Albania itself, resulting in a crisis of inter-state dimensions, the likes of which have been unthinkable to date. It is also likely that the EC has maintained the illusion of an equivalent treatment between Serbs and Croatians to avoid this new twist. Another conflict would imply a much more massive European action, this time military, if nothing more than to satisfy public opinion. In the case of Macedonia, the issue involves Greece, followed by Bulgaria, which recognized the declaration of sovereignty of the Yugoslavian republic, a primarily defensive measure aimed at underlining neutrality. Greece, as an EC member endeavouring to accentuate her pressure on Serbia, may find common interest with Belgrade to keep Macedonia from becoming independent, as she absolutely denies any state the right to bear the historic name of Macedonia. Recent military manoeuvres carried out in northern Greece, in Aegean Macedonian, were called "Phillip II". And finally Greece, who has always considered herself the poor relation of the EC, has suddenly discovered she is rich compared to Albania or Bulgaria. The demolition of the Iron Curtain has forced Greece to reconsider her regional political environment. She is directly affected when regional conflicts carry on. However, I do not have available sufficient data to analyze the anti-Greek rhetoric of certain Macedonian political groups.

Conclusion: the geopolitical representations involved

Where Croatia is concerned, its relationship to Europe depends on the ideal image of "sacrificing people for the benefit of the Christian Western world". This is the *Antemurale Christianitas* argument, from the ramparts of the Christian western world, that is, a Catholic one. But we are dealing with an ideological border region resulting from seventeenth-century counter-reform. A nation permanently battling against "schismatic" Serbs as well as an experiment in cohabitation with other people inside the Austro–Hungarian Empire. That is the reason they came up with the idea of Yugoslavia (a result of the wave of Illyrism).

On the other hand, directly opposed, a Serbian national spirit and memory resulting from:
- the Byzantine heritage
- struggles against Turkish influence, including domination and forced conversion, and
- a past riddled with insurrections (and autonomy for Montenegro): the first people of the Balkan Peninsula to revolt against the Ottomans.

For them, there was one historical mission: free the Slav-populated south from the Turks (in other words the Serbs, starting with Kosovo and

Sandjak). However, unlike the Croatians they had the historic experience of a strong state, and had never lived alongside other southern Slavic people, the Croatians in particular. They found themselves forced to defend the new state: a sort of piedmont role taking into account only the Serbian wish for unification, and leaving aside pro-Yugoslavian elements in the two northern nations. The former found natural allies among German and Austrian Catholics, and negotiated their "return to Europe". For the latter, the idea of Europe is a largely foreign concept (particularly for the Orthodox Church) they wish only to count on their fierce national determination.

The effects of the Yugoslavian crisis on the EC

The EC is acting as a mediator; its influence is not negligible, but it seems unable to put an end to the civil war. Among the reasons for its limited action are the differing opinions of member-states, and, I might add, of nations within. The question, then, is whether the Balkan issue is a test of European common foreign policy, or whether it is instead a battlefield for more or less hidden rivalries between EC states. The crisis has sped up thought on foreign policy and security. Jacques Delors likened this process to "a teenager having to deal with adult problems". And the crisis has shown that neither NATO nor the ECSC are able to act. Likewise, regional structures such as the Balkan conference and the Hexagonale have proved inadequate.

The EC's field of action has suddenly grown. The EC, however, despite the ECSC mandate, feels overwhelmed by this extension. Yugoslavia is also a "laboratory for testing the EC's managerial capacities' according to a recent SWP report (Ebenhausen, October 1991, which mentions Yugoslavia as an "Entwicklungslabor").

The EC may play a part in redefining Yugoslavian territory, provided it can see its way clearly.

But differences in opinion are striking. German public opinion made its choice from the outset. Why?

- devotion to the principle of self-determination, from which the Germans themselves benefited
- old, historic and religious affinities between south Germans, Slovenes and Croatians
- the importance of Yugoslavian workers in south Germany, many of them Croatians
- and finally, a pan-European political view, ever conscious of preventing the crisis from spreading (preoccupation with a more efficiently organized ECSC, the fear of a massive exodus, and nuclear danger . . .).

In Germany – and here I am referring in particular to analyses made by the SWP in Ebenhausen – it is felt that several EC states have a different approach attributable to their own minority problems (UK, France, Greece,

Italy). With the result, they explain, that everyone agreed to defuse the crisis, but disagreed as to how it should be done. Opinion in France is, I feel, indifferent, and those factions that are most involved all agree with the Croatian cause. The powers that be have maintained a middle-of-the-road approach, which is, however, evolving, first in favour of Yugoslavian unity, but then accepting the reality expressed by the northern republics, all the while hoping that a flexible global structure might be maintained. In Germany, a new structure with three states – Slovenia, Croatia and Serbia – is preferred. Upcoming German decisions will be made with reference to electoral considerations, and will take into account the feelings of the Christian Democrat groups. However, the importance of this goes beyond Germany. It is also present in Italy, Holland and France. In my opinion, it consists of elaborating a view of Europe enlarged to include nearby Catholic states and nations, and to encourage the emergence of "small nations". The travels and speeches made by the Pope bear this out. For the Serbs it is no more than a plot. The crisis has also revealed how differently prepared the various states are where crisis handling is concerned. The UK and France are better equipped and more familiar with this than other EC states. From this angle, the crisis also appears as the first test of German capability in carrying out foreign policy within the new European context. (Reunification was a special case, as it was brought about with global strategic constraints in mind).

Divergences obviously still exist in Europe. Germany insists more on self-determination and minorities; France stresses the stability of borders, but is now working on the rights of the minorities. We are then, heading for a compromise with *de facto* recognition of these new republics' independence and, later on, a system to link the right to economic aid to durable economic union and respect for the rights of minorities. The only point of agreement seems to be that existing national borders should be maintained, unless bordering states agree otherwise.

The problem is: Can the EC be anything other than an "official receiver" (in French, "*syndic de faillité*", which would, in any case, find itself in the unfortunate position of paying for reconstruction? Or can it still affect the redefinition of Yugoslavia? In this respect, the arbitration commission's decision will be very important where principles are concerned.

And finally, it is obvious that pursuing the construction of Europe has become a goal in itself, and that this objective influences the attitude of EC governments. I am also convinced that the end of a common threat to the EC will reveal national differences in western Europe with regard to the organization of the whole of Europe. The Balkan crisis is, then, also a very serious and unprecedented challenge for western Europe.[1]

---

1. This chapter is clearly a statement in time. Nevertheless, it remains an astute analysis of the geopolitcal remifications of the Balkans crisis as it existed during late 1991.

CHAPTER NINE

The return of the Macedonian Question
GEORGE PREVELAKIS

La vallée du Vardar, continuée par la Morava serbe, trace en effet la grande voie qui, des plaines et des mers du Nord, conduit à l'Archipel. Attirés par le soleil vers la mer souriante, vers les plaines fertiles et bien arrosées, vers les coteaux chargés de vignes, vers les îles enchantées, les peuples d'autrefois se sont pressés et poussés sur cette route, et les invasions ont succédé aux invasions. Les peuples d'aujourd'hui portent encore plus loin leurs regards et leurs désirs. Par delà Salonique, et la mer, et les îles, la route pour eux s'allonge encore jusqu'au détroit nouveau, porte de l'Orient, jusqu'au canal, artère du commerce moderne. De Port-Saïd à Vienne ou à Hambourg, Salonique sera quelque jour la grande escale, l'entrepôt de l'Allemagne et de l'Inde.   Victor Bérard (1897: 15–16)

Introduction

Few areas in the world are as interesting to political geographers as Macedonia. The ethnic mix of her populations, her situation at a major strategic crossroads, her troubled history, the struggle of the Balkan states for the control of the Macedonian territories – all have contributed to making Macedonia a laboratory for political geography.

For this reason, the geographical literature on Macedonia is very rich. Before the Second World War, almost all of the major political geographers had written on Macedonia. Extensive references to the Macedonian question can be found in the works of Isaiah Bowman (1921), Jean Brunhes (Brunhes & Vallaux 1921), Otto Maull (1915, 1922), Marion Newbigin (1915), Alan Ogilvie (1920, 1921) and Lothar Schüttel (1935). Jacques Ancel (1930a), the French geopolitician and specialist of the Balkans, dedicated a whole book on Macedonia. In this book he studied the changes brought about in the population and the economy of the region after the Balkan Wars (ibid. 1930b). The most influential personality in the geographical literature on Macedonia has undoubtedly been the Serb, Jovan Cvijić (1906, 1916, 1918), who made excellent use of his skills and influence as a geographer to serve the interests of his country (see Wilkinson 1951; Taylor 1993:

131

209–12). Together with the case of Isaiah Bowman (Prevelakis 1994), the personality of Cvijić illustrates to what extent geographers could influence the drafting of the political map in the beginning of our century. The Greek and Bulgarian geographers, historians and publicists have been mobilized to answer to the argumentation of Cvijić (e.g. Colocotronis 1919, Ischirkov 1916, 1918, Ivanof 1920).

We find the two last important geographical contributions concerning the Macedonian question during the period of the Greek Civil War and immediately after it. The first contribution is a PhD dissertation on Macedonia submitted to Clark University in 1947 by Huey Louis Kostanick (Kostanick 1947). The second contribution is the book of by H. R. Wilkinson (1951). Its purpose has been to show how the ethnographic cartography of the beginning of our century had contributed in depriving the Bulgarians of their "fair" share of Macedonia. Both books have to be interpreted in the political context of their period. Kostanick had served in the US Army in the Balkans during the Second World War and had been a research analyst at the Balkan Section of the Department of State after the end of the war. His motivation came from his direct experience of the importance of the Macedonian question on the eve of the Cold War, but, as in 1947 the USA had not yet intervened in the Greek Civil War, his style is more or less neutral and objective. Wilkinson, on the other hand, published his book after the end of the Greek Civil War and the failure of the Communist Bloc to take control of Macedonia. Yugoslavia had been expelled from the Cominform three years earlier, so, among the three states involved in the struggle for Macedonia, Bulgaria was the only representative of communist orthodoxy; this probably explains the author's more or less sympathetic attitude towards the Bulgarian aspirations. Independently of the political background, Wilkinson's book is most interesting and extremely well illustrated.

The Greek Civil War has been one of the causes of the confrontation between east and west. Its last battles were fought in the mountains of Macedonia. With the end of the Greek Civil War in 1949, the Macedonian question was closed, at least temporarily. Thus, the rich literature on the political geography of Macedonia ends abruptly with the beginning of the Cold War. The only notable exception is the article by Myron Weiner (Weiner 1971), in which the author uses the Macedonian question as the basis for constructing a geopolitical model.

For the first time since the emergence of the Eastern Question, the Cold War created stability in the Balkans, since to challenge the European territorial status quo could start a new world war. However, the freezing of the geopolitical situation for 40 years did not solve problems deeply rooted in history. On the other hand, important economic, political, cultural and demographic changes have taken place during this period. Thus, although, as the Yugoslav crisis has shown, the potential for conflict has not disappeared, today's situation differs in many ways from those of the past.

The structure of Macedonian geopolitics

The definition of Macedonia: geography and history

There is no consensus as to the geographical limits of Macedonia. During the nineteenth and twentieth centuries, Greeks, Serbs, Bulgarians and Macedonians have defined and redefined Macedonia according to what each nation considered to be its strong point. Thus, not only do the definitions vary according to the national point of view, but we also have differing definitions by each nation at different times. The Greeks, for example, had a very wide vision of Macedonia in the middle of the nineteenth century, when they considered that they would be able to annex an area much larger than today's Greek Macedonia. However, after 1870, when the influence of the Greek Church started to wane as a result of the activity of the Bulgarian Exarchate and when pan-Slavism put Greek expansionism under serious threat, a less ambitious definition has been adopted, based on the so-called *historical* Macedonia; that is, the state of Philip II and of Alexander the Great (see Wilkinson 1951: 1–6).

For our purposes, we can follow the definition of Macedonia as the area covering the Greek region of Macedonia, the territory of the former Yugoslav Republic of Macedonia and the Bulgarian region around Blagoevgrad (Kofos 1964: 3).

Table 9.1 The territory of Macedonia and the three Balkan states.

	Greece	Former Yugoslavia	Bulgaria	Total
Territory of the state (km^2)	132,000	256,000	111,000	499,000
Macedonian territory of the state (km^2)	34,600	25,700	6,800	67,100
The state's share of Macedonia (B/499,000%)	51.1	38.3	10.1	100
Macedonian territory in respect to total national territory (B/A%)	26.2	10.0	6.1	13.4
Macedonia in comparison to national territory (67,100/A%)	50.9	26.2	60.4	100

Sources: Kofos (1964: 3) and National Statistical Service of Greece (1967: 373).

This is of course a conventional definition. If we wished to enter into a more substantial discussion of the meaning of Macedonia, it would be necessary to study the use of the name as a political or administrative term in the states or empires of the past. Such a research, which is outside the scope of this chapter, would show that the extent of Macedonia has varied substantially through time. Thus, for example, in the Roman Empire, the province of Macedonia covered not only the geographical Macedonia as we have defined it, but also all of southern Greece, as well as the territories of Albania.

The population of the Greek and the former Yugoslavia parts of Macedonia are approximately the same, a little more than 2 million each, whereas the population of the Bulgarian part of Macedonia is considerably smaller, about 400,000. The total population of Macedonia is therefore between 4.5 and 5 million.

The Macedonian crossroads

As a geographical entity, Macedonia is, as Kostanick pointed out, "essentially an area of transition, both physically and culturally" (Kostanick 1947: 2). Wilkinson was even more explicit when he stated that:

> This region (Macedonia) is distinctive not on account of any physical unity or common political experiences but rather on account of the complexity of the ethnic structure of its population. It is a zone where the Albanian, Greek, Bulgarian and Serbian linguistic provinces meet and overlap, and where in addition exclaves of Romanian and Turkish speech are found; it is a region where the concept of national sentiment, associated with language, exists side by side with the perhaps older concept of community based on religious affinity; it is a region where many influences, economic, cultural and political, emanating from different parts of Europe, Asia and Africa, meet and mingle but where the process of fusion has not always taken place. (Wilkinson 1951: 3)

Probably the most concise description of the ethnological and political complication of Macedonia in the beginning of our century is the following, taken from a British Military Handbook of 1916: "The nationality of the population is the subject of endless dispute. The most exhaustive studies are those of avowed partisans. A Serbian map shows the whole of Slav Macedonia to be Serbian; a Bulgarian map, Bulgarian; and if an attempt is made from an impartial point of view to learn the facts, the reply is that there are no established facts, except that a Greek population inhabits the coast region and that beyond this region the people are Slavs, whereas there are also a certain number of Turks, Romanians, Albanians and – at Salonica – Spanish Jews. It is the Slavs who are in dispute, and their nationality can be determined according to the basis upon which a conclusion is founded, whether it be race, language, domestic customs, religion or existing national sentiment. The Serb bases his claim on Serbian predominance in the fifteenth century (later than any Bulgarian predominance), on folksongs, certain social customs, etc.; the Bulgar on the feeling of the people today and on the fact that the language used employs the terminal article peculiar to the Bulgarian tongue among Slav languages. He further maintains that his contention is admitted by the Treaty of San Stefano of 1878, and the Treaty of Serbia of 29 February 1912. As to religion, whole districts have belonged, according to the degree of ecclesiastical vigour of one set of propaganda or the persecuting intensity of another, to the Greek, the Bulgarian, the Serbian and again the Bulgarian Church. To give an instance of the confusion, the French forces on the Crna River, relying on the Serbian maps, were surprised to find the villagers eager to help the Bulgarian invaders. The matter is complicated by the fact that, the population having belonged half a century ago to the Greek Church, a section of Slavs calls itself Greek, although speaking Bulgarian. Although the Greek insists that these are "Bulgarophone Greeks", and the Bulgarian that they are Bulgars deterred from joining the national Church by Greek threats of excommunication, the Serbs may insist that the same people are racially and potentially Serbs. In some cases the purest Slav may be the keenest Greek, just as the keenest Turks (the Pomaks, who are Mohammedan Slavs) are often the purest Bulgars in blood.' (Admiralty War Staff, Intelligence Division 1916: 73–4).

Traditionally, geographers have explained the ethnic mosaic of Macedonia by the fragmentation of the territory into a series of small regions separated from one another by natural obstacles. The difficulties of circulation and the lack of accessibility were supposed to have protected the various ethno-cultural groups from assimilation. It is true that groups threatened by invaders or persecuted by imperial forces could find refuge in the mountains. However, the space of Macedonia cannot be assimilated to a series of separate territorial entities. The nomadic shepherds (for example the Vlachs) moved around Macedonia and even farther without losing their cultural identity. The resistance of the iconographies – in the sense of the term that Jean Gottman has given to it, that is the set of symbols and other cultural elements that link together a group of people and relate them to a territory (Gottman 1951, 1952a, 1952b) – can be explained by the possibilities of defence offered by a mountainous territory, but also by the need of social and political cohesion in an environment dominated by insecurity. The ethnic mosaic can be interpreted through the factor of circulation at least as well as through the influence of fragmentation (Prévélakis 1994).

Macedonia is structured around two elements dedicated to circulation. The first is the valley of the Vardar (in Greece Axios), the southern part of the Morava–Vardar corridor, which is a direct route from the Danube River to the Aegean Sea. The second is Salonica (Thessaloniki), an excellent port on the Aegean Sea, the most important crossroads of the Balkans, a point of convergence of the Roman *Via Egnatia*, the road towards Athens, the road towards Istanbul and the Morava–Vardar corridor.

Those two elements have played an antagonistic as well as a complementary role. In periods of peace and prosperity, when the whole region was part of a much wider empire (the Byzantine or the Ottoman), the influence of Salonica was predominant. The city organized a region whose limits stopped where the influence of other centres began: of Istanbul to the east, of Belgrade to the north. On the contrary, in periods of insecurity and war, the Vardar corridor became the dominant feature, bringing barbarian invasions and alien influences.

As a crossroads and a corridor, Macedonia has attended to a constant merging of populations until the period after the Second World War. This mixed character of the population has been reinforced by the imperial power, in a typical policy of "divide and rule". Thus, the Ottoman Empire systematically introduced new elements into the population of the area, each time one single element seemed to become predominant.

Past conflicts over Macedonia

In the struggle between order and chaos, between polarization and disruption, between centripetal and centrifugal forces, the latter have usually won. During the nineteenth century, when the decline of the central power in the Ottoman Empire and the penetration of the ideas in the Enlightment created an atmosphere favourable to the development of nationalism in the Balkans, Macedonia has not been able to become a core region of a state. The mixture of populations, the shadow of Istanbul, the cosmopolitan character of Salonica and the backwardness of the rural areas made it such that no strong Macedonian nationalism could emerge parallel to the Greek, Serbian or Bulgarian movements.

In addition, the strategic value of the area was too important to be left to the control of local forces. Salonica has always been a "second" city: under the shadow of Constantinople or Istanbul during the Byzantine and Ottoman Empires, under the shadow of Athens in modern Greece. Even in periods of prosperity, she has been unable to develop her own iconography. The most important ideological movement in modern Turkey, the New Turk movement, saw the light in Salonica, but only to be absorbed by the capital.

Thus, in the second half of the nineteenth century, Macedonia found herself at the intersection of the spheres of influence of the three cores of nationalism that had been formed in the southern Balkans: Greek, Serbian and Bulgarian. The demise of the Ottoman Empire created a situation of vacuum. Each of the three national cores perceived this vacuum as an opportunity and as a threat: as an opportunity when the geopolitical situation created hopes that the annexation of Macedonia was possible, as a threat when the geopolitical situation seemed to favour one of the other two nations.

Until the Cold War, the basic structure of the Macedonian conflict has been triangular (Greece–Serbia/Yugoslavia–Bulgaria). This form can lead

Table 9.2   Conflicts over Macedonia.

Nature of the conflict	Greece	Serbia/ Yugo.	Bulgaria	Outcome
Linguistic/religious strife (end of 19th century)	–	+	+	Shrinkage of Greek influence
Second Balkan War	+	+	–	Bulgarian territorial losses
First World War	+	+	–	Bulgarian territorial losses
Second World War	–	+	–	Bulgarian territorial losses
Greek Civil War until 1948	–	+	+	Communist guerrillas win
Greek Civil War from 1948	+	+	–	Communist guerillas lose
Political and diplomatic confrontation during the Cold War	+	–	+	Isolation of Yugoslavia

to three forms of alliances (Greece and Serbia–Yugoslavia against Bulgaria, Serbia–Yugoslavia and Bulgaria against Greece, Bulgaria and Greece against Serbia–Yugoslavia).

This table seems to indicate that each time two powers united against the third, the outcome was in favour of the first party. However, the situation is more complicated, because the three states were not the only actors and they usually served not only their own, but also aims of other, greater, powers. The Macedonian problem is like a set of concentric circles. At the centre we find Macedonia with its composite population. In the first circle around the core are situated three nations in competition for its control, that is, Greece, Serbia and Bulgaria. In the second circle, we find Turkey, Albania and Romania, three states that have had strong geopolitical interests in Macedonia. Turkey ruled Macedonia until the Balkan Wars. Albania has a common border with Macedonia and an Albanian minority lives in its western part. Even the Romanians raised irredentist claims on Macedonia (as well as on Thrace and Epirus), based on the presence of a population of Latin vernacular, the Vlachs or Aromouns, who practised transhumance in the mountains of these areas. With sedentarization and urbanization, this population has been absorbed into the other nations. The lack of a common border of Romania with Macedonia has been a serious handicap for Romanian aspirations.

At a third layer, we find the major European powers or the superpowers with their strategies: Germany–Austria and the *Drang nach Osten*, Italy and the *Mare Nostrum*, the Russian/Soviet search of an outlet to the warm seas, the English and the French interest for the Middle East and the Arab World, and the American policy of containment. Although the actors and the forms of intervention changed, the strategic interest of Macedonia remained.

137

All those layers interact in ways difficult to predict. What seems at first as a relatively simple combination of three elements proves thus to be a much more complex situation, once we take into consideration all the degrees of external influence attributable to strategic importance, to the economic value and, last but not least, to the symbolic content of Macedonia in the national iconographies that condition to a large extent the position of the three main protagonists. The local, the regional and the international conflicts are "interiorized" in the Macedonian question. This superimposition of three different levels of geopolitical tension can make Macedonia one of the hottest spots in the world. The combination of different geographical scales, which is necessary for analyzing the Macedonian situation, is one more reason for considering Macedonia as one of the most interesting case studies for political geography.

The starting-point of the Macedonian question can be considered to be the year 1878. After the defeat of Turkey by Russia and with Russian troops outside Istanbul, the Ottomans signed the Treaty of San Stefano (3 March 1878) that provided for the creation of a Greater Bulgaria of $160,000 \text{km}^2$ including almost all of Macedonia (except Salonica). Considered as a triumph of Russia, this treaty provoked reaction from Great Britain and Austria–Hungary, who managed to impose a new negotiation under the presidency of Bismarck. Thus, on 13 July, a new treaty, the Treaty of Berlin, was signed, creating a much smaller Bulgarian principality. The Bulgarians were disillusioned, and since then they have nurtured a dream to recreate Greater Bulgaria. On the other hand, the Greeks realized in 1878 that they did not have the monopoly of irredentism in Macedonia and Thrace, and that they had to turn against Bulgarian aspirations. The Serbians finally started also to look towards Macedonia as a possible exit to the sea after another provision of the Treaty of Berlin, the occupation of Bosnia–Herzegovina by the Austro–Hungarians, frustrated their hopes for an exit to the Adriatic Sea.

Thus, in 1878 a period of strife started against the Ottoman Empire but also among the three Balkan states. Its main episodes are the war of the Komitadjis (irregular bands supported by either Bulgaria, Greece or Serbia) in Ottoman Macedonia, the two Balkan Wars and the First and Second World Wars. The outcome of this period has been the division of Macedonia among the three states more or less on the lines of today's apportionment. The struggle for Macedonia created deep wounds in the relations between the Balkan nations, because of the opportunistic diplomacy of their governments and even more because of the horrors of a series of fratricidal wars (for the description of the atrocities during the Balkan Wars, see the *Carnegie Endowment for International Peace 1914*).

However, in the period between the two world wars, the Balkan states managed to make considerable progress towards an understanding. In 1930 the first Balkan Conference was held in Athens, paving the way towards the Balkan Pact of 1934, which linked together Greece, Turkey, Romania and Yugoslavia. Bulgaria joined the "Balkan Entente" in 1938. However, the aims of Italian and German expansionism broke this process by diplomacy, secret services and, finally, by military action. Thus, the fate of the Balkans to be overrun by far stronger external forces was confirmed once again (Rousek 1946: 374–5).

During the Second World War, Bulgaria, as an ally of the Axis powers, annexed or occupied all of Macedonia. "Liberated" by the Red Army and ruled by George Dimitrov, a prominent Comintern figure, Bulgaria could however count on Soviet support after the war. She has thus been able to avoid the worst, but still could not possibly keep her newly acquired Macedonian territories. Once again, as in 1878, in 1913 (Treaty of Bucharest, 10 August 1913, the result of the defeat of Bulgaria during the Second Balkan War, according to which Serbia and Greece divided western and central Macedonia between themselves) and in 1918 (in 1918 the Bulgarian army was defeated by the Entente army and, with the Treaty of Neuilly of 27 November 1919, she not only abandoned the territories she had held but also territories that had been annexed as a result of the Balkan Wars) Bulgaria saw her Macedonian trophy taken out of her hands.

Greece, although among the victors of the Second World War, was weakened by the Civil War. The strongest power on the Balkan scene was Tito's Yugoslavia. Tito's plan had been to extend the Yugoslav federation and to include Bulgaria as a seventh republic. The three Macedonians, the Greek ("Macedonia of the Aegean"), the Bulgarian ("Macedonia of the Pirin") and the Yugoslav ("Macedonia of the Vardar"), would be united to form one big "Republic of Macedonia", also to be included in the new Union. Thus, the old national problems of the Balkans were supposed to find their solution according to the federal model of the Soviet Union. The Bulgarian and the Greek communist parties had accepted Tito's plans. The resistance of the Greek nationalist government, supported by the British and after 1947 by the Americans, as well as the Stalin/Tito dispute, stopped these projects from being realized.

The occupation of large parts of Greek and Yugoslav Macedonia by the Bulgarian nationalists during the war, the danger for Greece of losing her share of Macedonia during the Civil War, the wave of refugees from Greece into the communist countries after the defeat of the Greek left wing, and so on, had re-animated the old suspicions, hatreds and fears. The Iron Curtain again divided Macedonia, and the three Macedonians started living their separate lives: of capitalism in Greek Macedonia, of orthodox communism in Bulgarian Macedonia, and of a specific form of communism in Yugoslav Macedonia.

In Greece, the exchange of populations after the First World War had caused a dramatic change in the ethnic composition of the northern provinces. Most of the refugees from Asia Minor and the coasts of the Black Sea had been established in Macedonia and Thrace. According to a report of the Society of Nations:

The result of the settlement in Macedonia of about 500,000 rural and 300,000 urban refugees, followed by the emigration in 1923 of 348,000 Moslems under the Treaty of Lausanne for the Exchange of Greek and Turkish Populations, has been radically to change the ethnic composition of the population of Greek Macedonia and definitely to hellenize that province. (League of Nations 1926: 264; cited by Wilkinson 1951: 264)

Wilkinson considers that this judgement, as well as the ethnographic map published in the same report, was strongly influenced by the Greek point of view. However, the fact remains that a dramatic change in the ethnography of Greek Macedonia took place, a change that created out of an area that was notoriously of mixed ethnic character a practically homogeneous Greek region.

During the Greek Civil War, the so called "Slavophones" (Slav-speaking population) of Greek Macedonia had been estimated to be about 90,000 (Kofos 1964: 172). A significant portion of them participated in guerrilla warfare on the side of the Democratic (communist-led) army. Many of them left the country in 1949 to find refuge in Yugoslavia or in Bulgaria and other communist countries. According to the 1951 population census, 41,000 Slavophones remained in Greece (ibid.: 185). The fact is that in the isolated mountainous areas two or more languages were spoken and the limits of nationality were often unclear. Under the more or less authoritarian regimes that followed the Civil War in Greece, even if more "Slavophones" had remained in Greece, they had no interest in manifesting their presence. In any case, after the defeat of the communists, few possibilities remained in Greece for political activity on the Macedonian question. The Greek communist party, outlawed and accused of high treason, had to abandon its former positions in respect of Macedonia.

In Bulgaria the situation also remained calm. The population of the "Macedonia of the Pirin" had little difficulty in accepting Bulgarian national identity after the annexation of this region by Bulgaria. In Yugoslavia, however, the situation was more difficult and this led Tito to devise a specific policy in order to cope with the Macedonian problem.

The new form of an old question

The Macedonian ethnogenesis

In Ottoman Macedonia at the end of the nineteenth century, much of the urban population had a Greek *national* identity because of the influence of the Greek nationalism and of the Greek state. In the cities there was also a large Jewish *sepharade* community. The Turks were naturally present and there were also persons conscious of a Bulgarian or a Serbian identity. However, most of the rural masses of the population had not yet developed a definite *national* identity. They had a *religious* identity of *rum* (that is, Orthodox Christians) and they spoke dialects that were often a mixture of Greek, Albanian, Vlach and Slavonic elements. For many observers of that period, this rural Macedonian population was therefore malleable and could accept any of the three dominant Balkan national identities based on Orthodoxy (Greek, Serbian, Bulgarian). The purpose of the *Komitadji* struggle had been to impose by force one of the national identities so as to facilitate the annexation of the territory by this or the other state. The idea that it was possible to integrate the Macedonian population into one of the existing national identities found its confirmation in Bulgaria, where the Slav-speaking Macedonians did accept Bulgarian identity, whereas the Greek-speaking Macedonians of the Bulgarian territories were obliged to leave. Greece solved the problem of its "Slavophones" in a similar way by the exchange of populations with Bulgaria, a form of "civilized" ethnic cleansing. However, Yugoslavia was unsuccessful in her efforts to turn her Macedonian population into Serbs during the period between the two world wars. In Bulgaria there were many refugees from Yugoslav Macedonia, who revitalized the Macedonian revolutionary organization (IMRO – Internal Macedonian Revolutionary Organization or, in Slavonic, VMRO). Created in 1893 in Salonica, IMRO was at the origin of the Ilinden (St Elijah's Day) uprising of August 1903. Between the two world wars, IMRO had a considerable de-stabilizing influence on Bulgarian political life and was responsible for the assassination of the moderate Bulgarian premier, Alexander Stamoliski, in 1923 (for an interesting parallel between the de-stabilizing role of IMRO in Bulgaria and that of the Palestinians in Lebanon and Jordan, see Weiner 1971: 678–9). Thus, Yugoslav Macedonia turned into a difficult problem for Belgrade and contributed to the bad relations between Yugoslavia and Bulgaria during this period.

The strategy of Tito towards the Macedonian problem has been contrary to that of pre-war Yugoslavia. Instead of trying to turn the reluctant and Bulgarophile population of Yugoslav Macedonia into Serbs, he proclaimed the existence of a separate Macedonian nation with the right to form its own republic inside Yugoslavia. He combined two ideas: the idea of a Macedonian state, and the idea of a Macedonian nation.

The idea of a Macedonian state can be traced back to the original IMRO. The independent Macedonia that some of the first leaders of IMRO wanted to create was not and could not be a national state, since the Macedonian population was a mixture of different ethnic groups. In the same way, the Macedonian state advocated by the Communist International could not be founded on the basis of a Macedonian *ethnic* nation, since it was supposed to comprise territories with homogeneous Greek populations together with the territories inhabited by Slav Macedonians.

The idea of a Macedonian *nation* has its origin in certain ethnographic maps from the beginning of this century and has been developed by the well known Serb geographer Jovan Cvijić. Cvijić made use of the category of "Macedonian Slavs" or "Macedo-Slavs" in the sense of a non-Greek Macedonian population, which, however, was neither Serb nor Bulgarian. He wanted thus to challenge the then-prominent idea that most of the population of Macedonia were Bulgars. Knowing that it would be difficult to assert persuasively that the population of Macedonia were Serbs, he presented the idea that they constituted a distinct group, suggesting thus that their territories should not be granted automatically to Bulgaria. As Wilkinson states, "Cvijić's conception of the Macedo-Slavs ... neatly robbed the Bulgarians of their strongest claim to Macedonia – the claim that its inhabitants were mostly Bulgarians ... The beauty of Cvijić's conception was that on the surface it appeared to be a compromise between extreme Serbian and extreme Bulgarian ideas ... Thus by its very moderation it commended itself to public opinion as impartial' (Wilkinson 1951: 149–50). Although Cvijić introduced the new notion of (Slav) Macedonians, he was not a proponent of a Macedonian state. He considered that the valley of the Vardar was an indispensable element of Yugoslavia from a geopolitical point of view, and that therefore the Macedo-Slavs had to be integrated into the Yugoslav Nation.

By declaring the existence of a Macedonian national group, Tito applied and extended the anti-Bulgarian strategy of Cvijić, which proved most useful especially after Tito's conflict with Stalin, when Bulgaria went from being ally to adversary. By forming a Macedonian Republic, he recuperated the most radical elements of the pre-war IMRO and won the sympathy of many former Bulgarophiles. His policy concentrated on the newer generations, to which he tried to instil the new Macedonian patriotism. Thus, a Macedonian iconography has been created. The new Macedonian national myth is not different from other national myths, a mix of truths and fallacies. The Macedonian linguists have forged the rules of a Macedonian language based on Macedonian dialects as distant as possible from the Bulgarian language. A Macedonian literature has also been produced. The Macedonian historians have assembled elements of the history of the peoples that have left their mark on the region and melted them into a unified history of Macedonia, marked by heroes like the "Greeks" Alexander the Great and Aristotle, Cyrill and Methodius (claimed by the Greeks, the Serbians and the Bulgarians), the "Bulgarian" Tsar Samuel (991–1014), and so on.

Thus, after the end of the Cold War, the structure of the Macedonian Question had changed from triangular to quadrangular: Macedonian nationalism has been added to Greek, Serbian and Bulgarian nationalism.

History versus geography

The contradictory national icons

Before the nineteenth century, all of the Christian Orthodox populations of the Ottoman Empire considered themselves members of the same family, of the *rum milliet*. The Western idea of the national identity was introduced for the first time in the Ottoman Empire by Greek nationalism. The success of the Greeks in obtaining support from the European powers for their nation-state is attributable to a large extent to the prestige of Ancient Greece and to the Philhellene movement of which Lord Byron was the most prominent representative. The other Balkan nationalisms tried to follow the Greek example. History has been considered as a political capital that could ensure outside help and reinforce internal cohesion. Thus, there was competition between the Balkan nations for the appropriation of a history that, in most cases, had a common heritage. This competition took the form of conflicting national historiographies. The educational system of each Balkan state was responsible for diffusing to the population the historiographic model created in the capitals, whereas the main task of the national academies has been to demonstrate the validity of the national interpretation of history and to denounce the other nations for "deformations" of history.

During the second half of the nineteenth century, the idea that nations are basically linguistic groups made substantial progress in Europe. In order to reinforce the national homogeneity, the national intelligentsia developed purified and normalized versions of the national language (like the Greek *katharevousa*) that were taught systematically to the populations living in the territory of each state. The diversity of the dialects has been replaced by the homogeneity of the official language. The principle of national self-determination that also started to be accepted during the same period, led to the belief that, together with history, language was an important arena in the struggle for territory. Since the treaty of San Stefano in 1878, when the ethnographic map of Kiepert (Kiepert 1876) had been used to trace the borders of Greater Bulgaria, language became thus a major issue in the geopolitics of Macedonia.

In the struggle for a larger share of territory, each national core combined the old element of religious identity with the newer and Western-inspired ideological elements. The Greeks emphasized the role of history. A first reason for that was the heritage of Ancient Greece, which, as the Greeks argued, gave them inalienable rights on Macedonia (or, at least, on *historical* Macedonia). A second reason has been that the Greek-speaking population of Macedonia was concentrated on the coasts; thus, it was difficult for the Greeks to insist on the ethno-linguistic factor without legitimizing the claims of either the Serbians or the Bulgarians. Finally, for a long time, there has been a confusion between the Greek *national* identity and the Greek *religious* (or *rum*) identity. This confusion allowed to the Greeks to hope for territorial expansion that covered the whole of the Balkan peninsula as well as part of Asia Minor. The Greeks preferred not to give a precise carto-graphic expression of their territorial claims in order to leave open as many options as possible. Thus, the Greek perception of space has been extremely vague. The absence of a geographical vision in Greek iconography is bal-anced by an over-growth of history: everywhere where Greek culture has played an important role, the territory is potentially Greek.

The Macedonian iconography is diametrically opposed to the Greek vision. It is founded on the idea of a Macedonian region with a personality of its own. Macedonian history is made up of events that happened and of the personalities that lived in the space of Macedonia. The most brilliant part of Macedonian history is the period of Alexander the Great. A geo-graphical myth (Macedonia) leads to the appropriation of history, whereas, in the Greek vision, an historical myth (the continuity of Greeks) legitimizes the appropriation of territory. The misunderstanding between Greeks and Macedonians is easy to explain. In a symmetrical way, they both perceive the other as a robber. The Macedonians consider that the Greeks have broken the *geographical* unity of Macedonia by annexing the *region* of Mac-edonia of the Aegean, whereas the Greeks consider that the Macedonians have damaged the *historical* unity of Greece by claiming the *period* of the Macedonian state and empire.

Typical of this contradiction of perceptions is the dialogue of the deaf between Greeks and Macedonians. Many Macedonians have made exten-sive use of the symbol of unified Macedonia (which, as noted, has a central position in Macedonian iconography), that is a map of the geographical region of Macedonia. The Greeks have interpreted the use of this symbol as an expression of irredentism, since the map of a unified Macedonia includes Greek Macedonian territories. They have responded to this "prov-ocation" by the *mot d'ordre* "Macedonia is Greek", by which they mean that the name – as well as the Greek part – of Macedonia cannot become the object of Macedonian irredentism. However, for non-Greeks, this phrase (which was on a poster that the foreign tourist found in front of him on arrival at Athens airport) can have only one interpretation: that the Greeks consider the former Yugoslav Republic of Macedonia's territory as Greek!

The perception of the Bulgarians is inspired essentially by the ethno-linguistic principle. They declare that there is no Macedonian language and that the Slavonic dialects spoken in Macedonia are simply branches of Bulgarian. They then argue that the Macedonian identity is "artificial" and does not really exist. This idea of the artificiality of the Macedonian nation, which many Greek commentators also accept, relies on the assumption of a national *substance* to be found in "natural" nations, and lacking from the Macedonians. There is therefore no Macedonian Nation and the so-called

Macedonians are in fact Bulgars. For this reason, the Bulgarian attitude towards the Macedonians is that of a "big brother" who waits patiently for his younger brother to come to his senses (Gorev 1994).

The Serbs have combined the Greek and Bulgarian strategies by invoking both history and language. However, they are weaker than either the Greeks or the Bulgarians on those two grounds. Their main argument is in fact geopolitical: they need to control the corridor towards the Aegean Sea to secure their communications. Instead of being a handicap, the weak position of the Serbs at the symbolic and iconographic level has turned into an advantage. Not restricted by a doctrinaire position, their leaders have managed to find compromises and thus to set up alliances either with the Greeks against the Bulgarians or with the Macedonians against both Bulgarians and Greeks.

The current tensions

As long as Belgrade kept the Yugoslav federation strongly together, the dangers of a new explosion were limited. The Macedonian question was part of a Yugoslav strategy of internal federal politics and the rare outbursts belonged to the tactical arsenal of diplomatic pressures towards Greece or Bulgaria. Belgrade knew that the Macedonian issue could find little echo in either Greek or Bulgarian Macedonia. The USA supported Yugoslavia and obliged the Greek governments to overlook the process of the Macedonian ethnogenesis and the utilization of Greek national symbols. The Bulgarians had also to comply with the discipline of the Cold War and did not try to raise the Macedonian question in any substantial way.

The first indications of a nationalist and irredentist Macedonian movement appeared outside the Balkans in the early 1980s. The nationalist non-Greek Macedonian émigrés in Australia and Canada accused first the Greeks and Bulgarians and then also the Yugoslavs of oppressing the "Macedonian Nation" and of occupying its lands. The Greek Macedonians in the same diaspora lands responded by organizing counter-manifestos to underline the Greek character of Macedonian history. If such confrontations had remained at a safe distance from Macedonia, they could be viewed as interesting cases of cultural geography (for the story of the various "brands" of Macedonian identity, among which we find the new brands of "Macedono-Australian" and "Macedono-Canadian"; see Kofos 1990: 132–5). However, towards the end of communist rule, information about the feelings of the population in Yugoslavian Macedonia started to become more and more alarming. Thus, in an article published in 1990 and titled "The wakening of the Komitadjis" a French journalist described his impressions from a visit to the region. The author reported the re-establishment of IMRO. One of its leaders, Venko Vetchkov, expressed its aims and strategy in the following words:

145

We are living in very important times. Macedonia is waking up after forty years of communist lethargy . . . There is an absolute necessity to share a social and cultural identity to attain economic prosperity . . . When you know for whom you are working, in what space, in what cultural identity, things are much more simple for everybody. Today, with three Macedonians, nothing good can come out . . . In spite of all the things the communists have said about IMRO, people have remained firm on its original ideals with respect for individuals and cultures in a unified territory.

Journalist: And IMRO violence, has it disappeared?

Venko: If the democratic process fails, we will not stop people from revolting. It is written in black and white on our program (in the author's translation from the French, Nothias 1990: 152, 155).

In fact during the 1980s, two new elements had influenced the situation in Yugoslav Macedonia. First, after Tito's death, Yugoslavia entered into a period of ethnic strife and growth of nationalistic attitudes. Secondly, the Balkans became de-stabilized by the end of the Cold War. Together with so many other demons of the past, the Macedonian question started again to cause friction among the Balkan states. Macedonian nationalism, from an element of cohesion of Yugoslavia, became, in the context of the Yugoslav crisis (although, it is true, much less than the Croatian, the Slovene or the Bosnian nationalism), one of the factors that led to the disruption of former Yugoslavia. In September 1991, 90 per cent of the Macedonian voters chose the creation of an independent state. The elections that took place in the same year confirmed the return of IMRO, which won 31 per cent of the seats and became the strongest party in the Macedonian parliament. At the same time, another nationalism appeared, that of the Albanian Macedonians, who won 20 per cent of the seats in Parliament (Chiclet 1992).

Since then, the Macedonian question has become a European and an international issue. Greece has used all the diplomatic means at her disposal and has mobilized her diaspora of about 5 million persons around the world in order to prevent the recognition of the new state under the name of Macedonia. Only in April 1993 did the United Nations recognize it, but with a *provisional* (Former Yugoslav Republic of Macedonia) and without a flag, as Greece reacted to the use of the symbol of the ancient Macedonian kings – the Star of the Vergina – on the flag of the new state. The embargo imposed by the socialist government of Andreas Papandreou since the beginning of 1994 on all Macedonian imports and exports passing through Thessaloniki has worsened an already difficult economic situation.

The leader of the new Macedonian state, President Kiro Gligorov, an experienced politician, has managed to keep a balance between the diverging tendencies in his state and to manoeuvre quite efficiently at the

146

diplomatic level. Thus, Macedonia, although potentially one of the most dangerous spots in the Balkans, has been peaceful until now, the only former Yugoslav republic that has not been involved in armed conflict. In October 1994 Kirov Gligorov was re-elected as President of the Former Yugoslav Republic of Macedonia.

A region of conflict or a crossroads of co-operation?

The opportunities

After the end of the Cold War, the political and economic difficulties in eastern and western Europe have created a climate of "Europessimism" that often leads us to forget the enormous possibilities created by the end of the dichotomy of our continent.

The Balkans have many important assets for becoming one of the leading world regions of the twenty-first century. The situation of the Balkan peninsula, between Europe, Asia and Africa, is again becoming a great advantage. The Balkan states hold natural resources that lay dormant in the past because of lack of capital or of appropriate technologies. The spectacular growth of Greek commercial agriculture during the past two decades is a good example of the possibilities created by a combination of transport and agronomic innovation. In many Balkan areas, easily accessible from the big west European as well as by the growing east European and CIS markets, there is a largely undeveloped potential for tourism. However, the greatest asset of the Balkans is its human capital. The cultural environment of this area did not prepare its populations for industrial employment and therefore constituted an obstacle to growth during the past century, but now Balkan culture becomes an advantage. What is today so important is not so much a massive and well disciplined workforce, but rather an active population that is mobile, enterprising and receptive to the messages of the international economic environment. In such a context, the Balkan nations, together with the networks of their diasporas, have important relative advantages because of their history, their geographical situation and their culture. Even the relative backwardness of the Balkan economies has a positive aspect, since they can adapt to a global economic environment "on the move" much more rapidly than those of the relatively rigid industrialized European nations.

From the point of view of opportunity, few European areas have the advantages of Macedonia, situated at the very heart of the Balkans, at the intersection of the major axes of circulation. In a world in which the barriers to circulation tend to fall, the role of a crossroads, which offered to Macedonia its economic successes before the "Balkanization of the Balkans", will serve again as a course of progress and prosperity. Thus, the structural geographical characteristics of Macedonia encourage an optimistic view of the future in a medium- to long-term perspective. However, before Macedonia (and the Balkans in general) can grasp the opportunities of the post-Cold War world, they have to solve the geopolitical problems that they have inherited from their late history. Just as Macedonia is the point of convergence for Balkan opportunities, in the same way it can be considered as the crucible of almost all Balkan geopolitical contradictions.

An approaching storm?

Many Albanians and Bulgarians continue to have an irredentist attitude towards Macedonia. There were only two possible solutions to the Macedonian question according to the Bulgarians: either the annexation of the largest part of Macedonia by Bulgaria, or the recognition of the independent Macedonia as a second Bulgarian state. As the Greeks saw the independence of Cyprus as a first step towards *enosis* (union with Greece), in the same way the Bulgarians perceived the Macedonian state as a stepping-stone towards a Greater Bulgaria. After the declaration of Macedonian independence, Bulgaria has recognized the Macedonian state but has refused to recognize the Macedonian nation. She has not stated officially that Macedonians are Bulgars, but has left all doors open for doing so in due time. During a conference organized on 8 March 1994 in Paris by the French Institute for International Relations (IFRI), the Bulgarian president Zhelev declared that "it is up to the inhabitants of this area [meaning the Former Yugoslav Republic of Macedonia] to decide what they really are", letting his audience understand that they had not yet done so. The Bulgarian strategy seems to rely on an imminent internal Macedonian crisis to cause some of the Macedonians to turn to Bulgaria for help. Bulgaria would then be legitimized to intervene in Macedonia (and eventually to annex the non-Albanian part of the Former Yugoslav Republic of Macedonia), using as a pretext the protection of a population that returned at last to its "real" (Bulgarian) identity. The objective of Albania can also be a territorial expansion to the western, Albanian inhabited, areas of Macedonia. In comparison with the Bulgarian situation, the Albanian case is simpler, because there is no substantial difference between the Albanian language as spoken in Tirana and as spoken in Macedonia. In any case, there is a common interest linking together Bulgaria and Albania against the territorial integrity of the Former Yugoslav Republic of Macedonia, which creates the basis for an alliance.

Another similarity between Albania and Bulgaria is that their potential territorial claims are not limited to Macedonia but extend to neighbouring areas. For Bulgaria, an exit to the Aegean Sea has been a permanent aim, an objective that seemed to her to be dictated by geography itself. A Bulgarian corridor through Greek Thrace would give a great geopolitical advantage to Bulgaria, since circulation from the Black Sea to the Mediterranean would be made possible only through Bulgarian territory. The straits would lose much of their importance, and Bulgaria would obtain a good bargaining position towards Russia and other countries. Thus, the question of Macedonia is part of a wider issue of the constitution of a Greater Bulgaria. The area of Macedonia inhabited by Albanians is similar to that of Kosovo. Kosovo is part of Serbia, but it is inhabited by a majority of ethnic Albanians. An explosion of ethnic trouble in either of the two areas would probably provoke a more general destabilization. In such a climate, Albania could hope to obtain from the international community the constitution of a Greater Albania, by making an appeal to the principle of self-determination. As the Serbians seem for the time being to control the Kosovar Albanians, a revolt of the Macedonian Albanians seems more probable.

In the case of a Macedonian crisis, Albania and Bulgaria would have a serious opportunity to share the territory of the Former Yugoslav Republic of Macedonia. However, such a change of the *status quo* cannot be accepted easily by Greece and Serbia. Both countries consider the corridor that links them together through Macedonia as a vital economic and strategic issue. For Greece the Morava–Vardar axis is her main territorial link with western Europe and, for Serbia, the port of Thessaloniki is a very important access to the sea, especially after the break-up of Yugoslavia and the difficulties to ensure a valid exit to the Adriatic Sea. As Albania and Bulgaria have been enemies of Greece and Serbia in the past and as Albanian relations with both Greece and Serbia are bad because of the conflict over the Greek minority living in southern Albania ("Northern Epirus" to the Greeks) and the Kosovo dispute, the control of the Vardar valley by those countries would be perceived as a threat to the vital interests of Greece and Serbia. Would they contribute passively to a growing danger of separation from one another? Already in 1992, some Serbians had suggested to Greece a preventive common military action to create a common Greece/Serbia border (*Amyna kai Diplomatia* 1993). Greece can thus find herself with a large dilemma in the future: either to accept Albanian and Bulgarian expansion in Macedonia, which will surround her with enemies, or to get involved in a war of a very uncertain outcome.

In fact, Turkey would not be indifferent to a Greek action in Macedonia. There is a strong feeling in Turkey that the Balkan Muslims are threatened with extermination and that there is a Turkish responsibility to protect those former subjects of the Ottoman Empire. In addition, the destabilization of an area from Albania to Thrace can appear to many Turks as an opportunity to seize the Greek part of western Thrace, which has an important Muslim community more and more under Turkish influence.

One can easily imagine how the whole Balkan area can get into very serious trouble from an explosion in the Former Yugoslav Republic of Macedonia. The prospect of a third Balkan War, involving Greece and Serbia on the one side, and Albania, Bulgaria and Turkey on the other, is worrying the strategic analysts more and more. Thus, the stability of Macedonia becomes a crucial international issue. Macedonia is the most recent nation-state to arrive on the Balkan scene. One can have doubts about the consistency of the Macedonian ethnogenesis as time is an important factor in the consolidation of identities. The ethnic mix that continues to characterize the population of the Former Yugoslav Republic of Macedonia introduces a contradiction between the idea of Macedonian nation and that of a Macedonian state. The Albanians of Macedonia, who represent at least one-fifth of the population, cannot accept the Slav-Macedonian identity, since their language is not Slavonic. If the Macedonian *state* identity were founded on the Slav-Macedonian *ethnic* identity, the Albanians would be turned into an ethnic minority. In such a case the dangers of secession would be even greater than today. For this reason, the Macedonian state needs to underline an *historical* rather than an *ethnic* Macedonian identity. The reference to Macedonian ancient history, in which the Albanian-Macedonians have as many (or as few) rights as the Slav-Macedonians, solves the problem of the Albanian community, but creates even more difficulties with Greece. In fact the Greeks could accept, as a compromise, a denomination of the new state based on the notion of the Slav-Macedonians (like "the Slav Republic of Macedonia"), an idea that the Gligorov government cannot embrace without destroying the fragile *modus vivendi* with the Albanian community.

Greece is in a most awkward position when confronted with the Macedonian state, not knowing what to wish. An eventual disappearance of Macedonia as a state will open a Pandora's box of a diplomatic and/or military disaster. On the other hand, it is true that irredentism is inherent in the Macedonian iconography, which is based, as we saw, on the idea of the indivisibility of a geographical Macedonia. A consolidated Macedonian state will, sooner or later, make some kind of claim on Greek and Bulgarian Macedonia. However, it is difficult to imagine the conditions under which such claims could find satisfaction, since the population of the "Macedonia of the Aegean" is almost 100 per cent Greek, and the inhabitants of the "Macedonia of the Pirin" have been Bulgarized. However, the perplexity of the Greek political and intellectual leaders has offered to the most irresponsible elements of Greek public life the possibility of rousing public opinion. The policy of the embargo (abandoned at the end of 1995), which has worsened the economic, social and political situation in Macedonia and has brought the danger of a crisis a step nearer, has been the result of pressure by the press and public opinion on a weak Greek government. Greece, politically and intellectually unprepared for a complex geopolitical situation, has made again, as in the case of the Cyprus crisis, the wrong moves on the chessboard of Balkan politics. In fact, even if there is a contradiction between the national iconographies of Greece and Macedonia that may create problems in the future, the two countries have a vital common interest that concerns the present: to preserve peace.

Europe and the Macedonian Gordian Knot

After the Yugoslav crisis, the old idea that the violence, which is character-istic of the modern history of the Balkans, stems from some inherent traits of the Balkan peoples, has started to come to the surface again. However, what happens in the Balkans is the result of two sets of conditions. The first set concerns internal Balkan factors: the tensions that have accumulated during the decades of communist rule, the difficulties of the transition from communism to capitalism, the friction created by the new conditions of circulation between countries that were separated for four decades, the traumas of the past, and conflicting national aspirations. The second set concerns the geopolitical environment of the Balkan states. As long as this environment was stable, the Balkan scene remained calm and the "old demons" remained asleep. This shows that the determining factors of con-flict in the Balkans are not the internal, but the external. With the end of the Cold War, the geopolitical equilibrium of Europe disappeared. The Balkan peoples realized that an era of transition had started and that during this new period everything was possible again. The nationalist passions that have exploded in former Yugoslavia are the expression of deep anxieties created by European instability. Europe and the international community did not manage to dissipate those fears. The contradictory messages of European diplomacy on the one hand, and the embargo and the threats of a military intervention on the other, have increased the feeling of living in an unpredictable, insecure and threatening world. In the Balkan cultural and political context, such anxieties lead to a "regression" to aggressive behaviour. Thus, the old demons have woken up again.

The forces of disruption, although substantial, are not the only ones present on the Balkan scene. The opportunities created by the reunification of European space can constitute an important counterweight to the awak-ening of the old demons of nationalism. However, as long as they remain undeveloped, they stay inactive, and meanwhile the forces of disruption gain territory. The role of the international environment and more specifi-cally of the European Union can be decisive in turning the tide. However, Europe, after failing to cope with the Yugoslav crisis, seems to resign her-self to a passive attitude confronted with the danger of new conflicts in the Balkans. In front of the inefficiency (which seems to be succeeded by indif-ference) of Europe, perhaps the European attitude towards the Balkans should not be interpreted as the last act of the drama of Western domina-tion on a space that used to belong to the Ottoman Empire (in this respect it is worth reading again Toynbee 1922). In any case, if, by some miracle, the political will to act in the Balkans returns to the European Union, Mac-edonia could be an ideal case for constructive intervention.

The basic geographical characteristics of Macedonia lend themselves to a policy that fits in with the basic objective of the European Union: free cir-culation of people and goods in a unified European space. As noted earlier, the structural element of the region is the Vardar–Thessaloniki crossroads. At present, traffic along the Morava–Vardar corridor is at a standstill. Even before the break-up of Yugoslavia, its economic potential was underdeveloped. The road and railway lines were completely insufficient to carry traffic that was developing rapidly. The economic development of the areas around these axes, and especially in Yugoslav Macedonia, was extremely low.

The Morava–Vardar corridor can function as the spinal cord of a stabilized Balkan space, if its economic potential is developed. The European Union should take the initiative to propose to Serbia, Macedonia and Greece an ambitious project of trans-state regional development based on the possibilities of this corridor, linking central Europe with the eastern Mediterranean. The stabilizing effect of such a project would come from a series of factors, and first of all from its psychological effect. With such a gesture, Europe would show its concern about the region and dissipate fears that the European powers are playing again the old game of spheres of influence. The attention of the Balkan elites would be diverted from destructive militancy towards the management of new economic possibilities. The European Union would dispose of an efficient instrument of pressure towards the governments of the Balkan states. Such pressures, exerted through priorities in economic options, would prove much more effective in containing nationalism than the threats of embargo or of military intervention.

There are some obvious obstacles in realizing such a project. The relationship of the European Union to Serbia would have to be re-examined and some concessions from the Serbian part would have to be conceded. A compromise solution would have to be found in the dispute between Greece and the Former Yugoslav Republic of Macedonia. Those problems can be solved if Europe shows a determination to promote the region's economic take-off. The benefits from the upgrading of Thessaloniki as a port would be an important argument for persuading Greece to adopt a more understanding attitude towards the problems of political stability in the Former Yugoslav Republic of Macedonia. In the same way, if Serbia were reassured that the road to Thessaloniki will always be open to its traffic, she will be less fearful of being landlocked, and therefore may be more conciliatory in respect to the Bosnian question.

On the economic scale, the difficulties are limited in comparison to the benefits. An important investment will be needed. However, if the European Union leads the way and offers sufficient guarantees, there would certainly be a substantial financing from Greek private sources, such as the ship-owning community, especially if the Greek state plays an important role in managing the whole project. The natural resources for industrial, agricultural and tourist development, the low cost and the high quality of the manpower in the area, the knowledge of Serbs and Greeks, are important assets that guarantee a rapid take-off.

The Macedonians of the Former Yugoslav Republic of Macedonia cannot fail to see the way out of their present difficulties in a project that will turn their region into an international crossroads. For the Bulgarians and for the Albanians it would be an important step towards integration in Europe, since their main axes of communication are linked to the Morava–Vardar axis and, in any case, the success of the Morava–Vardar regional plan would lead to its extension towards its Albanian and Bulgarian branches. For the Greeks, finally, it would be an excellent opportunity to become the instrument of the European Union's policy and to profit from a dramatic growth in the importance of Thessaloniki as a major port of the Balkans and of the eastern Mediterranean. In addition to the geopolitical aim of stabilization in a critical area, such a project makes economic sense in a region that has a great potential for development and constitutes one of the zones of expansion of the European economy.

Such a positive scenario changes the image of Macedonia, completely. It becomes again that of an area of co-operation, of contact and of understanding among peoples with different origins and cultures, as when the Balkans were under one *imperium*, that of the Ottoman Empire. A dream like that can become reality only if the European Union really approves of unifying the European space of which the Balkans are an integral part. The success of such a project as the one described could be an important step in that direction and, on the contrary, if the negative scenario for Macedonia were confirmed, this would have the most demoralizing effect not only in the Balkans but all over Europe. Those European politicians who adopt a passive stance towards the Balkan problems, counting on a fragmentation of the Balkan space that will make easier the penetration of certain west European economic and political interests, should be reminded of Winston Churchill's naming the Balkans as the soft underbelly of Europe.

The Macedonian question is like the Gordian knot. In Macedonia and more generally in the Balkans, the European Union has tried until now to unite the various strands of nationalism, territorial disputes, iconographies, and so on, only to find out that it is impossible. Will the European Union decide at last to imitate Alexander the Great and cut the Gordian knot? Unfortunately, for the time being, nothing seems to encourage such a hope.

References

Amyna kai Diplomatia 1993. O diamelismos to Skopion tha statheropoiouse ta Valkania. *Amyna kai Diplomatia* **27**, 6–7.

Admiralty War Staff, Intelligence Division 1916. *A handbook of Macedonia and surrounding territories*. London.

Ancel, J. 1930a. *Peuples et nations des Balkans*. Paris: A. Colin.

— 1930b. *La Macédoine, étude de colonisation contemporaine*. Paris: Librarie Delagrave.

Bérard, V. 1897. *La Macédoine*. Paris: C. Lévy.

Bowman, I. 1921. *The New World, problems in political geography*. New York: World Book Company.

Brunhes, J. & C. Vallaux 1921. *La géographie de l'histoire: géographie de la paix et de la guerre sur terre et sur mer*. Paris: Librairie Félix Alcan.

Carnegie Endowment for International Peace 1914. *Report of the International Commission to inquire into the causes and conduct of the Balkan Wars*. Washington: Carnegie Endowment for International Peace.

Chiclet, C. 1992. La Macédoine menacée d'étouffement. *Le Monde Diplomatique* (6 September), 6.

Colocotronis, V. 1919. *La Macédoine et l'Hellénisme, étude historique et ethnologique*. Paris: Berger–Levrault.

Cvijić , J. 1906. *Remarks on the ethnography of the Macedonian Slavs*. London.

— 1916. Les bases géographiques de la question macédonienne. In *Questions Balkaniques*, Jovan Cvijić , 29–41. Paris: Attinger.

— 1918. *La Péninsule Balkanique: géographie humaine*. Paris: A. Colin.

Gorev, G. 1994. Nos frères macédoniens. Proposition pour une unification singulière. *Courrier International* **206**, 212 [translation from the Bulgarian of an article published in *Douma* in Sofia].

Gottman, J. 1951. Geography and international relations. *World Politics* III(2), 153–73.

— 1952a. *La politique des états et leur géographie*. Paris: Arman Colin.

— 1952b. The political partitioning of our world: an attempt at analysis. *World Politics* IV(4), 512–19.

Ivanoff, I. 1920. *La question macédonienne au point de vue historique, ethnographique et statistique*. Paris: Librairie J. Gamber.

Ischirkov, A. 1916. *Les confins occidentaux des terres bulgares*. Lausanne: Librairie Nouvelle.

— 1918. *Le nom de Bulgare: éclaircissement d'histoire et d'ethnographie*. Lausanne: Librairie Centrale des Nationalités.

Kiepert, H. 1876. *Ethnographische Ubersichtskarte des Europäischen Orients*. Berlin: D. Reimer.

Kofos, E. 1964. *Nationalism and communism in Macedonia*. Salonica: Institute for Balkan Studies.

— 1990. National heritage and national identity in nineteenth and twentieth century Macedonia. In *Modern Greece: nationalism and nationality*, M. Blinkhorn & Th. Veremis (eds), 103–142. Athens: Sage–ELIAMEP.

Kostanick, H. L. 1947. *Macedonia – a study in political geography* [mimeo.]. School of Geography, Clark University, Worcester, Massachusetts.

League of Nations 1926. *Greek Refugee Settlement*. Geneva.

Maul, O. 1915. Kultur und politische geographische Entwicklung und Aufgaben des heutigen Griechenlands. *Mitteilungen der Geographischen Gesellschaft in München* X(2).

— 1922. *Griechisches Mittelmeergebiet*. Breslau: Ferdinard Hirt.

National Statistical Service of Greece 1967. *Statistical yearbook of Greece*. Athens: The National Statistical Service of Greece.

Newbigin, M. 1915. *Geographical aspects of Balkan problems*. London: Putnam.

Nothias, J-C. 1990. Le révei des Comitadjis. *L'autre Journal* (October), 143–55.

Olgivie, A. 1920. A contribution to the geography of Macedonia. *Geographical Journal* LV(1), 1–7.

— 1921. Physiography and settlements in Macedonia. *Geographical Review* XI(1), 172–93.

Prévélakis, G. 1994. *Les Balkans, cultures et géopolitique*. Paris: Nathan.

— 1994. Isaiah Bowman, adversaire de la Geopolitik, *L'Espace Géographique* **1**, 78–89.

Rousek, J. S. 1946. The geopolitics of the Balkans. *The American Journal of Economics and Sociology* 5(3), 365–77.

Schüttel, L. 1935. Die makedonische Frage. *Zeitschrift für Geopolitik* (1–6), 176–82.

Taylor, P. 1993. *Political geography: world economy, nation-state and locality*, 3rd edn. London.

REFERENCES

Toynbee, A. 1922. *The Western Question in Greece and Turkey: a study in the contact of civilisations.* London: Constable.

Weiner, M. 1971. The Macedonian syndrome: an historical model for international relations and political development. *World Politics* XXIII(4), 665–83.

Wilkinson, H. R. 1951. *Maps and politics: a review of ethnographic cartography of Macedonia.* Liverpool: Liverpool University Press.

CHAPTER TEN

Minorities and boundaries in the Balkans
HUGH POULTON

Introduction

The current violent disintegration of Yugoslavia and the probable south-ward extension and internationalization of the conflict has put Balkan boundary problems once more centre stage. Geographical features and the Ottoman heritage have historically resulted in compartmentalized communities and as a result the peoples of the Balkans managed to retain their separate identities and cultures. Also, for many of them it meant, retaining a sense of former glorious history when they controlled particular areas – often at the expense of their neighbours, who likewise make historical claims to the territory in question. This is most dramatically shown by the competing claims of the Serb Vojislav Šešelj and the Croat Dobroslav Paraga.

This inability easily to draw clear cut boundaries that could satisfy at least most of the participants, combined with a feeling that, after the two world wars (the first, of course, sparked off in the Balkans) and the ensuing decades of Cold War "stability", boundaries were and are sacrosanct. Perhaps they could have been drawn better in the past to reduce such huge minority problems as the Kosovo Albanian one, but that was viewed as history. To reopen the dread border question was seen as unthinkable, with such problems as Bosnia and Macedonia to contend with. However, after the Serbian nationalist revival of the mid-1980s, sparked by Kosovo and hijacked by Milošević , and the 1990 elections, which saw the former communists blatantly using the rampant Serbian nationalism to hide their economic bankruptcy, winning in the Serbian centre (including Monte-negro), and anti-communist nationalists winning elsewhere, Yugoslavia had to most seriously observe to run its course. The problems facing it were insurmountable in its old form, but the "West" was extremely reluctant to recognize the new realities. Incredibly, the Yugoslav crisis appeared to catch the Western governments unaware, as did the break-up of the USSR, where the West again, backing Gorbachev, pushed for the increasingly unlikely option of preserving the USSR in form.

European Community observers always appear to be behind events. In Slovenia they were monitoring the cease-fire and Federal Army withdrawal while the real action was in Croatia. Now *current* negotiations concentrate almost exclusively on the Serb/Croat crisis, with no apparent planning for the probably more serious troubles to come (although the *current* proposals to send in UN peace-keeping troops may change this). The crisis is bound to move on to Bosnia and potentially to extend internationally with Kosovo and Macedonia. Whereas the Serb/Croat hostilities and future Serb/Croat/Muslim hostilities in Bosnia are bloody but essentially internal matters, this is not so for the Albanian and Macedonian problems. The Serb authorities and the Serbian-dominated Federal Army are unlikely to watch Kosovo detach itself, neither will Serb public opinion (one of the latest public opinion polls in Serbia puts Šešeljs Serbian Radical Party second in popularity, with 15% of the vote behind Milošović's Socialist Party with 30%).

Will Albania stand by when the tanks roll in to crush their brothers and sisters over the border? Will Bulgaria stand by if a similar situation develops in Macedonia? Have the EC or the UN any policy on this? This is not idle speculation but a distinct probability. We have seen Slovenia secede despite EC disapproval and refusal to accept the reality right up to the last minute, and now probably the same situation will apply to Croatia. What about Kosovo – so much a truncated nation that it is almost half the "mother" nation.

It is somewhat ironic that, as western Europe slowly heads towards greater political unity, eastern Europe is threatened with ethnic fragmentation, and nowhere more so that in the Balkans. However, the two are connected. Whereas it is perhaps easily understandable why, for example, Slovenia wants to separate from a Yugoslavia where the main partner is Milošević's Serbia, what on Earth can they hope to gain that they have not enjoyed already under the federal system? The answer lies in the emerging Europe. All the players on the new stage want to "join Europe" as quickly as possible. The point is that small submerged nations want to join a future federal Europe in their own right, *not* as a junior partner in a federation already, which would remove them one step from the decision-making process. Thus, it is the truly multinational former federal states of the USSR and Yugoslavia, that face disintegration and raise acute immediate boundary problems.

In the other countries, the nationalist forces that have filled the power vacuum vacated by the discredited former ideology of Marxist–Leninism raise the issue of the treatment of their own sizeable minorities within boundaries that appear to be reasonably secure; the exceptions to this relate to the Yugoslav Albanian and possibly the Macedonian questions, which inevitably transgress national boundaries (see below). It seems possible that, whereas in the 1980s individual human rights became the yardstick by which the regimes were judged (and found wanting), in the 1990s and beyond, minority rights are the new criteria.

In Yugoslavia the Gordian knot remains Bosnia–Herzegovina, where the population mix points to a worst-case scenario of "Lebanonization" and there appears no easy solution. The heritage of the Ottoman *millet* system – which resulted in the largest group there, the Muslims, encouraged by the Tito regime to defend itself not on ethnic–national criteria but on religious criteria – has left an intractable problem. The Muslims needed Yugoslavia to remain in some form if they were to maintain their position. With Slovenia gone and a Croatia, however large, certain to follow, the future looks grim. The espoused aim of Izetbegović and his party, of turning Bosnia–Herzegovina into a Swiss-type "sovereign" multinational polity, is a non-starter. Partition of one sort or another appears likely between Croatia and Serbia, up and including total incorporation into a Greater Serbia by whatever name. The October Sandžak referendum of Muslims in Serbia demanding autonomy is unlikely to result in any boundary changes, although it points to another future acute inter-ethnic problem to add to the Serbs in Croatia (if any remain in what is left of Croatia) and the Bosnia–Herzegovina mix. The Hungarian minority in the north is also unlikely to be instrumental in any border changes, similarly the small number of Italians in the northwest. These problems, some of them acute and potentially violent, are likely to remain internal ones and there is an urgent priority is to set up mechanisms for resolving such potential inter-ethnic conflicts within the boundaries that are eventually determined.

And what are the boundaries to be? Some Western politicians appear to imply, like Tudjman, that for example Croatia's borders are unchangeable, even God given. Why? This appears to be an extension of the above-noted refusal to countenance boundary changes; that is, if Yugoslavia is to collapse, then better it should split along the "accepted" republican boundaries. This poses no problem with relatively homogenous Slovenia, but rather overlooks the fact that Milošović and the Serbs had already torn up Tito's boundaries by removing all autonomy from Kosovo and Vojvodina and not to accept many of the others that remained. The Serbs rightly point out that the Tito division was somewhat arbitrary and was probably designed to keep them from totally dominating the old Yugoslav state. However, the Serbs cannot claim rights for its members outside Serbia while denying fundamental rights to its won more numerous Albanians.

The old Yugoslavia has definitely gone and with its going it has opened up many other boundary questions in the Balkans – some of which relate to problems originating within Yugoslavia and involving her neighbours, others being independent. The main ones are the Albanians in Yugoslavia, the "Macedonian Question", and the potential irredenta of the Turks in Greece and Bulgaria, and the Greeks in Albania. On the fringes of the

Balkans there is also the Moldovan–Romanian question and the deteriorating relations between Hungary and Romania in Transylvania, although these are outside the scope of this chapter.

The Albanians in Yugoslavia

The Albanians in Yugoslavia remain probably the most acute problem in terms of boundaries. It is inevitable that the 2 million or so Albanians will move to at least republican independence, and Serb irrationality is greatest over Kosovo. The Belgrade intellectuals' "genocide" petition of January 1986, which signalled the real beginning of the rise of the Serbian nationalism that Milošović has been so successful in riding, specifically accused the then authorities of condoning national treason and "genocide" against the Serb minority in Kosovo. The new Serbian authorities led by Milošović progressively moved against all forms of Albanian autonomy, which under the 1974 Constitution was *de facto* a republic. By mid-1990, Serbia had completed its dominance over the province and officially withdrew its autonomy. Mass dismissals of Albanian functionaries and their replacement by Serbs continued and the former province has remained under virtual military rule. Albanian language broadcasting on Priština television and radio was stopped and, in August 1990, *Rilindja* (the main Albanian language newspaper published in Priština) was banned altogether until further notice. The Albanians responded by boycotting elections and by trying to block the new Serbian Constitution, but to no avail, and the Kosovo assembly was dissolved on 5 July 1990, with the Kosovo presidency resigning in protest. On 7 September 1990 a two-thirds majority of Kosovo deputies met in secret at Kačanak and declared Kosovo to be a republic. The Serb authorities arrested those they could find. On 21 October 1991 Tanjug announced that tuition in Albanian in Kosovo's schools had been postponed "for an indefinite period".

The Albanians in Kosovo have remained surprisingly quiet as the Yugoslav crisis has developed. A referendum held by the Albanians, despite Serbian obstruction in late October 1991, saw a claimed 87.01 per cent vote (940,802 out of a potential 1,051,357 eligible) of whom 99.87 per cent (913,707) voted for a sovereign independent Kosovo Republic and a Provisional Government was elected led by Dr Bujar Bukoshi. Needless to say, the Serbian authorities have shown no inclination to accept any of this and, although the situation remains extremely tense, in Kosovo there has mercifully not yet been any "national uprising". It appears that the Kosovo Albanians are awaiting developments in the north, although there have been reports of criticism of this "wait and see" policy, associated with more cautious leaders such as Ibrahim Rugova, by more radical elements such as Adem Demaqi (the "Kosovo Mandela").

Either way the Kosovo Albanians will not acquiesce in continual Serbian repression; in the short term, in the absence of outside pressure, it seems unlikely that the Serbs and the Serbian Federal Army will idly stand by and watch Kosovo detach itself. In Albania proper, all shades of public and official opinion recognize the rights of the Kosovo Albanians to republican status and, with the current desperate internal problems, the temptation to intervene in the event of large-scale military operations in Kosovo by the Federal Army will be very strong. International conflict is thus a distinct possibility.

In the long term it is apparent that Serbia cannot rule Kosovo by force for ever. The population is (and is becoming more so) overwhelmingly Albanian and will remain so despite the empty rhetoric of a Serbian repopulation programme. Serbs (and for that matter Albanians) are emigrating from the area for economic reasons as well as in response to heightened ethnic tension. It also appears that the experience of escalating repression in the 1980s, which saw even the arrest and imprisonment of such loyal Titoists as Azem Vllasi, has poisoned inter-ethnic relations between Albanians and Serbs in Kosovo to such an extent that any rapprochement between them in the immediate future appears remote. Appeals to ancient history are not enough. If and when the Albanians of Kosovo are allowed, or take, real autonomy, it is likely that the exodus of Serbs from the area will accelerate and may even disappear completely. The outside world should be impressing on the Serbs that the situation in Kosovo – which for many years has been the disgrace of Europe – cannot continue. This is not a small minority amid a Serb majority, akin to the situation in the Vojvodina. With Yugoslavia falling apart, the Kosovo Albanian cause appears unanswerable. The boundaries of Serbia should not and probably cannot contain Kosovo. Whether the Kosovo Albanians will join Albania in a Greater Albania (a possibility) should be up to them to decide between themselves.

Although the above argument calling for a probable redrawing of national frontiers is perhaps radical, it is not too problematic in minority nationality terms – or even perhaps in economic terms, given the old Titoist system of the republican–autonomous provincial economic units. Problems arise with the Yugoslav Albanians outside Kosovo – in Serbia proper, in Montenegro and more problematically in Macedonia. In Serbia proper and Montenegro, boundary changes to incorporate overwhelming majority Albanian areas adjoining Kosovo will be resisted and are possibly unnecessary if a Kosovo republic of Greater Albania is created. (Interestingly, the redrawing of Serbia's internal administrative boundaries in April 1991, so as to "carve-up" Kosovo, could actually be seen to enlarge it in the form of the three units of Metohija, Kosovo and Pčinja, the last of which includes the Albanian dominated Opštinas of Bujanovac and Preševo.) However, even if such changes happen, which is perhaps unlikely, they are most minor adjustments to the remaining Serbian heartlands (including Montenegro). This is not the case for Macedonia, which with Bosnia remains the hardest minority problem to suggest solutions.

Any form of Kosovo republic will inevitably attract the up to 20 per cent Albanian population of Yugoslav Macedonia who live in compact areas in the west of the republic. A greater Albania will attract them even more. Either way, these areas may want to move out of Macedonia and join with their neighbouring fellow nationals in Kosovo. This would severely truncate the Macedonian republic and question even further its continued existence as a separate unit without the umbrella protection of the former Yugoslav state. Tensions between the Albanians and Macedonian Slavs have been acute in the past and continue to this day, compounded by uncertainty within the political spectrum of the Macedonian majority. The Albanians in Macedonia have in the past followed events in Kosovo closely, with demonstrations in Macedonia mirroring demonstrations in Kosovo and strong links between the two areas.

The largest party in the republican assembly, with 37 seats out of 120 – the Internal Revolutionary Organization-Democratic Party of National Unity (VMRO–DPMNE) – is strongly nationalistic and anti-Albanian, and its leader Ljupco Georgievski resigned as Vice-President of the Republic in October 1991. The new Constitution has been met by protests from VMRO–DPMNE for not being more explicitly Macedonian in orientation. On 14 November VMRO–DPMNE demonstrators from the Albanian-inhabited western regions gathered outside the assembly chanting anti-Albanian slogans and calling for the resignation of the President, Kiro Gligorov, whereas within the assembly the VMRO–DPMNE deputies called for an amendment to the Constitution to make "Macedonia the mother state of the Macedonian people". Rival deputies from the Party of Democratic Prosperity (PDP) – the Albanian party and third largest in the assembly, with 25 seats – wanted the Albanian language to have equal status with Macedonian, and a formulation that would specifically include the Albanians as an integral component. The amendments from both sides were defeated and the Constitution came into force.

In the long term, the dissatisfaction of the Albanians may prove more relevant and the language issue in and out of schools remains. Despite appeals and petitions from ethnic Albanians for parallel tuition in Albanian in the Albanian western regions, the authorities have remained adamant that Macedonia is for the Macedonian people, instead of the pre-1989 formulation as "a state of the Macedonian People and the Albanian and Turkish minorities". Given these attitudes, the possibilities of the Macedonians coming to an agreed *modus vivendi* with the Albanians does not look promising. As before, events in Kosovo will be crucial.

The Macedonian Question

The "Macedonian Question" has historically been the most contentious in the whole area and is likely to remain so. Who are the Macedonians? Are they a distinct people? And even if they are, is a "sovereign independent Macedonia" economically feasible at all (especially given the above possibility of secession of the western Albanian inhabited areas)? And, if it is feasible, will it attract fellow Macedonians in Bulgaria, Albania and Greece.

Prospects for Macedonia as a separate unit may not look promising in the face of hostility from almost all sides. Serbian nationalists such as Šešelj do not recognize them; virtually all Bulgarians regard them as Bulgarians, and official Greece has never recognized them. However, what seems incontestable is that there are many Slavs in Yugoslavia (and for that matter in Bulgaria, Greece and Albania) who live in the geographical area of Macedonia and who see themselves as Macedonian in identity. Whether this is purely or partly the result of the full weight of the bureaucracy and education system instilling this in a process of ethnogenesis is irrelevant. If they are not a separate nation, then from language, cultural and historical reasons they are Bulgarians – not Serbs and certainly not Greeks – and although viewing the concept of an independent Macedonia with some distaste, the Bulgarians prefer this option to that of total Serbian domination of what is now Yugoslav Macedonia. Vuk Drašković , leader of the Serbian Renaissance Movement – previously Milošević 's main rival, but currently apparently eclipsed by the even more nationalistic Šešelj – explicitly told the Bulgarian media in November 1990 that Macedonia would be re-absorbed by Serbia if Yugoslavia became a confederation, and events have since moved beyond a Bulgarian involvement. Drašković also at the same time called for a partition of Yugoslav Macedonia between Serbia and Bulgaria. In a way similar to the Muslims of Bosnia, it appears that the Macedonians initially looked to Yugoslavia to retain their position, and their demands on behalf of Macedonians in neighbouring countries, especially Greece and Bulgaria, are in fact a sign of weakness.

The number of Slav Macedonians in Albania is unclear, with claims varying from a few thousand to over 100,000 (the latter figure inevitably originating from Skopje – 10,000–20,000 appears more likely). Some minority rights were granted to Albania's minorities (in contrast to Greece and Zhivkov's Bulgaria; see below), albeit within the Albanian framework of extreme individual repression. In the new Albania, it is possible for the minorities to organize, and a Macedonian political association held its first conference in October 1991 in Pustec village in Korçë district. Albania appears not to be threatened by its Slav minorities, whether Macedonian or Serb and Montenegrin in the north.

Bulgaria is far more ambivalent. As noted above, she has reluctantly recognized Skopje's declarations by once more reiterating the widespread view in Bulgaria that all Macedonians are of course Bulgarians and always will be, but that Bulgaria is not seeking to redraw any boundaries and thus a separate Macedonia is preferable to its incorporation into a Greater Serbia. As regards the Macedonians in Pirin in southwest Bulgaria, any organized form of expression of a Macedonian identity separate from the Bulgarian has been proscribed, as have activists from the main organization espousing such a view. They have been harassed and threatened with imprisonment. How popular Ilinden UMO is in Pirin is hard to say, but it is clear that here are some in Pirin who do see themselves as distinct from Bulgarians in ethnicity (similarly, there are some in Yugoslav Macedonia who see themselves as Bulgarians). The relaxation following the fall of Zhivkov (previously all manifestations of Macedonian activity separate from Bulgarian were heavily penalized) has allowed such people to become more open in their activities, activities that all shades of mainstream political opinion in Bulgaria see as part of a Yugoslav (Serbian) plot against Bulgaria in continuation of old historical enmity for Macedonia. The Bulgarian Ilinden UMO, who allege that the organization is funded and controlled by Yugoslavia to detach Pirin from Bulgaria, and that the mass media in Yugoslav Macedonia is directly financed (and therefore controlled) by Belgrade. (Ironically, Serbs such as Ivan Stoilković , a leading Serb from Kumanovo, complain of "Bulgarophilia" and intolerance of Serbia by Yugoslav Macedonians!)

In Greece the Greek authorities have, from the outset of the modern Greek state, consistently denied the existence of the Slav Macedonians as a separate people from the Greeks and instead officially refer to them as Slavaphone Greeks. In fact, the Greek authorities have been and continue to be very hostile to any notion of ethnic minorities living in Greece, whether they be Slavs, Vlachs, Albanians, Gypsies or Turks, and they only recognize religious minorities. This is a heritage from the Ottoman *millet* system, which the Greek authorities have consciously used deliberately to confuse the concepts of citizenship, nationality and religion. As such they have over a long period subjected all Orthodox Christian minorities in Greece to sustained assimilatory pressures. This has been amplified this century by settling large numbers of Greeks from Turkey in the northern areas, where before the Slavs were the largest group.

This policy of assimilation by pressure and massive influx to Hellenize the north has been in the main successful, and many Orthodox Slav, Vlachs and Albanians have become unquestionably Hellenicized over the years. However, not all have, and there have been recent internal manifestations of Macedonian nationalism, which the Greek authorities view with hostility. Although Greece is an EC member-state, she has until now avoided adverse criticism for her dismal treatment of minorities. With the collapse of communism, perhaps she will come under greater scrutiny, and, to Greece's fury, the US State Department report on human rights adversely mentioned the treatment of her Macedonian minority. However, it is unlikely that border changes will result from any pressure from Macedonians in Greece.

The Turks in Greece

The 100,000 or so Turks in Greece also face severe pressure and the situation appears to be becoming more serious with increased polarization of the communities in western Thrace. Turkey is Greece's traditional enemy and the example of Cyprus is obviously a worrying one for Greeks. As noted above, the authorities do not accept national minorities in Greece, only religious ones, and, although the Greek state has been very successful in assimilating its Orthodox minorities, it has so far been less successful with its Muslims, whether Turks of Pomaks (Islamic Slavs). Moreover, its repeated concentration on religious criteria over ethnic–linguistic ones has resulted in a tendency for the Pomaks to identify with the Turks. (This is a common feature in the Balkans, where religion has been and continues to be an important factor in self-identification.) Smaller Islamic minorities such as the Pomaks have tended to become assimilated by larger Islamic groups within the relevant countries – the Turks in Bulgaria and Greece, or in Yugoslavia the Macedonia Albanians; they have also tended to assimilate the Turks there, resulting in the authorities encouraging these smaller Islamic groups to assert their separate identities to combat the growth of Albanian nationalism. Similarly, in Kosovo. Of course, this does not apply where Muslim Slavs are the majority Islamic group (e.g. the Muslims in Bosnia).

The Greek authorities have put the Turkish minority under pressure. In the vital field of education they have steadily increased teaching in Greek at the expense of Turkish and, since 1968, only graduates from a special academy in Thessaloniki can be qualified to teach in Turkish schools. Critics claim that the academy deliberately relies on an outdated religious curriculum to create an incompetent Hellenic education system in western Thrace, isolated from the mainstream of modern Turkish culture. The implementation in 1985 of a law requiring graduate examination from Turkish secondary and high schools to be in Greek has resulted in a dramatic decline in secondary school students from 227 in Xanthi and 305 in Komotini in 1983–4 to 1985 and 42 respectively in 1986–7. The authorities have also prohibited the use of the adjective "Turkish" minority in Greece in election campaigns, thus allegedly "spreading an atmosphere of terror".

The authorities have continued to try and impose their official candidates as muftis and on community boards, despite the adverse wishes of the population. The situation has deteriorated and inter-communal violence broke out in early 1991. Unrest flared up again in August on the dismissal of the Mufti of Xanthi, who had been selected by the Turkish community, and his replacement by a government appointee. Over a long period there had been complaints from the Turkish community about official obstructions in building permits and, in September, unease continued after Greek police destroyed Turkish shanty houses with allegedly unnecessary violence and giving the occupants no time to remove their possessions. The Greek authorities' actions appear actually to be creating the possibility of a problem akin to Cyprus, by alienating the population and by repeated persecution reinforcing the position of such people as Dr Ahmet as leaders of the community.

The Turks of Bulgaria

By contrast, the situation of the Turks in Bulgaria has dramatically improved since the fall Zhivkov in November 1989. The ludicrous assimilation campaign of 1984–5, with its Greek-like denial of the existence of any Turks in Bulgaria, and its brutal repression eventually resulting in the mass exodus of 1989, has been buried for good. The desperate economic situation, aggravated by the mass exodus, has combined with the fears of sections of the Bulgarian population, especially those living in cities surrounded by areas dominated by ethnic Turks, to produce a virulent Bulgarian nationalism that is openly anti-Turk. Faced with this, the authorities have been forced to move more slowly than they would have liked in restoring, for example, education rights to ethnic Turks.

There is also an anti-Turk vein in some sections of the intelligentsia, which combines with a general feeling of unease that Bulgaria, a small country with a small population of which the Slav element has a far lower (actually negative) growth rate compared to her large minorities of Turks and Gypsies, may actually be swamped. The new Constitution specifically forbids political parties based on ethnicity. This ruling has prevented the Gypsy organizations from gaining a political voice, but the Turkish political party, the Movement for Rights and Freedoms (DPS), has managed so far to circumvent this despite protests from leading politicians, including even indirect censure from President Zhelev, who in October 1991 announced that the Constitutional Court should decide on the matter. Despite this and the continuing boycott by Turks of schools (they want four periods a week of Turkish in Turkish areas, whereas the government has compromised with the DPS does not appear to be a party of confrontation and, with the partial exception of the Macedonian activists in Pirin – always a special case for the Bulgarians (see above) – the minority situation in Bulgaria appears relatively hopeful and there seems no short-term danger of conflict that might result in border changes. In contrast to Greece and Serbia, the bulk of the Bulgarian intelligentsia were never in favour of its government's chauvinistic policies towards its minorities and, despite the deep wounds and large-scale suffering caused by Zhivkov's disastrous minority policies, both the government and the DPS leadership appear willing to work constructively together to overcome past legacies.

The Greeks of Albania

Although the Greeks have consistently denied the existence of any ethnic minorities in Greece, they claim a huge number of ethnic Greeks in southern Albania, with emigré sources claiming some 400,000. Such estimates are based on the tendency noted above to claim all Orthodox subjects in the area as ethnic Greeks, and it includes all those who are Greek Orthodox by religion – Slavs (Macedonians and Montenegrins), Albanians and Vlachs, as well as Greeks. A more realistic figure may well be 60,000, although this is still unclear. As noted above, the Albanian state, despite its extreme denial of individual rights, did allow minority rights, and Greek schools were allowed, although emigré reports stated that such schools were being closed down. There has been pressure in the past to Albanianize minorities, but not on the scale seen in Greece of Zhivkov's Bulgaria. The minority has its publications and political associations, and there are recent reports of Greek nationals co-operating with Albanians in opening new private businesses in the Gjirokaster and Sarandë districts.

Despite the huge numbers of Greeks in Albania claimed by Greek circles, and the current acute economic crisis in Albania, there appears to be no real sign of mass movement by ethnic Greeks to secede, which casts doubt on the veracity of emigré Greek claims. For the present, border changes appear unlikely. (Albanian organizations in Albania respond to Greek claims by accusing the Greeks of discriminatory treatment of Albanians in Chamuria – northern Greece).

Conclusion

In the Balkan states, apart from the former Yugoslavia and Albania regarding the Yugoslav Albanians, the impetus for major boundary changes does not appear to be present. In Yugoslavia, however, the junior partners in the previous federation, similarly to those in the USSR, have shown their desire to take greater control of their situations by declarations of sovereignty or independence. However, the position of the Muslims of Bosnia, and possibly also the Macedonians, is unlikely to be strong enough to survive without the umbrella Yugoslavia and, despite their declarations, the future is not promising for them. The Serbs (including the Montenegrins as Serbs), although not a numerical majority, have effectively been a power majority in post-war Yugoslavia, shown in their overrepresentation outside their own republic in the Communist Party, the army and the police. The 1990 elections tended to confirm this, and the current civil war further reinforces this view. A Greater Serbia is being created now by force of arms. Boundaries of the new states in the Balkans have to be agreed and outside influences from EC and UN should be applying pressure so as to avoid as much bloodshed as possible. If the new boundaries are left to be decided by internal force of arms alone, then the results will be catastrophic. The three crucial questions are Bosnia–Herzegovina, the Yugoslav Albanians in Kosovo, and Macedonia itself.

Regarding the myriad minorities that remain and will remain within states – and this includes the many members of non-territorial minorities, particularly the Gypsies who are currently suffering a spate of racist attacks in several countries in eastern Europe, especially Romania, and also the Vlachs and the Pomaks – there has to be a wider European context and generally agreed rules and procedures governing minority matters that all participants in the new Europe agree and abide by. The Paris summit in November 1990 made a good start. Minority rights have been neglected in favour of individual rights until now. This was understandable and probably correct. However, as noted above, we are moving into a new era where minority rights will become more important. To widen the stage a little the problems are not confined to eastern Europe or the Balkans – Britain, Spain and prospective EC member Turkey have similar acute problems. The idealized "nation-state" has shown itself to be inadequate in solving acute minority problems such as those in Northern Ireland or involving the Basques. Romania is unlikely on current showing to "solve" the problems of her Hungarian minority in Transylvania within the strict nation-state confines. A European framework might.

Thus, the new states of eastern Europe have to be brought into at least part of the west European framework as quickly as possible. German unification showed the enormous economic dislocation suffered by what was the strongest east European economy on entering the EC. The economics are problematic in the extreme. Spain made the change from long-lasting dictatorship to full EC membership fairly easily, but she never had the problems now facing the former communist regimes. There is an argument that western Europe should push on with greater union, politically and economically, without the others, as bringing them in now would cause huge problems, as German unification showed. Economically, this might be attractive, but politically it is a mistake. Eastern Europe, and especially the Balkans, cannot be left to their own devices and allowed to fall into violence and chaos. Yugoslavia has shown what is at stake.

Afterword

Although this chapter was written in November 1991, much of it still remains valid in 1992. The problems of Bosnia–Herzegovina, Macedonia and the whole "Albanian question" remain as acute as before. Within Serbia, nationalism is still at a premium, with the success of Milošović and Šešelj in the elections. In Croatia, the Tudjman regime displays a nationalism as fierce as any in the area. Ethnic states are the norm, with all the associated problems of irredentism on one hand and the position of minorities within the new states on the other.

In the event, the "West", in an attempt to avert the inevitable bloodshed, disastrously recognized Bosnia–Herzegovina as a unitary independent state, while giving strong signals that international force would not be used to protect it from Serbian aggression. The result has been a barbarous war, with murder and terror used against whole populations to "solve" the problems of dividing the intricate ethnic mix of the territory – the so-called "ethnic cleansing" measures. There is little doubt that the Serbian side, which now controls some 70 per cent of the territory, bears the brunt of blame for a majority of these outrages, but in this appalling situation excesses have been carried out by all sides. The propaganda battle has even seen allegations of Serbs bombing Serbs and Muslims bombing Muslims, in attempts to demonize the other side and win favourable international opinion. In the southwest of the republic where Croats predominated, the Serb minorities have been expelled or have fled, and a self-styled Croatian government led by Mate Boban has proclaimed itself in control of so-called "Herzeg–Bosnia". Similarly, and more dramatically, the Serbs have systematically cleared large areas of non-Serbs to link with Serbia proper the Serbian areas of the west of the republic, and those of the Serb-populated and -controlled Krajinas of Croatia. A *de facto* "Greater Serbia" is emerging along with a changed Croatia. As foreseen, the Muslims have been the real losers. Forced into an uneasy alliance with a dubious ally, Croatia, they have physically been ghettoized into two main enclaves – one north of Bihać and surrounded by Serbian-controlled and "cleansed" territory, the other larger area comprising a triangle of territory, with Travnik, Sarajevo and Tuzla approximately at the corners.

The violent disintegration of Yugoslavia has resulted in massive population movements, with over 2 million displaced people. Along with "ethnic cleansing" measures, there has been a large-scale movement of Serbs from Croatia, outside of the Krajinas, and Croats from Serbia. They have left in part because of psychological pressures (stigmatization with "collective guilt") and in part as a result of actual physical pressure (e.g. hand grenades thrown into Croatian-owned property in the Vojvodina). Either way, throughout the area the populations have become more homogenized – albeit by brutal methods. It appears unlikely, given the barbarism, that these people will return to their homes, many of which have been deliberately burned or forcibly requisitioned. Most probably will not return.

The international community still recognizes Bosnia–Herzegovina as an entity, despite the progressive stages of incorporation (e.g. joint currency, media, legal systems, etc.) of Serbian areas of Croatia (the Krajinas) and Bosnia, both to themselves and to Serbia. A similar "gleichanschaltung" has taken place between "Herzeg–Bosnia" and Croatia. It is probable that a new Serb/Croat war will break out in 1993 over control of the Krajinas, in part because of the pressure on the Tudjman administration by Croatian refugees from the Krajinas. The most likely option still appears to be some form of "Greater Serbia", probably remaining an international paria for some time, and a differently shaped Croatia – that is, losing the Krajinas but gaining "Herzeg–Bosnia". For the Muslims, the highly unsatisfactory result looks to be some kind of rump Muslim state, in contingency to the new Croatia and probably dependent on it, and possibly guaranteed by the UN. In this scenario, the Muslims in the enclave north of Bihać, would remain controlled by Serbian forces and be in a position similar to those in the eastern Sandžak region – another area of great inter-ethnic tension.

The other areas of possible border changes remain connected to the whole question of Albania's borders, all of which look increasingly fragile. The problem of Kosovo remains essentially as before, although the international community has at last awoken to the threat of a third Balkan War over this issue. The Serbs constitute a majority in the northeast of the province in Depošavić district, and a rational solution would be to recognize an independent Kosovo with this part remaining with Serbia and allowing all those who want to leave voluntarily to do so – possibly in exchange for Albanians in Montenegro and Serbia proper. However, in Serbian opinion, rationality over Kosovo has not been evident for a long time. Three other options remain.

The first is a return to autonomy akin to the 1974 set-up. Although this may appeal to outsiders, it seems certain to be rejected by both sides. The Serbian side has pursued and continues to pursue a relentless centralization, and Kosovo was the issue by which Milošević rose to power in the first place. With the eclipse of the maverick Milan Panićas, a rival to Milošević, such a return seems very unlikely to be accepted by the Serbs. Similarly, the Kosovo Albanians' basic unchangeable demand is separation from Serbian control. The second option is a continuing of the present situation. This appears unlikely in the long term, as there are already strong pressures within the Albanian side for more resolute action in place of Rugova'a avowed pacificism, and the Serbs have repeatedly stated that they want to change the ethnic composition of Kosovo and are attempting to attract Serbian refugees into the province. The third option is a seemingly inevitable bloodbath, probably sparked off by an incident or incidents involving the heavily armed Serbian–Montenegrin minority, with attendant attempted "ethnic cleansing" measures by the Serbs. With such known culprits of such measures as Željko Ražnatović (a.k.a. Arkan) voted in as an MP for Kosovo, the future looks bleak. The West has started to say it will militarily intervene to prevent such a scenario, which would probably lead to international war. Such intervention, if it occurred, would be militarily more feasible in Kosovo than in Bosnia because Kosovo is ethnically more homogenized (90% Albanian) and less mountainous. However, such an intervention would need a radical change in the existing attitude of the international community to boundary changes.

What was not foreseen in the original paper was the extent of the dramatic rise of Greek nationalism over the Macedonian issue, which may well see military intervention by Greek forces if either the Macedonian Albanian problem (still as problematic as before, despite the apparent Macedonian–Albanian coalition government) or Kosovo explodes. For Macedonia itself, the "Albanian Question" remains paramount. The republic remains beleaguered: unrecognized by the EC because of Greece's veto, blockaded by Greece to the south, with a hostile Serbia to the north and a small Serbian minority radicalized by the likes of Šešelj, and rising tension and the appearance of armed groups in the west on the Albanian/Macedonian ethnic divide. As foreseen, it has become steadily closer to the old friend/enemy, Bulgaria. Some form of union in the future, especially if the Albanians in the west of the republic secede and Greece actively intervenes, cannot be ruled out. International recognition is vital for its future.

As regards Albania, the original paper also underestimated the weakness of the southern border. The apparent collapse of central control, and the rise of near anarchy in parts of Albania itself, has seen the Greek consulates in Sarandë and Gjirokaster almost replacing Tirana as loci of power and authority for local residents. Many inhabitants in the south have changed their names to Greek forms, and huge numbers have gone to Greece in search of employment. With Greek nationalism running so high, the calls have risen for the occupation of southern Albania – termed by Greek nationalists as "northern Epirus".

Elsewhere the situation regarding possible changes has not radically changed. Bulgaria, despite a new wave of mass emigration of Turks in the south to Turkey, mainly for economic reasons, remains a beacon of relative ethnic stability. The situation of the Turks in Greece has improved a little, but problems still remain. However, Turkey remains cautious in foreign policy matters in the Balkans, despite Demirel being a descendant from a Bosnian emigrant family (his grandfather emigrated from Bosnia this century), and the likelihood of boundary changes involving the Turkish communities remains very slim.[1]

---

1. This chapter was written in November 1991 and updated in 1992. The piece is interesting as a statement in time and still has relevance in many parts. Inevitably, some sections have been superseded by events. The author, at the time of writing, could not have envisaged the contemporary strength of Croatia, now a major regional power due to Western armament and Serbia's relative, sanctions-induced weakness.

CONCLUSION
The two scenarios

Before the agreement that was initialled in Dayton, Ohio, the editors had offered an alternative choice of future scenarios. This seemed to suggest itself from the varied contributions that this book had offered the reader.

The worst scenario

Perhaps the worst scenario would visualize a Balkan future plagued by continued anxiety among a patchwork of impoverished states. At the local level, if the Serbs continue a policy of territorial expansion on an ad hoc basis, the time might come when the Yugoslav rump will stretch to the Adriatic Sea; inevitably Croatia will disintegrate in defeat, and Europe may well be faced with a large refugee problem. Meanwhile the purified ethnic areas would include some autonomous regions that might suffer troubled links with any new centralized administration. Alternatively, any idea of a "canton" patchwork in Bosnia, whether under a confederation or a federation, could lead to future antagonism.

At the regional level, something of the domino theory might occur, whereby the conflagration in Bosnia could spread via the Sandzak, Kosovo and Macedonia into a wider area of conflict. This might then involve Bulgaria, leading to a wider Balkan–Mediterranean war. In turn, such actions might inflame Greek sentiments and could encourage Turkish involvement. An already weakened or outmoded NATO would then place unbearable pressure on European Community members to solve the crisis peacefully.

At the international level, one could assume that Russia would openly support its fellow Orthodox Serbs or Bulgaria. Former Communist hardliners might then see openings for counter-revolution, giving Russia an excuse to obtain a Balkan foothold. Insecurity would follow and, should the West object to Russian encroachments, this could once again turn the Balkans into a hotspot for great power rivalry.

The best scenario

The Ohio agreement, if implemented in full, will unquestionably mark a step forwards in shaping the future of the Balkans by outside, as opposed to internal Balkan, forces. It is likely to mark a drastically curbed programme for the expansion of Serbia, and it may well deter other Balkan powers with expansionist ambitions from repeating the tragedy of ex-Yugoslavia, and Bosnia in particular. It is the result, without doubt, of the remarkable success of the army of Croatia in Krajina (now no longer Serbia, either politically or ethnically) and in western Bosnia. On the other hand, the short-term nature of this agreement is likely to achieve very limited success in healing the ethnic divide and subduing the ethnic hatreds which, however contrived, have now become a fact of life in the Balkans. The desire for revenge, as in the Northern Ireland question and in the varied conflicts that have dominated the Middle East for centuries, has revealed itself as a permanent state of mind. This holds out little hope that the changing face of the Balkans is likely to have a fixed expression, a cheerful countenance or a scar-free skin. Current protests and bellicose speeches in and around Sarajevo make the position clear to all. Outside the Balkans, the successor to Boris Yeltsin may yet wish to change the face of both the Caucasus and the Balkans. The very presence of US personnel, in large numbers, amid a semi-refugee society, will bring about its own changing face to this region. The bizarre metamorphosis of a city, such as Tuzla, from an "Oriental Ottoman town" to a drab skyscraper city of Socialist Utopian dreams to a city whose haunts will satisfy the requirements of an occupying army, however welcome it may be, is a facet of Balkan life that has few precedents over such a short space of time in its past. The editors can offer no solace for the future. It is enough to trace events to a point where the future of the Balkans is at a crossroads quite unlike any other that typified its wild mountains and lush valleys way back into the distant past and before its tumultuous tribal history began.

Index